SECOND EDITION

Learning JavaScript Design Patterns

A JavaScript and React Developer's Guide

Addy Osmani

Beijing · Boston · Farnham · Sebastopol · Tokyo

Learning JavaScript Design Patterns

by Addy Osmani

Published by O'Reilly Media, Inc., 1005 Gravenstein Highway North, Sebastopol, CA 95472.

O'Reilly books may be purchased for educational, business, or sales promotional use. Online editions are also available for most titles (*http://oreilly.com*). For more information, contact our corporate/institutional sales department: 800-998-9938 or *corporate@oreilly.com*.

Acquisitions Editor: Amanda Quinn
Development Editor: Michele Cronin
Production Editor: Clare Laylock
Copyeditor: Stephanie English
Proofreader: Rising Sun Technologies

Indexer: Sue Klefstad
Interior Designer: David Futato
Cover Designer: Karen Montgomery
Illustrator: Kate Dullea

August 2012:   First Edition
April 2023:   Second Edition

Revision History for the Second Edition
2023-04-28:   First Release

See *http://oreilly.com/catalog/errata.csp?isbn=9781098139872* for release details.

978-1-098-13987-2

[LSI]

Table of Contents

Preface

The world of JavaScript has come a long way since I wrote the first edition of *Learning JavaScript Design Patterns* over 10 years ago. At that time, I was working on large-scale web applications and found that the lack of structure and organization in JavaScript code made it difficult to maintain and scale those applications.

Fast forward to today, and the web development landscape has changed dramatically. JavaScript has become one of the most popular programming languages in the world and is used for everything from simple scripts to complex web applications. The JavaScript language has evolved to include modules, promises, and `async`/`await`, which has heavily influenced how we architect applications. The way developers write components, such as with React, has also significantly impacted how they think about maintainability. This has resulted in the need for modern patterns that take these new changes into account.

With the rise of modern libraries and frameworks like React, Vue, and Angular, developers are now building applications that are more complex than ever before. I recognized the need for an updated version of *Learning JavaScript Design Patterns* to reflect the changes in JavaScript and web application development.

In this second edition of *Learning JavaScript Design Patterns*, I aim to help developers apply modern design patterns to their JavaScript code and React applications. The book covers more than 20 design patterns essential for building maintainable and scalable applications. The book is not just about design patterns but also about rendering and performance patterns, which are critical to the success of modern web applications.

The first edition of this book focused on classical design patterns, such as the Module pattern, the Observer pattern, and the Mediator pattern. These patterns are still important and relevant today, but the web development world has evolved significantly in the past decade, and new patterns have emerged. This new edition covers these new patterns, such as promises, `async`/`await`, and the newer variations of the

Module pattern. We also cover architectural patterns such as MVC, MVP, and MVVM and discuss where modern frameworks fit with these architectural patterns.

Today's developers are exposed to many library-specific or framework-specific design patterns. React's matured ecosystem and utilization of newer JS primitives provide an excellent launchpad to talk about best practices and patterns in the framework or library context. In addition to classic design patterns, this book covers modern React patterns, such as Hooks, Higher-Order Components, and Render Props. These patterns are specific to React and essential for building modern web applications using this popular framework.

This book is not just about patterns; it's also about best practices. We cover topics such as code organization, performance, and rendering, which are crucial for building high-quality web applications. You will learn about dynamic imports, code-splitting, server-side rendering, hydration, and Islands architecture, all of which are essential for building fast and responsive web applications.

By the end of this book, you will have a deep understanding of design patterns and how to apply them to your JavaScript code and React applications. You will also know which patterns are relevant to the modern web and which are not. This book is not just a reference for patterns; it's also a guide to building high-quality web applications. You will learn how to structure your code for maximum maintainability and scalability and how to optimize your code for performance.

Structure of the Book

This book is organized into 15 chapters, designed to walk you through JavaScript design patterns from a modern perspective, incorporating updated language features and React-specific patterns. Each chapter builds upon the previous one, enabling you to grow your knowledge incrementally and apply it effectively:

- Chapter 1, "Introduction to Design Patterns": Get acquainted with the history of design patterns and their significance in the programming world.
- Chapter 2, ""Pattern"-ity Testing, Proto-Patterns, and the Rule of Three": Understand the process of evaluating and refining design patterns.
- Chapter 3, "Structuring and Writing Patterns": Learn the anatomy of a well-written pattern and how to create one.
- Chapter 4, "Anti-Patterns": Discover what anti-patterns are and how to avoid them in your code.
- Chapter 5, "Modern JavaScript Syntax and Features": Explore the latest JavaScript language features and their impact on design patterns.

- Chapter 6, "Categories of Design Patterns": Delve into the different categories of design patterns: creational, structural, and behavioral.

- Chapter 7, "JavaScript Design Patterns": Study over 20 classic design patterns in JavaScript and their modern adaptations.

- Chapter 8, "JavaScript MV* Patterns": Learn about architectural patterns like MVC, MVP, and MVVM and their significance in modern web development.

- Chapter 9, "Asynchronous Programming Patterns": Understand the power of asynchronous programming in JavaScript and various patterns for handling it.

- Chapter 10, "Modular JavaScript Design Patterns": Discover patterns for organizing and modularizing your JavaScript code.

- Chapter 11, "Namespacing Patterns": Learn various techniques for namespacing your JavaScript code to avoid global namespace pollution.

- Chapter 12, "React.js Design Patterns": Explore React-specific patterns, including Higher-Order Components, Render Props, and Hooks.

- Chapter 13, "Rendering Patterns": Understand different rendering techniques like client-side rendering, server-side rendering, progressive hydration, and Islands architecture.

- Chapter 14, "Application Structure for React.js": Learn how to structure your React application for better organization, maintainability, and scalability.

- Chapter 15, "Conclusions": Wrap up the book with key takeaways and final thoughts.

Throughout the book, practical examples are provided to illustrate the patterns and concepts discussed. By the end of your journey, you'll have a solid understanding of JavaScript design patterns and be equipped to write elegant, maintainable, and scalable code.

Whether you're a seasoned web developer or just starting out, this book will provide the knowledge and tools you need to build modern, maintainable, and scalable web applications. I hope that this book will be a valuable resource for you as you continue to develop your skills and build amazing web applications.

Conventions Used in This Book

The following typographical conventions are used in this book:

Italic
    Indicates new terms, URLs, email addresses, filenames, and file extensions.

`Constant width`

Used for program listings, as well as within paragraphs to refer to program elements such as variable or function names, databases, data types, environment variables, statements, and keywords.

`Constant width italic`

Shows text that should be replaced with user-supplied values or by values determined by context.

This element signifies a tip or suggestion.

This element signifies a general note.

Using Code Examples

Supplemental material (code examples, exercises, etc.) is available for download at *https://github.com/addyosmani/learning-jsdp*.

If you have a technical question or a problem using the code examples, please send email to *bookquestions@oreilly.com*.

This book is here to help you get your job done. In general, if example code is offered with this book, you may use it in your programs and documentation. You do not need to contact us for permission unless you're reproducing a significant portion of the code. For example, writing a program that uses several chunks of code from this book does not require permission. Selling or distributing examples from O'Reilly books does require permission. Answering a question by citing this book and quoting example code does not require permission. Incorporating a significant amount of example code from this book into your product's documentation does require permission.

We appreciate, but generally do not require, attribution. An attribution usually includes the title, author, publisher, and ISBN. For example: "*Learning JavaScript Design Patterns*, 2nd ed., by Addy Osmani (O'Reilly). Copyright 2023 Adnan Osmani, 978-1-098-13987-2."

If you feel your use of code examples falls outside fair use or the permission given above, feel free to contact us at *permissions@oreilly.com*.

O'Reilly Online Learning

O'REILLY® For more than 40 years, *O'Reilly Media* has provided technology and business training, knowledge, and insight to help companies succeed.

Our unique network of experts and innovators share their knowledge and expertise through books, articles, and our online learning platform. O'Reilly's online learning platform gives you on-demand access to live training courses, in-depth learning paths, interactive coding environments, and a vast collection of text and video from O'Reilly and 200+ other publishers. For more information, visit *https://oreilly.com*.

How to Contact Us

Please address comments and questions concerning this book to the publisher:

O'Reilly Media, Inc.
1005 Gravenstein Highway North
Sebastopol, CA 95472
800-998-9938 (in the United States or Canada)
707-829-0515 (international or local)
707-829-0104 (fax)

We have a web page for this book, where we list errata, examples, and any additional information. You can access this page at *https://oreil.ly/js_design_patterns_2e*.

Email *bookquestions@oreilly.com* to comment or ask technical questions about this book.

For news and information about our books and courses, visit *https://oreilly.com*.

Find us on LinkedIn: *https://linkedin.com/company/oreilly-media*

Follow us on Twitter: *https://twitter.com/oreillymedia*

Watch us on YouTube: *https://youtube.com/oreillymedia*

Acknowledgments

I would like to thank the amazing reviewers for the second edition, including Stoyan Stefanov, Julian Setiawan, Viswesh Ravi Shrimali, Adam Scott, and Lydia Hallie.

The first edition's passionate, talented technical reviewers included Nicholas Zakas, Andrée Hansson, Luke Smith, Eric Ferraiuolo, Peter Michaux, and Alex Sexton. They—as well as members of the community at large—helped review and improve this book, and the knowledge and enthusiasm they brought to the project was simply amazing.

A special thanks to Leena Sohoni-Kasture for her contributions and feedback to the editing of the second edition.

Finally, I would like to thank my wonderful wife, Elle, for all of her support while I was putting together this publication.

CHAPTER 1

Introduction to Design Patterns

Good code is like a love letter to the next developer who will maintain it!

Design patterns provide a common vocabulary to structure code, making it easier to understand. They help enhance the quality of this connection to other developers. Knowledge of design patterns helps us identify recurring themes in requirements and map them to definitive solutions. We can rely on the experience of others who have encountered a similar problem and devised an optimized method to address it. This knowledge is invaluable as it paves the way for writing or refactoring code to make it maintainable.

Whether on the server or client, JavaScript is a cornerstone of modern web application development. The previous edition of this book focused on several popular design patterns in the JavaScript context. Over the years, JavaScript has significantly evolved as a language in terms of features and syntax. It now supports modules, classes, arrow functions, and template literals that it did not previously. We also have advanced JavaScript libraries and frameworks that have made life easy for many web developers. How relevant, then, are design patterns in the modern JavaScript context?

It's important to note that traditionally, design patterns are neither prescriptive nor language-specific. You can apply them when you think they fit, but you don't have to. Like data structures or algorithms, you can still apply classic design patterns using modern programming languages, including JavaScript. You may not need some of these design patterns in modern frameworks or libraries where they are already abstracted. Conversely, the use of specific patterns may even be encouraged by some frameworks.

In this edition, we are taking a pragmatic approach to patterns. We will explore why specific patterns may be the right fit for implementing certain features and if a pattern is still recommended in the modern JavaScript context.

As applications got more interactive, requiring a large amount of JavaScript, the language came under constant criticism for its negative impact on performance. Developers are continuously looking for new patterns that can optimize JavaScript performance. This edition highlights such improvements wherever relevant. We will also discuss framework-specific patterns such as React Hooks and Higher-Order Components that have become increasingly popular in the age of React.js.

Going back a step, let us start by exploring the history and importance of design patterns. If you're already familiar with this history, feel free to skip to "What Is a Pattern?" on page 3 to continue reading.

History of Design Patterns

Design patterns can be traced back to the early work of an architect named Christopher Alexander (*https://oreil.ly/LxYgk*). He often wrote about his experiences in solving design issues and how they related to buildings and towns. One day, it occurred to Alexander that certain design constructs lead to a desired optimal effect when used repeatedly.

Alexander produced a pattern language in collaboration with two other architects, Sara Ishikawa and Murray Silverstein. This language would help empower anyone wishing to design and build at any scale. They published it in 1977 in a paper titled "A Pattern Language," later released as a complete hardcover book (*https://oreil.ly/Cy0DR*).

Around 1990, software engineers began to incorporate the principles Alexander had written about into the first documentation about design patterns to guide novice developers looking to improve their coding skills. It's important to note that the concepts behind design patterns have been around in the programming industry since its inception, albeit in a less formalized form.

One of the first and arguably the most iconic formal works published on design patterns in software engineering was a book in 1995 called *Design Patterns: Elements of Reusable Object-Oriented Software*—written by Erich Gamma, Richard Helm, Ralph Johnson, and John Vlissides. Most engineers today recognize this group as the Gang of Four (GoF).

The GoF publication (*https://oreil.ly/xj66Y*) was particularly instrumental in pushing the concept of design patterns further in our field. It describes several development techniques and pitfalls and provides 23 core object-oriented design patterns frequently used worldwide today. We will cover these patterns in more detail in Chapter 6, and they also form the basis for our discussion in Chapter 7.

What Is a Pattern?

A pattern is a reusable solution template that you can apply to recurring problems and themes in software design. Similar to other programming languages, when building a JavaScript web application, you can use the template to structure your JavaScript code in different situations where you think it will help.

Learning and using design patterns is mainly advantageous for developers because of the following:

Patterns are proven solutions.
> They are the result of the combined experience and insights of developers who helped define them. They are time-tested approaches known to work when solving specific issues in software development.

Patterns can be easily reused.
> A pattern usually delivers an out-of-the-box solution you can adopt and adapt to suit your needs. This feature makes them quite robust.

Patterns can be expressive.
> Patterns can help express elegant solutions to extensive problems using a set structure and a shared *vocabulary*.

Additional advantages that patterns offer include the following:

Patterns assist in preventing minor issues that can cause significant problems in the application development process.
> When you use established patterns to build code, you can relax about getting the structure wrong and focus on the quality of the overall solution. The pattern encourages you to write more structured and organized code naturally, avoiding the need to refactor it for cleanliness in the future.

Patterns provide generalized solutions, documented in a fashion that doesn't require them to be tied to a specific problem.
> This generalized approach means you can apply design patterns to improve code structure regardless of the application (and, in many cases, the programming language).

Some patterns can decrease the overall code file-size footprint by avoiding repetition.
> Design patterns encourage developers to look more closely at their solutions for areas where they can achieve instant reductions in duplication. For example, you can reduce the number of functions performing similar processes in favor of a single generalized function to decrease the size of your codebase. This is also known as making code more *dry*.

Patterns add to a developer's vocabulary, which makes communication faster.
Developers can reference the pattern when communicating with their team, when discussing it in the design patterns community, or indirectly when another developer later maintains the code.

Popular design patterns can be improvised further by harnessing the collective experiences of developers using those patterns and contributing back to the community.
In some cases, this leads to the creation of entirely new design patterns, while in others, it can lead to improved guidelines on the usage of specific patterns. This can ensure that pattern-based solutions continue to become more robust than ad hoc ones.

Patterns are *not* exact solutions. The role of a pattern is merely to provide us with a solution scheme. Patterns don't solve all design problems, nor do they replace good software designers. You still need sound designers to choose the correct patterns that can enhance the overall design.

An Everyday Use Case for Design Patterns

If you have used React.js, you have probably come across the Provider pattern. If not, you may have experienced the following situation.

The component tree in web applications often needs access to shared data such as user information or user access permissions. The traditional way to do this in JavaScript is to set these properties for the root level component and then pass them down from parent to child components. As the component hierarchy deepens and becomes more nested, you drill down it with your data, resulting in the practice of prop drilling. This leads to unmaintainable code where the property setting and passing will get repeated in every child component, which relies on that data.

React and a few other frameworks address this problem using the Provider pattern. With the Provider pattern, the React Context API can broadcast the state/data to multiple components via a context provider. Child components needing the shared data can tap into this provider as a context consumer or use the useContext Hook.

This is an excellent example of a design pattern used to optimize the solution to a common problem. We will cover this and many such patterns in a lot of detail in this book.

Summary

With that introduction to the importance of design patterns and their relevance to modern JavaScript, we can now deep dive into learning JavaScript design patterns. The first few chapters in this book cover structuring and classifying patterns and identifying anti-patterns before we go into the specifics of design patterns for JavaScript. But first, let's see what it takes for a proposed "proto-pattern" to be recognized as a pattern in the next chapter.

CHAPTER 2

"Pattern"-ity Testing, Proto-Patterns, and the Rule of Three

From the moment a new pattern is proposed to its potential widespread adoption, a pattern may have to go through multiple rounds of deep inspection by the design community and software developers. This chapter talks about this journey of a newly introduced "proto-pattern" through a "pattern"-ity test until it is eventually recognized as a pattern if it meets the *rule of three*.

This and the next chapter explore the approach to structuring, writing, presenting, and reviewing nascent design patterns. If you'd prefer to learn established design patterns first, you can skip these two chapters for the time being.

What Are Proto-Patterns?

Remember that not every algorithm, best practice, or solution represents what might be considered a complete pattern. There may be a few key ingredients missing, and the pattern community is generally wary of something claiming to be one without an extensive and critical evaluation. Even if something is presented to us which *appears* to meet the criteria for a pattern, we should not consider it as one until it has undergone suitable periods of scrutiny and testing by others.

Looking back upon Alexander's work once more, he claims that a pattern should be both a process and a "thing." This definition is obtuse as he follows by saying that it is the process that should create the "thing." This is why patterns generally focus on addressing a visually identifiable structure; we should be able to visually depict (or draw) a picture representing the structure resulting from placing the pattern into practice.

The "Pattern" Tests

You may often come across the term "proto-pattern" when studying design patterns. What is this? Well, a pattern that has not yet conclusively passed the "pattern"-ity tests is usually referred to as a proto-pattern. Proto-patterns may result from the work of someone who has established a particular solution worthy of sharing with the community. However, due to its relatively young age, the community has not had the opportunity to vet the proposed solution suitably.

Alternatively, the individual(s) sharing the pattern may not have the time or interest in going through the "pattern"-ity process and might release a short description of their proto-pattern instead. Brief descriptions or snippets of this type of pattern are known as *patlets*.

The work involved in comprehensively documenting a qualified pattern can be pretty daunting. Looking back at some of the earliest work in the field of design patterns, a pattern may be considered "good" if it does the following:

Solves a particular problem
> Patterns are not supposed to just capture principles or strategies. They need to capture solutions. This is one of the most essential ingredients of a good pattern.

Does not have an obvious solution
> We can find that problem-solving techniques often attempt to derive from well-known first principles. The best design patterns usually provide solutions to issues indirectly—this is considered a necessary approach for the most challenging problems related to design.

Describes a proven concept
> Design patterns require proof that they function as described, and without this proof, the design cannot be seriously considered. If a pattern is highly speculative in nature, only the brave will attempt to use it.

Describes a relationship
> In some cases, it may appear that a pattern describes a type of module. Despite what the implementation looks like, the official description of the pattern must describe much deeper system structures and mechanisms that explain its relationship to code.

We would be forgiven for thinking that a proto-pattern that fails to meet guidelines isn't worth learning from; however, this is far from the truth. Many proto-patterns are actually quite good. I am not saying that all proto-patterns are worth looking at, but there are quite a few useful ones in the wild that could assist us with future projects. Use your best judgment with the above list in mind, and you'll be fine in your selection process.

Rule of Three

One of the additional requirements for a pattern to be valid is that it displays some recurring phenomenon. You can often qualify this in at least three key areas, referred to as the rule of three. To show recurrence using this rule, one must demonstrate the following:

Fitness of purpose
How is the pattern considered successful?

Usefulness
Why is the pattern considered successful?

Applicability
Is the design worthy of being a pattern because it has broader applicability? If so, this needs to be explained. When reviewing or defining a pattern, it is vital to keep these areas in mind.

Summary

This chapter has shown how every proposed proto-pattern may not always be accepted as a pattern. The next chapter shares the essential elements and best practices for structuring and documenting patterns so that the community can easily understand and consume them.

CHAPTER 3

Structuring and Writing Patterns

The success of a new idea depends on its utility and also on how you present it to those it is trying to help. For developers to understand and adopt a design pattern, it should be presented with relevant information about the context, circumstances, prerequisites, and significant examples. This chapter applies to those trying to understand a specific pattern and those trying to introduce a new one because it provides essential information on how patterns are structured and written.

The Structure of a Design Pattern

Pattern authors would be unable to successfully create and publish a pattern if they cannot define its purpose. Similarly, developers will find understanding or implementing a pattern challenging if they do not have a background or context.

Pattern authors must outline a new pattern's design, implementation, and purpose. Authors initially present a new pattern in the form of a *rule* that establishes a relationship between:

- A context
- A system of forces that arises in that context
- A configuration that allows these forces to resolve themselves in context

With this in mind, let's now summarize the component elements for a design pattern. A design pattern should have the following, with the first five elements being the most important:

Pattern name
A unique name representative of the purpose of the pattern.

Description
A brief description of what the pattern helps achieve.

Context outline
The contexts in which the pattern effectively responds to its users' needs.

Problem statement
A statement of the problem addressed so that we understand the pattern's intent.

Solution
A description of how the user's problem is solved in an understandable list of steps and perceptions.

Design
A description of the pattern's design and, in particular, the user's behavior in interacting with it.

Implementation
A guide to how developers would implement the pattern.

Illustrations
Visual representations of classes in the pattern (e.g., a diagram).

Examples
Implementations of the pattern in a minimal form.

Corequisites
What other patterns may be needed to support the use of the pattern being described?

Relations
What patterns does this pattern resemble? Does it closely mimic any others?

Known usage
Is the pattern being used in the wild? If so, where and how?

Discussions
The team's or author's thoughts on the exciting benefits of the pattern.

Well-Written Patterns

Understanding the structure and purpose of a design pattern can help us gain a deeper appreciation for the reasoning behind why a pattern is needed. It also helps us evaluate the pattern for our own needs.

A good pattern should ideally provide a substantial quantity of reference material for end users. Patterns should also provide evidence of why they are necessary.

Just having an overview of a pattern is not enough to help us identify them in the code we may encounter day-to-day. It's not always clear if a piece of code we're looking at follows a set pattern or accidentally resembles one.

If you suspect that the code you see uses a pattern, consider writing down some aspects of the code that fall under a particular existing pattern or set of patterns. It may be that the code follows sound principles and design practices that coincidentally overlap with the rules for a specific pattern.

 Solutions in which neither interactions nor defined rules appear are not patterns.

Although patterns may have a high initial cost in the planning and write-up phases, the value returned from that investment can be worth it. Patterns are valuable because they help to get all the developers in an organization or team on the same page when creating or maintaining solutions. If you're considering working on a pattern of your own, research beforehand, as you may find it more beneficial to use or extend existing, proven patterns rather than starting afresh.

Writing a Pattern

If you're trying to develop a design pattern yourself, I recommend learning from others who have already been through the process and done it well. Spend time absorbing the information from several different design pattern descriptions and take in what's meaningful to you. Explore structure and semantics—you can do this by examining the interactions and context of the patterns you're interested in to identify the principles that assist in organizing those patterns together in valuable configurations.

You can utilize the *existing* format to write your own pattern or see if there are ways to improve it by integrating your ideas. An example of a developer who did this in recent years is Christian Heilmann, who took the existing *Module* pattern (see Figure 7-2) and made some fundamentally valuable changes to it to create the *Revealing Module* pattern (see "The Revealing Module Pattern" on page 51).

Adhering to the following checklist would help if you're interested in creating a new design pattern or adapting an existing one:

How practical is the pattern?
Ensure that the pattern describes proven solutions to recurring problems rather than just speculative solutions that haven't been qualified.

Keep best practices in mind.
Our design decisions should be based on principles we derive from understanding best practices.

Our design patterns should be transparent to the user.
Design patterns should be entirely transparent to the end-user experience. They primarily serve the developers using them and should not force changes to the expected user experience.

Remember that originality is not key in pattern design.
When writing a pattern, you do not need to be the original discoverer of the documented solutions, nor do you have to worry about your design overlapping with minor pieces of other patterns. If the approach is strong enough to be broadly applicable, it has a chance of being recognized as a valid pattern.

Patterns need a strong set of examples.
A good pattern description needs to be followed by an equally effective set of examples demonstrating the successful application of the pattern. To show broad usage, examples that exhibit sound design principles are ideal.

Pattern writing is a careful balance between creating a design that is general, specific, and, above all, useful. Try to ensure that you comprehensively cover all possible application areas when writing a pattern.

Whether you write a pattern or not, I hope this brief introduction to writing patterns has given you some insights that will assist your learning process and help you rationalize the patterns covered in the following sections of this book.

Summary

This chapter painted a picture of the ideal "good" pattern. It is equally important to understand that "bad" patterns exist, too, so we can identify and avoid them. And that is why we have the next chapter about "anti-patterns."

CHAPTER 4

Anti-Patterns

As engineers, we may run into situations when we are on a deadline to deliver a solution or where code gets included as a series of patches without a code review. The code in such cases may not always be well thought out and may propagate what we call *anti-patterns*. This chapter describes what anti-patterns are and why it is essential to understand and identify them. We also look at some typical anti-patterns in JavaScript.

What Are Anti-Patterns?

If a pattern represents a best practice, an anti-pattern represents the lesson learned when a proposed pattern goes wrong. Inspired by the GoF's book *Design Patterns*, Andrew Koenig first coined the term anti-pattern in 1995 in his article in the *Journal of Object-Oriented Programming*, Volume 8 (*https://oreil.ly/Megyr*). He described anti-patterns as:

> An antipattern is just like a pattern, except that instead of a solution, it gives something that looks superficially like a solution but isn't one.

He presented two notions of anti-patterns. Anti-patterns:

- Describe a *bad* solution to a particular problem that resulted in an unfavorable situation occurring
- Describe *how* to get out of the said situation and go to a good solution

On this topic, Alexander writes about the difficulties in achieving a good balance between good design structure and good context:

These notes are about the process of design; the process of inventing physical things which display a new physical order, organization, form, in response to function. ... Every design problem begins with an effort to achieve fitness between two entities: the form in question and its context. The form is the solution to the problem; the context defines the problem.

Understanding anti-patterns is as essential as being aware of design patterns. Let us qualify the reason behind this. When creating an application, a project's lifecycle begins with construction. At this stage, you are likely to choose from the available *good* design patterns as you see fit. However, after the initial release, it needs to be maintained.

Maintenance of an application already in production can be particularly challenging. Developers who haven't worked on the application before may accidentally introduce a *bad* design into the project. If these *bad* practices have already been identified as anti-patterns, developers will recognize them in advance and avoid the known common mistakes. This is similar to how knowledge of design patterns allows us to recognize areas where we could apply *known* and *helpful* standard techniques.

The quality of the solution as it evolves will either be *good* or *bad*, depending on the skill level and time the team has invested in it. Here, *good* and *bad* are considered in context—a "perfect" design may qualify as an anti-pattern if applied in the wrong context.

To summarize, an anti-pattern is a bad design that is worthy of documenting.

Anti-Patterns in JavaScript

Developers sometimes knowingly opt for shortcuts and temporary solutions to expedite code deliveries. These tend to become permanent and accumulate as technical debt that is essentially made up of anti-patterns. JavaScript is a weakly typed or untyped language that makes taking certain shortcuts easier. Following are some examples of anti-patterns that you might come across in JavaScript:

- Polluting the global namespace by defining numerous variables in the global context.
- Passing strings rather than functions to either `setTimeout` or `setInterval`, as this triggers the use of `eval()` internally.
- Modifying the `Object` class prototype (this is a particularly bad anti-pattern).
- Using JavaScript in an inline form, as this is inflexible.

- The use of `document.write` where native Document Object Model (DOM) alternatives such as `document.createElement` are more appropriate. `document.write` has been grossly misused over the years and has quite a few disadvantages. If it's executed after the page has been loaded, it can overwrite the page we're on, which makes `document.createElement` a far better choice. Visit this link (*https://oreil.ly/kc1c0*) for a live example of this in action. It also doesn't work with XHTML, which is another reason opting for more DOM-friendly methods such as `document.createElement` is favorable.

Knowledge of anti-patterns is critical for success. Once we learn to recognize such anti-patterns, we can refactor our code to negate them so that the overall quality of our solutions improves instantly.

Summary

This chapter covered patterns that could cause problems known as anti-patterns and examples of JavaScript anti-patterns. Before we cover JavaScript design patterns in detail, we must touch upon some critical modern JavaScript concepts that will prove relevant to our discussion on patterns. This is the subject of the next chapter, which introduces modern JavaScript features and syntax.

CHAPTER 5

Modern JavaScript Syntax and Features

JavaScript has been around for many decades now and has undergone multiple revisions. This book explores design patterns in the modern JavaScript context and uses modern ES2015+ syntax for all the examples discussed. This chapter discusses ES2015+ JavaScript features and syntax essential to further our discussion of design patterns in the current JavaScript context.

Some fundamental changes were introduced to JavaScript syntax with ES2015 that are especially relevant to our discussion on patterns. These are covered well in the BabelJS ES2015 guide (*https:// oreil.ly/V09r_*).

This book relies on modern JavaScript syntax. You may also be curious about TypeScript. TypeScript, a statically typed superset of JavaScript, offers several language features that JavaScript does not. These features include strong typing, interfaces, enums, and advanced type inference and can also influence design patterns. To learn more about TypeScript and its benefits, consider checking out some O'Reilly books such as *Programming TypeScript* by Boris Cherny.

The Importance of Decoupling Applications

Modular JavaScript allows you to logically split your application into smaller pieces called modules. A module can be imported by other modules that, in turn, can be imported by more modules. Thus, the application can be composed of many nested modules.

In the world of scalable JavaScript, when we say an application is *modular*, we often mean it's composed of a set of highly decoupled, distinct pieces of functionality stored in modules. Loose coupling facilitates easier maintainability of apps by removing *dependencies* where possible. If implemented efficiently, it allows you to see how changes to one part of a system may affect another.

Unlike some more traditional programming languages, the older iterations of JavaScript until ES5 (Standard ECMA-262 5.1 Edition (*https://oreil.ly/w2WxN*)) did not provide developers with the means to organize and import code modules cleanly. It was one of the concerns with the specifications that had not required great thought until more recent years when the need for more organized JavaScript applications became apparent. AMD (Asynchronous Module Definition) (*https://oreil.ly/W5XPd*) and CommonJS (*https://oreil.ly/lgw0w*) modules were the most popular patterns to decouple applications in the initial versions of JavaScript.

Native solutions to these problems arrived with ES6 or ES2015 (*https://oreil.ly/rPxFL*). TC39 (*https://oreil.ly/GJduA*), the standards body charged with defining the syntax and semantics of ECMAScript and its future iterations, had been keeping a close eye on the evolution of JavaScript usage for large-scale development and was acutely aware of the need for better language features for writing more modular JS.

The syntax to create modules in JavaScript was developed and standardized with the release of ECMAScript modules in ES2015. Today, all major browsers support JavaScript modules. They have become the de facto method of implementing modern-day modular programming in JavaScript. In this section, we'll explore code samples using the syntax for modules in ES2015+.

Modules with Imports and Exports

Modules allow us to separate our application code into independent units, each containing code for one aspect of the functionality. Modules also encourage code reusability and expose features that can be integrated into different applications.

A language should have features that allow you to `import` module dependencies and `export` the module interface (the public API/variables we allow other modules to consume) to support modular programming. The support for JavaScript modules (also referred to as ES modules) (*https://oreil.ly/kd-pu*) was introduced to JavaScript in ES2015, allowing you to specify module dependencies using an `import` keyword. Similarly, you can use the `export` keyword to export just about anything from within the module:

- `import` declarations bind a module's exports as local variables and may be renamed to avoid name collisions/conflicts.

- export declarations declare that a local binding of a module is externally visible such that other modules may read the exports but can't modify them. Interestingly, modules may export child modules but can't export modules that have been defined elsewhere. We can also rename exports so that their external name differs from their local names.

 .mjs is an extension used for JavaScript modules that helps us distinguish between module files and classic scripts (*.js*). The *.mjs* extension ensures that corresponding files are parsed as a module by runtimes and build tools (for example, Node.js (*https://oreil.ly/E9oRS*), Babel (*https://oreil.ly/fkQAL*)).

The following example shows three modules for bakery staff, the functions they perform while baking, and the bakery itself. We see how functionality that is exported by one module is imported and used by the other:

```
// Filename: staff.mjs
// =========================================
// specify (public) exports that can be consumed by other modules
export const baker = {
    bake(item) {
        console.log( `Woo! I just baked ${item}` );
    }
};

// Filename: cakeFactory.mjs
// =========================================
// specify dependencies
import baker from "/modules/staff.mjs";

export const oven = {
    makeCupcake(toppings) {
        baker.bake( "cupcake", toppings );
    },
    makeMuffin(mSize) {
        baker.bake( "muffin", size );
    }
}

// Filename: bakery.mjs
// =========================================
import {cakeFactory} from "/modules/cakeFactory.mjs";
cakeFactory.oven.makeCupcake( "sprinkles" );
cakeFactory.oven.makeMuffin( "large" );
```

Typically, a module file contains several related functions, constants, and variables. You can collectively export these at the end of the file using a single export statement followed by a comma-separated list of the module resources you want to export:

```
// Filename: staff.mjs
// =======================================
const baker = {
  //baker functions
};
const pastryChef = {
  //pastry chef functions
};
const assistant = {
  //assistant functions
};

export { baker, pastryChef, assistant };
```

Similarly, you can import only the functions you need:

```
import {baker, assistant} from "/modules/staff.mjs";
```

You can tell browsers to accept <script> tags that contain JavaScript modules by specifying the type attribute with a value of module:

```
<script type="module" src="main.mjs"></script>
<script nomodule src="fallback.js"></script>
```

The nomodule attribute tells modern browsers not to load a classic script as a module. This is useful for fallback scripts that don't use the module syntax. It allows you to use the module syntax in your HTML and have it work in browsers that don't support it. This is useful for several reasons, including performance. Modern browsers don't require polyfilling for modern features, allowing you to serve the larger transpiled code to legacy browsers alone.

Module Objects

A cleaner approach to importing and using module resources is to import the module as an object. This makes all the exports available as members of the object:

```
// Filename: cakeFactory.mjs

import * as Staff from "/modules/staff.mjs";

export const oven = {
    makeCupcake(toppings) {
        Staff.baker.bake( "cupcake", toppings );
    },
    makePastry(mSize) {
        Staff.pastryChef.make( "pastry", type );
    }
}
```

Modules Loaded from Remote Sources

ES2015+ also supports remote modules (e.g., third-party libraries), making it simplistic to load modules from external locations. Here's an example of pulling in the module we defined previously and utilizing it:

```
import {cakeFactory} from "https://example.com/modules/cakeFactory.mjs";
// eagerly loaded static import

cakeFactory.oven.makeCupcake( "sprinkles" );
cakeFactory.oven.makeMuffin( "large" );
```

Static Imports

The type of import just discussed is called static import. The module graph needs to be downloaded and executed with static import before the main code can run. This can sometimes lead to the eager loading of a lot of code up front on the initial page load, which can be expensive and delay key features being available earlier:

```
import {cakeFactory} from "/modules/cakeFactory.mjs";
// eagerly loaded static import

cakeFactory.oven.makeCupcake( "sprinkles" );
cakeFactory.oven.makeMuffin( "large" );
```

Dynamic Imports

Sometimes, you don't want to load a module up-front but on demand when needed. Lazy-loading modules allows you to load what you need when needed—for example, when the user clicks a link or a button. This improves the initial load-time performance. Dynamic import (*https://oreil.ly/fqR6v*) was introduced to make this possible.

Dynamic import introduces a new function-like form of import. `import(url)` returns a promise for the module namespace object of the requested module, which is created after fetching, instantiating, and evaluating all of the module's dependencies, as well as the module itself. Here is an example that shows dynamic imports for the `cakeFactory` module:

```
form.addEventListener("submit", e => {
  e.preventDefault();
  import("/modules/cakeFactory.js")
    .then((module) => {
      // Do something with the module.
      module.oven.makeCupcake("sprinkles");
      module.oven.makeMuffin("large");
    });
});
```

Dynamic import can also be supported using the `await` keyword:

```
let module = await import("/modules/cakeFactory.js");
```

With dynamic import, the module graph is downloaded and evaluated only when the module is used.

Popular patterns like Import on Interaction and Import on Visibility can be easily implemented in vanilla JavaScript using the dynamic import feature.

Import on Interaction

Some libraries may be required only when a user starts interacting with a particular feature on the web page. Typical examples are chat widgets, complex dialog boxes, or video embeds. Libraries for these features need not be imported on page load but can be loaded when the user interacts with them (for example, by clicking on the component facade or placeholder). The action can trigger the dynamic import of respective libraries followed by the function call to activate the desired functionality.

For example, you can implement an onscreen sort function using the external `lodash.sortby` module (*https://oreil.ly/VUgnM*), which is loaded dynamically:

```
const btn = document.querySelector('button');

btn.addEventListener('click', e => {
  e.preventDefault();
  import('lodash.sortby')
    .then(module => module.default)
    .then(sortInput()) // use the imported dependency
    .catch(err => { console.log(err) });
});
```

Import on Visibility

Many components are not visible on the initial page load but become visible as the user scrolls down. Since users may not always scroll down, modules corresponding to these components can be lazy-loaded when they become visible. The IntersectionObserver API (*https://oreil.ly/wXwgi*) can detect when a component placeholder is about to become visible, and a dynamic import can load the corresponding modules.

Modules for the Server

Node (*https://oreil.ly/4Bh_O*) 15.3.0 onward supports JavaScript modules. They function without an experimental flag and are compatible with the rest of the npm package ecosystem. Node treats (*https://oreil.ly/q1Jzl*) files ending in *.mjs* and *.js* with a top-level type field value of module as JavaScript modules:

```
{
  "name": "js-modules",
  "version": "1.0.0",
  "description": "A package using JS Modules",
  "main": "index.js",
  "type": "module",
  "author": "",
  "license": "MIT"
}
```

Advantages of Using Modules

Modular programming and the use of modules offer several unique advantages. Some of these are as follows:

Modules scripts are evaluated only once.
> The browser evaluates module scripts only once, while classic scripts get evaluated as often as they are added to the DOM. This means that with JS modules, if you have an extended hierarchy of dependent modules, the module that depends on the innermost module will be evaluated first. This is a good thing because it means that the innermost module will be evaluated first and will have access to the exports of the modules that depend on it.

Modules are auto-deferred.
> Unlike other script files, where you have to include the `defer` attribute if you don't want to load them immediately, browsers automatically defer the loading of modules.

Modules are easy to maintain and reuse.
> Modules promote decoupling pieces of code that can be maintained independently without significant changes to other modules. They also allow you to reuse the same code in multiple different functions.

Modules provide namespacing.
> Modules create a private space for related variables and constants so that they can be referenced via the module without polluting the global namespace.

Modules enable dead code elimination.
> Before the introduction of modules, unused code files had to be manually removed from projects. With module imports, bundlers such as webpack (*https://oreil.ly/37e9F*) and Rollup (*https://oreil.ly/rUWiB*) can automatically identify unused modules and eliminate them. Dead code may be removed before adding it to the bundle. This is known as tree-shaking.

All modern browsers support module import (*https://oreil.ly/IauTK*) and export (*https://oreil.ly/NubAY*), and you can use them without any fallback.

Classes with Constructors, Getters, and Setters

In addition to modules, ES2015+ also allows defining classes with constructors and some sense of privacy. JavaScript classes are defined with the class keyword. In the following example, we define a class Cake with a constructor and two getters and setters:

```
class Cake{

    // We can define the body of a class constructor
    // function by using the keyword constructor
    // with a list of class variables.
    constructor( name, toppings, price, cakeSize ){
        this.name = name;
        this.cakeSize = cakeSize;
        this.toppings = toppings;
        this.price = price;
    }

    // As a part of ES2015+ efforts to decrease the unnecessary
    // use of function for everything, you will notice that it is
    // dropped for cases such as the following. Here an identifier
    // followed by an argument list and a body defines a new method.

    addTopping( topping ){
        this.toppings.push( topping );
    }

    // Getters can be defined by declaring get before
    // an identifier/method name and a curly body.
    get allToppings(){
        return this.toppings;
    }

    get qualifiesForDiscount(){
        return this.price > 5;
    }

    // Similar to getters, setters can be defined by using
    // the set keyword before an identifier
    set size( size ){
        if ( size < 0){
            throw new Error( "Cake must be a valid size: " +
                                    "either small, medium or large");
        }
        this.cakeSize = size;
    }
}

// Usage
let cake = new Cake( "chocolate", ["chocolate chips"], 5, "large" );
```

JavaScript classes are built on prototypes and are a special category of JavaScript functions that need to be defined before they can be referenced.

You can also use the extends keyword to indicate that a class inherits from another class:

```
class BirthdayCake extends Cake {
  surprise() {
    console.log(`Happy Birthday!`);
  }
}

let birthdayCake = new BirthdayCake( "chocolate", ["chocolate chips"], 5,
  "large" );
birthdayCake.surprise();
```

All modern browsers and Node support ES2015 classes. They are also compatible with the new-style class syntax (*https://oreil.ly/9c9jm*) introduced in ES6.

The difference between JavaScript modules and classes is that modules are imported (*https://oreil.ly/IauTK*) and exported (*https://oreil.ly/NubAY*), and classes are defined with the class keyword.

Reading through, one may also notice the lack of the word "function" in the previous examples. This isn't a typo: TC39 has made a conscious effort to decrease our abuse of the function keyword for everything, hoping it will help simplify how we write code.

JavaScript classes also support the super keyword, which allows (*https://oreil.ly/gYvxw*) you to call a parent class' constructor. This is useful for implementing the self-inheritance pattern. You can use super to call the methods of the superclass:

```
class Cookie {
  constructor(flavor) {
    this.flavor = flavor;
  }

  showTitle() {
    console.log(`The flavor of this cookie is ${this.flavor}.`);
  }
}

class FavoriteCookie extends Cookie {
  showTitle() {
    super.showTitle();
    console.log(`${this.flavor} is amazing.`);
  }
}

let myCookie = new FavoriteCookie('chocolate');
myCookie.showTitle();
```

```
// The flavor of this cookie is chocolate.
// chocolate is amazing.
```

Modern JavaScript supports public and private class members. Public class members are accessible to other classes. Private class members are accessible only to the class in which they are defined. Class fields are, by default, public. Private class fields (*https://oreil.ly/SXsES*) can be created by using the # (hash) prefix:

```
class CookieWithPrivateField {
  #privateField;
}

class CookieWithPrivateMethod {
  #privateMethod() {
    return 'delicious cookies';
  }
}
```

JavaScript classes support static methods and properties using the `static` keyword. Static members can be referenced without instantiating the class. You can use static methods to create utility functions and static properties for holding configuration or cached data:

```
class Cookie {
  constructor(flavor) {
    this.flavor = flavor;
  }
  static brandName = "Best Bakes";
  static discountPercent = 5;
}
console.log(Cookie.brandName); //output = "Best Bakes"
```

Classes in JavaScript Frameworks

Over the last few years, some modern JavaScript libraries and frameworks—notably React—have introduced alternatives to classes. React Hooks make it possible to use React state and lifecycle methods without an ES2015 class component. Before Hooks, React developers had to refactor functional components as class components so that they handle state and lifecycle methods. This was often tricky and required an understanding of how ES2015 classes work. React Hooks are functions that allow you to manage a component's state and lifecycle methods without relying on classes.

Note that several other approaches to building for the web, such as the Web Components (*https://oreil.ly/ndfeb*) community, continue to use classes as a base for component development.

Summary

This chapter introduced JavaScript language syntax for modules and classes. These features allow us to write code while adhering to object-oriented design and modular programming principles. We will also use these concepts to categorize and describe different design patterns. The next chapter talks about the different categories of design patterns.

Related Reading

- JavaScript modules on v8 (*https://oreil.ly/IEuAq*)
- JavaScript modules on MDN (*https://oreil.ly/OAL9O*)

CHAPTER 6

Categories of Design Patterns

This chapter documents the three main categories of design patterns and the different patterns that fall under them. While every design pattern addresses a specific object-oriented design problem or issue, we can draw parallels between the solutions based on how they solve these issues. This forms the basis for the categorization of design patterns.

Background

Gamma, Helm, Johnson, and Vlissides (1995), in their book, *Design Patterns: Elements of Reusable Object-Oriented Software* (*https://oreil.ly/viJe6*), describe a design pattern as:

> A design pattern names, abstracts, and identifies the key aspects of a common design structure that make it useful for creating a reusable object-oriented design. The design pattern identifies the participating classes and their instances, their roles and collaborations, and the distribution of responsibilities.

> Each design pattern focuses on a particular object-oriented design problem or issue. It describes when it applies, whether or not it can be applied in view of other design constraints, and the consequences and trade-offs of its use. Since we must eventually implement our designs, a design pattern also provides sample... code to illustrate an implementation.

> Although design patterns describe object-oriented designs, they are based on practical solutions that have been implemented in mainstream object-oriented programming languages....

Design patterns can be categorized based on the type of problem they solve. The three principal categories of design patterns are:

- Creational design patterns
- Structural design patterns
- Behavioral design patterns

In the following sections, we'll review these three with a few examples of the patterns that fall into each category.

Creational Design Patterns

Creational design patterns focus on handling object-creation mechanisms where objects are created in a manner suitable for a given situation. The basic approach to object creation might otherwise lead to added complexity in a project, while these patterns aim to solve this problem by *controlling* the creation process.

Some patterns that fall under this category are Constructor, Factory, Abstract, Prototype, Singleton, and Builder.

Structural Design Patterns

Structural patterns are concerned with object composition and typically identify simple ways to realize relationships between different objects. They help ensure that when one part of a system changes, the entire structure of the system need not change. They also assist in recasting parts of the system that don't fit a particular purpose into those that do.

Patterns that fall under this category include Decorator, Facade, Flyweight, Adapter, and Proxy.

Behavioral Design Patterns

Behavioral patterns focus on improving or streamlining the communication between disparate objects in a system. They identify common communication patterns among objects and provide solutions that distribute the responsibility of communication among different objects, thereby increasing communication flexibility. Essentially, behavioral patterns abstract actions from objects that take the action.

Some behavioral patterns include Iterator, Mediator, Observer, and Visitor.

Design Pattern Classes

Elyse Nielsen in 2004 created a "classes" table to summarize the 23 GoF design patterns. I found this table extremely useful in my early days of learning about design patterns. I've modified it where necessary to suit our discussion on design patterns.

I recommend using this table as a reference, but remember that we will discuss several other patterns not mentioned here later in the book.

 We discussed JavaScript ES2015+ classes in Chapter 5. JavaScript classes and objects will be relevant when you review the following table.

Let us now proceed to review the table:

Creational	Based on the concept of creating an object
Class	
Factory method	Makes an instance of several derived classes based on interfaced data or events
Object	
Abstract Factory	Creates an instance of several families of classes without detailing concrete classes
Builder	Separates object construction from its representation; always creates the same type of object
Prototype	A fully initialized instance used for copying or cloning
Singleton	A class with only a single instance with global access points

Structural	Based on the idea of building blocks of objects
Class	
Adapter	Matches interfaces of different classes so that classes can work together despite incompatible interfaces
Object	
Bridge	Separates an object's interface from its implementation so that the two can vary independently
Composite	A structure of simple and composite objects that makes the total object more than just the sum of its parts
Decorator	Dynamically adds alternate processing to objects
Facade	A single class that hides the complexity of an entire subsystem
Flyweight	A fine-grained instance used for efficient sharing of information that is contained elsewhere
Proxy	A placeholder object representing the true object

Behavioral	Based on the way objects play and work together
Class	
Interpreter	A way to include language elements in an application to match the grammar of the intended language
Template method	Creates the shell of an algorithm in a method, then defers the exact steps to a subclass
Object	
Chain of responsibility	A way of passing a request between a chain of objects to find the object that can handle the request
Command	A way to separate the execution of a command from its invoker

Iterator	Sequentially accesses the elements of a collection without knowing the inner workings of the collection
Mediator	Defines simplified communication between classes to prevent a group of classes from referring explicitly to each other
Memento	Captures an object's internal state to be able to restore it later
Observer	A way of notifying change to a number of classes to ensure consistency between the classes
State	Alters an object's behavior when its state changes
Strategy	Encapsulates an algorithm inside a class, separating the selection from the implementation
Visitor	Adds a new operation to a class without changing the class

Summary

This chapter introduced categories of design patterns and explained the distinction between creational, structural, and behavioral patterns. We discussed the differences between these three categories and GoF patterns in each category. We also reviewed the "classes" table that shows how the GoF patterns relate to the concepts of classes and objects.

These first few chapters have covered theoretical details about design patterns and some basics of JavaScript syntax. With this background, we are now in a position to jump into some practical examples of design patterns in JavaScript.

CHAPTER 7

JavaScript Design Patterns

The previous chapter provided examples of the three different categories of design patterns. Some of these design patterns are relevant or required in the web development context. I have identified a few timeless patterns that can be helpful when applied in JavaScript. This chapter explores JavaScript implementations of different classic and modern design patterns. Every section is dedicated to one of the three categories—creational, structural, and behavioral. Let us begin with creational patterns.

Choosing a Pattern

Developers commonly wonder whether there is an ideal pattern or set of patterns they should use in their workflow. There isn't a single correct answer to this question; each script and web application we work on will likely have distinct individual needs. We must consider whether a pattern can offer real value to an implementation.

For example, some projects may benefit from the decoupling benefits offered by the Observer pattern (which reduces how dependent parts of an application are on one another). At the same time, others may be too small for decoupling to be a concern.

That said, once we have a firm grasp of design patterns and the specific problems they are best suited to, it becomes much easier to integrate them into our application architectures.

Creational Patterns

Creational patterns provide mechanisms to create objects. We will cover the following patterns:

The Constructor Pattern

A constructor is a special method used to initialize a newly created object once the memory has been allocated for it. With ES2015+, the syntax for creating classes (*https://oreil.ly/TjEI1*) with constructors was introduced to JavaScript. This enables the creation of objects as an instance of a class using the default constructor (*https://oreil.ly/zNmUI*).

In JavaScript, almost everything is an object, and classes are syntactic sugar for JavaScript's prototypal approach to inheritance. With classic JavaScript, we were most often interested in object constructors. Figure 7-1 illustrates the pattern.

Object constructors are used to create specific types of objects—both preparing the object for use and accepting arguments to set the values of member properties and methods when the object is first created.

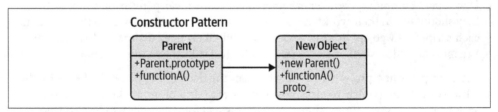

Figure 7-1. Constructor pattern

Object Creation

The three common ways to create new objects in JavaScript are as follows:

```
// Each of the following options will create a new empty object
const newObject = {};

// or
const newObject = Object.create(Object.prototype);
```

```
// or
const newObject = new Object();
```

Here, we have declared each object as a constant, which creates a read-only block-scoped variable. In the final example, the `Object` constructor creates an object wrapper for a specific value, or where no value is passed, it creates an empty object and returns it.

You can now assign keys and values to an object in the following ways:

```
// ECMAScript 3 compatible approaches

// 1. Dot syntax

// Set properties
newObject.someKey = "Hello World";

// Get properties
var key = newObject.someKey;



// 2. Square bracket syntax

// Set properties
newObject["someKey"] = "Hello World";

// Get properties
var key = newObject["someKey"];



// ECMAScript 5 only compatible approaches
// For more information see: http://kangax.github.com/es5-compat-table/

// 3. Object.defineProperty

// Set properties
Object.defineProperty( newObject, "someKey", {
    value: "for more control of the property's behavior",
    writable: true,
    enumerable: true,
    configurable: true
});

// 4. If this feels a little difficult to read, a short-hand could
// be written as follows:

var defineProp = function ( obj, key, value ){
  config.value = value;
  Object.defineProperty( obj, key, config );
};
```

```
// To use, we then create a new empty "person" object
var person = Object.create( null );

// Populate the object with properties
defineProp( person, "car",  "Delorean" );
defineProp( person, "dateOfBirth", "1981" );
defineProp( person, "hasBeard", false );


// 5. Object.defineProperties

// Set properties
Object.defineProperties( newObject, {

  "someKey": {
    value: "Hello World",
    writable: true
  },

  "anotherKey": {
    value: "Foo bar",
    writable: false
  }

});

// Getting properties for 3. and 4. can be done using any of the
// options in 1. and 2.
```

You can even use these methods for inheritance as follows:

```
// ES2015+ keywords/syntax used: const
// Usage:

// Create a race car driver that inherits from the person object
const driver = Object.create(person);

// Set some properties for the driver
defineProp(driver, 'topSpeed', '100mph');

// Get an inherited property (1981)
console.log(driver.dateOfBirth);

// Get the property we set (100mph)
console.log(driver.topSpeed);
```

Basic Constructors

As discussed earlier in Chapter 5, JavaScript classes were introduced in ES2015, allowing us to define templates for JavaScript objects and implement encapsulation and inheritance (*https://oreil.ly/VjSbn*) using JavaScript.

To recap, classes must include and declare a method named `constructor()`, which will be used to instantiate a new object. The keyword `new` allows us to call the constructor. The keyword `this` inside a constructor references the new object created. The following example shows a basic constructor:

```
class Car {
    constructor(model, year, miles) {
        this.model = model;
        this.year = year;
        this.miles = miles;
    }

    toString() {
        return `${this.model} has done ${this.miles} miles`;
    }
}

// Usage:

// We can create new instances of the car
let civic = new Car('Honda Civic', 2009, 20000);
let mondeo = new Car('Ford Mondeo', 2010, 5000);

// and then open our browser console to view the output of
// the toString() method being called on these objects
console.log(civic.toString());
console.log(mondeo.toString());
```

This is a simple version of the Constructor pattern but it suffers from some problems. One is that it makes inheritance difficult, and the other is that functions such as `toString()` are redefined for each new object created using the `Car` constructor. This isn't optimal because all of the instances of the `Car` type should ideally share the same function.

Constructors with Prototypes

Prototypes in JavaScript allow you to easily define methods for all instances of a particular object, be it a function or a class. When we call a JavaScript constructor to create an object, all the properties of the constructor's prototype are then made available to the new object. In this fashion, you can have multiple `Car` objects that access the same prototype. We can thus extend the original example as follows:

```
class Car {
    constructor(model, year, miles) {
        this.model = model;
        this.year = year;
        this.miles = miles;
    }
}
```

```
// Note here that we are using Object.prototype.newMethod rather than
// Object.prototype to avoid redefining the prototype object
// We still could use Object.prototype for adding new methods,
// because internally we use the same structure

Car.prototype.toString = function() {
    return `${this.model} has done ${this.miles} miles`;
};

// Usage:
let civic = new Car('Honda Civic', 2009, 20000);
let mondeo = new Car('Ford Mondeo', 2010, 5000);

console.log(civic.toString());
console.log(mondeo.toString());
```

All Car objects will now share a single instance of the toString() method.

The Module Pattern

Modules are an integral piece of any robust application's architecture and typically help keep the units of code for a project cleanly separated and organized.

Classic JavaScript had several options for implementing modules, such as:

- Object literal notation
- The Module pattern
- AMD modules
- CommonJS modules

We have already discussed modern JavaScript modules (also known as "ES modules" or "ECMAScript modules") in Chapter 5. We will primarily use ES modules for the examples in this section.

Before ES2015, CommonJS modules or AMD modules were popular alternatives because they allowed you to export the contents of a module. We will be exploring AMD, CommonJS, and UMD modules later in the book in Chapter 10. First, let us understand the Module pattern and its origins.

The Module pattern is based partly on object literals, so it makes sense to refresh our knowledge of them first.

Object Literals

In object literal notation, an object is described as a set of comma-separated name/ value pairs enclosed in curly braces ({}). Names inside the object may be either strings or identifiers followed by a colon. It would be best if you did not use a comma after the final name/value pair in the object, as this may result in errors:

```
const myObjectLiteral = {
    variableKey: variableValue,
    functionKey() {
        // ...
    }
};
```

Object literals don't require instantiation using the new operator but shouldn't be used at the start of a statement because the opening { may be interpreted as the beginning of a new block. Outside of an object, new members may be added to it using the assignment as follows myModule.property = "someValue";.

Here is a complete example of a module defined using object literal notation:

```
const myModule = {
    myProperty: 'someValue',
    // object literals can contain properties and methods.
    // e.g., we can define a further object for module configuration:
    myConfig: {
        useCaching: true,
        language: 'en',
    },
    // a very basic method
    saySomething() {
        console.log('Where is Paul Irish debugging today?');
    },
    // output a value based on the current configuration
    reportMyConfig() {
        console.log(
            `Caching is: ${this.myConfig.useCaching ? 'enabled' : 'disabled'}`
        );
    },
    // override the current configuration
    updateMyConfig(newConfig) {
        if (typeof newConfig === 'object') {
            this.myConfig = newConfig;
            console.log(this.myConfig.language);
        }
    },
};

// Outputs: What is Paul Irish debugging today?
myModule.saySomething();

// Outputs: Caching is: enabled
myModule.reportMyConfig();

// Outputs: fr
myModule.updateMyConfig({
```

```
      language: 'fr',
      useCaching: false,
});

// Outputs: Caching is: disabled
myModule.reportMyConfig();
```

Using object literals provided a way to encapsulate and organize code. Rebecca Murphey has written about this topic in depth (*https://oreil.ly/rAYcw*) should you wish to read into object literals further.

The Module Pattern

The Module pattern was initially defined to provide private and public encapsulation for classes in conventional software engineering.

At one point, organizing a JavaScript application of any reasonable size was a challenge. Developers would rely on separate scripts to split and manage reusable chunks of logic, and it wasn't surprising to find 10 to 20 scripts being imported manually in an HTML file to keep things tidy. Using objects, the Module pattern was just one way to encapsulate logic in a file with both public and "private" methods. Over time, several custom module systems came about to make this smoother. Now, developers can use JavaScript modules to organize objects, functions, classes, or variables such that they can be easily exported or imported into other files. This helps prevent conflicts between classes or function names included in different modules. Figure 7-2 illustrates the Module pattern.

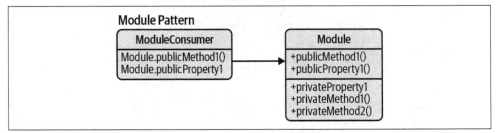

Figure 7-2. Module pattern

Privacy

The Module pattern encapsulates the "privacy" state and organization using closures. It provides a way of wrapping a mix of public and private methods and variables, protecting pieces from leaking into the global scope and accidentally colliding with another developer's interface. With this pattern, you expose only the public API, keeping everything else within the closure private.

This gives us a clean solution where the shielding logic does the heavy lifting while we expose only an interface we wish other parts of our application to use. The pattern uses an immediately invoked function expression (IIFE) (*https://oreil.ly/5gef1*) where an object is returned. See Chapter 11 for more on IIFEs.

Note that there isn't an explicitly true sense of "privacy" inside JavaScript because it doesn't have access modifiers, unlike some traditional languages. You can't technically declare variables as public or private, so we use function scope to simulate this concept. Within the Module pattern, variables or methods declared are available only inside the module itself, thanks to closure. However, variables or methods defined within the returning object are available to everyone.

A workaround to implement privacy of variables in returned objects uses `WeakMap()` (*https://oreil.ly/SmKvK*) discussed later in this chapter in "Modern Module Pattern with WeakMap" on page 48. `WeakMap()` takes only objects as keys and cannot be iterated. Thus, the only way to access the object inside a module is through its reference. Outside the module, you can access it only through a public method defined within it. Thus, it ensures privacy for the object.

History

From a historical perspective, the Module pattern was originally developed in 2003 by several people, including Richard Cornford (*https://oreil.ly/YTZeM*). Douglas Crockford later popularized it in his lectures. Another piece of trivia is that some of its features may appear quite familiar if you've ever played with Yahoo's YUI library. The reason for this is that the Module pattern was a strong influence on YUI when its components were created.

Examples

Let's begin looking at implementing the Module pattern by creating a self-contained module. We use the `import` and `export` keywords in our implementation. To recap our previous discussion, `export` allows you to provide access to module features outside the module. At the same time, `import` enables us to import bindings exported by a module to our script:

```
let counter = 0;

const testModule = {
  incrementCounter() {
    return counter++;
  },
  resetCounter() {
    console.log(`counter value prior to reset: ${counter}`);
    counter = 0;
  },
};

// Default export module, without name
export default testModule;
```

```
// Usage:

// Import module from path
import testModule from './testModule';

// Increment our counter
testModule.incrementCounter();

// Check the counter value and reset
// Outputs: counter value prior to reset: 1
testModule.resetCounter();
```

Here, the other parts of the code cannot directly read the value of our `incrementCounter()` or `resetCounter()`. The `counter` variable is entirely shielded from our global scope, so it acts just like a private variable would—its existence is limited to within the module's closure so that the two functions are the only code able to access its scope. Our methods are effectively namespaced, so in the test section of our code, we need to prefix any calls with the module's name (e.g., `testModule`).

When working with the Module pattern, we may find it helpful to define a simple template we can use to get started with it. Here's one that covers namespacing, public, and private variables:

```
// A private counter variable
let myPrivateVar = 0;

// A private function that logs any arguments
const myPrivateMethod = foo => {
  console.log(foo);
};

const myNamespace = {
  // A public variable
  myPublicVar: 'foo',

  // A public function utilizing privates
  myPublicFunction(bar) {
    // Increment our private counter
    myPrivateVar++;

    // Call our private method using bar
    myPrivateMethod(bar);
  },
};

export default myNamespace;
```

What follows is another example, where we can see a shopping basket implemented using this pattern. The module itself is completely self-contained in a global variable called `basketModule`. The basket array in the module is kept private, so other parts

---

of our application cannot directly read it. It exists only within the module's closure, and so the only methods able to access it are those with access to its scope (i.e., addItem(), getItem(), etc.):

```
// privates

const basket = [];

const doSomethingPrivate = () => {
  //...
};

const doSomethingElsePrivate = () => {
  //...
};

// Create an object exposed to the public
const basketModule = {
  // Add items to our basket
  addItem(values) {
    basket.push(values);
  },

  // Get the count of items in the basket
  getItemCount() {
    return basket.length;
  },

  // Public alias to a private function
  doSomething() {
    doSomethingPrivate();
  },

  // Get the total value of items in the basket
  // The reduce() method applies a function against an accumulator and each
  // element in the array (from left to right) to reduce it to a single value.
  getTotal() {
    return basket.reduce((currentSum, item) => item.price + currentSum, 0);
  },
};

export default basketModule;
```

Inside the module, you may have noticed that we return an object. This gets automatically assigned to basketModule so that we can interact with it as follows:

```
// Import module from path
import basketModule from './basketModule';

// basketModule returns an object with a public API we can use

basketModule.addItem({
```

```
  item: 'bread',
  price: 0.5,
});

basketModule.addItem({
  item: 'butter',
  price: 0.3,
});

// Outputs: 2
console.log(basketModule.getItemCount());

// Outputs: 0.8
console.log(basketModule.getTotal());

// However, the following will not work:

// Outputs: undefined
// This is because the basket itself is not exposed as a part of our
// public API
console.log(basketModule.basket);

// This also won't work as it exists only within the scope of our
// basketModule closure, not in the returned public object
console.log(basket);
```

These methods are effectively namespaced inside `basketModule`. All our functions are wrapped in this module, giving us several advantages, such as:

- The freedom to have private functions that can be consumed only by our module. They aren't exposed to the rest of the page (only our exported API is), so they're considered truly private.

- Given that functions are usually declared and named, it can be easier to show call stacks in a debugger when we're attempting to discover what function(s) threw an exception.

Module Pattern Variations

Over time, designers have introduced different variations of the Module pattern suited to their needs.

Import Mixins

This pattern variation demonstrates how you can pass globals (e.g., utility functions or external libraries) as arguments to a higher-order function in a module. This effectively allows us to import and locally alias them as we wish:

```
// utils.js
export const min = (arr) => Math.min(...arr);

// privateMethods.js
import { min } from "./utils";

export const privateMethod = () => {
  console.log(min([10, 5, 100, 2, 1000]));
};

// myModule.js
import { privateMethod } from "./privateMethods";

const myModule = () => ({
  publicMethod() {
    privateMethod();
  },
});

export default myModule;

// main.js
import myModule from "./myModule";

const moduleInstance = myModule();
moduleInstance.publicMethod();
```

Exports

This next variation allows us to declare globals without consuming them and could similarly support the concept of global imports seen in the last example:

```
// module.js
const privateVariable = "Hello World";

const privateMethod = () => {
  // ...
};

const module = {
  publicProperty: "Foobar",
  publicMethod: () => {
    console.log(privateVariable);
  },
};

export default module;
```

Advantages

We've seen why the Constructor pattern can be useful, but why is the Module pattern a good choice? For starters, it's a lot cleaner for developers coming from an object-oriented background than the idea of true encapsulation, at least from a JavaScript perspective. With import Mixins, developers can manage dependencies between modules and pass globals as needed, making the code more maintainable and modular.

Secondly, it supports private data—so, in the Module pattern, we have access to only the values that we explicitly exported using the export keyword. Values we didn't expressly export are private and available only within the module. This reduces the risk of accidentally polluting the global scope. You don't have to fear that you will accidentally overwrite values created by developers using your module that may have had the same name as your private value: it prevents naming collisions and global scope pollution.

With the Module pattern, we can encapsulate parts of our code that should not be publicly exposed. They make working with multiple dependencies and namespaces less risky. Note that a transpiler such as Babel is needed to use ES2015 modules in all JavaScript runtimes.

Disadvantages

The disadvantages of the Module pattern are that we access both public and private members differently. When we wish to change the visibility, we must make changes to each place we use the member.

We also can't access private members in methods we added to the object later. That said, in many cases, the Module pattern is still quite helpful and, when used correctly, certainly has the potential to improve the structure of our application.

Other disadvantages include the inability to create automated unit tests for private members and additional complexity when bugs require hot fixes. It's simply not possible to patch privates. Instead, one must override all public methods interacting with the buggy privates. Developers can't easily extend privates either, so it's worth remembering that privates are not as flexible as they may initially appear.

For further reading on the Module pattern, see Ben Cherry's excellent in-depth article (*https://oreil.ly/wfX1y*).

Modern Module Pattern with WeakMap

Introduced to JavaScript in ES6, the WeakMap (*https://oreil.ly/SmKvK*) object is a collection of key-value pairs in which the keys are weakly referenced. The keys must be objects, and the values can be arbitrary. The object is essentially a map where keys are held weakly. This means that keys will be a target for garbage collection (GC) if there is no active reference to the object. Examples 7-1, 7-2, and 7-3 look at an implementation of the Module pattern that uses the WeakMap object.

Example 7-1. Basic module definition

```
let _counter = new WeakMap();

class Module {
    constructor() {
        _counter.set(this, 0);
    }
    incrementCounter() {
        let counter = _counter.get(this);
        counter++;
        _counter.set(this, counter);

        return _counter.get(this);
    }
    resetCounter() {
        console.log(`counter value prior to reset: ${_counter.get(this)}`);
        _counter.set(this, 0);
    }
}

const testModule = new Module();

// Usage:

// Increment our counter
testModule.incrementCounter();
// Check the counter value and reset
// Outputs: counter value prior to reset: 1
testModule.resetCounter();
```

Example 7-2. Namespaces with public/private variables

```
const myPrivateVar = new WeakMap();
const myPrivateMethod = new WeakMap();

class MyNamespace {
    constructor() {
        // A private counter variable
        myPrivateVar.set(this, 0);
        // A private function that logs any arguments
        myPrivateMethod.set(this, foo => console.log(foo));
        // A public variable
        this.myPublicVar = 'foo';
    }
    // A public function utilizing privates
    myPublicFunction(bar) {
        let privateVar = myPrivateVar.get(this);
        const privateMethod = myPrivateMethod.get(this);
        // Increment our private counter
        privateVar++;
        myPrivateVar.set(this, privateVar);
```

```
        // Call our private method using bar
        privateMethod(bar);
    }
}
```

Example 7-3. Shopping basket implementation

```
const basket = new WeakMap();
const doSomethingPrivate = new WeakMap();
const doSomethingElsePrivate = new WeakMap();

class BasketModule {
    constructor() {
        // privates
        basket.set(this, []);
        doSomethingPrivate.set(this, () => {
            //...
        });
        doSomethingElsePrivate.set(this, () => {
            //...
        });
    }
    // Public aliases to a private function
    doSomething() {
        doSomethingPrivate.get(this)();
    }
    doSomethingElse() {
        doSomethingElsePrivate.get(this)();
    }
    // Add items to our basket
    addItem(values) {
        const basketData = basket.get(this);
        basketData.push(values);
        basket.set(this, basketData);
    }
    // Get the count of items in the basket
    getItemCount() {
        return basket.get(this).length;
    }
    // Get the total value of items in the basket
    getTotal() {
        return basket
            .get(this)
            .reduce((currentSum, item) => item.price + currentSum, 0);
    }
}
```

Modules with Modern Libraries

You can use the Module pattern when building applications with JavaScript libraries such as React. Let's say you have a large number of custom components created by your team. In that case, you can separate each component in its own file, essentially creating a module for every component. Here is an example of a button component customized from the *material-ui (https://oreil.ly/77tjD)* button component and exported as a module:

```
import React from "react";
import Button from "@material-ui/core/Button";

const style = {
  root: {
    borderRadius: 3,
    border: 0,
    color: "white",
    margin: "0 20px"
  },
  primary: {
    background: "linear-gradient(45deg, #FE6B8B 30%, #FF8E53 90%)"
  },
  secondary: {
    background: "linear-gradient(45deg, #2196f3 30%, #21cbf3 90%)"
  }
};

export default function CustomButton(props) {
  return (
    <Button {...props} style={{ ...style.root, ...style[props.color] }}>
      {props.children}
    </Button>
  );
}
```

The Revealing Module Pattern

Now that we are a little more familiar with the Module pattern, let's look at a slightly improved version: Christian Heilmann's Revealing Module pattern.

The Revealing Module pattern came about as Heilmann was frustrated that he had to repeat the name of the main object when he wanted to call one public method from another or access public variables. He also disliked switching to object literal notation for the things he wished to make public.

His efforts resulted in an updated pattern where we can simply define all functions and variables in the private scope and return an anonymous object with pointers to the private functionality we wished to reveal as public.

With the modern way of implementing modules (*https://oreil.ly/eMYvs*) in ES2015+, the scope of functions and variables defined in the module is already private. Also, we use `export` and `import` to reveal whatever needs to be revealed.

An example of the use of the Revealing Module pattern with ES2015+ is as follows:

```
let privateVar = 'Rob Dodson';
const publicVar = 'Hey there!';

const privateFunction = () => {
  console.log(`Name:${privateVar}`);
};

const publicSetName = strName => {
  privateVar = strName;
};

const publicGetName = () => {
  privateFunction();
};

// Reveal public pointers to
// private functions and properties
const myRevealingModule = {
  setName: publicSetName,
  greeting: publicVar,
  getName: publicGetName,
};

export default myRevealingModule;

// Usage:
import myRevealingModule from './myRevealingModule';

myRevealingModule.setName('Matt Gaunt');
```

In this example, we reveal the private variable `privateVar` through its public get and set methods, `publicSetName` and `publicGetName`.

You can also use the pattern to reveal private functions and properties with a more specific naming scheme:

```
let privateCounter = 0;

const privateFunction = () => {
    privateCounter++;
}

const publicFunction = () => {
    publicIncrement();
}

const publicIncrement = () => {
    privateFunction();
}

const publicGetCount = () => privateCounter;

// Reveal public pointers to
```

```
// private functions and properties
const myRevealingModule = {
    start: publicFunction,
    increment: publicIncrement,
    count: publicGetCount
};

export default myRevealingModule;

// Usage:
import myRevealingModule from './myRevealingModule';

myRevealingModule.start();
```

Advantages

This pattern allows the syntax of our scripts to be more consistent. It also makes it easier to understand at the end of the module which of our functions and variables may be accessed publicly, which eases readability.

Disadvantages

A disadvantage of this pattern is that if a private function refers to a public function, that public function can't be overridden if a patch is necessary. This is because the private function will continue to refer to the private implementation, and the pattern doesn't apply to public members, only to functions.

Public object members, which refer to private variables, are also subject to the no-patch rule.

As a result, modules created with the Revealing Module pattern may be more fragile than those created with the original Module pattern, and you should take care when using it.

The Singleton Pattern

The Singleton pattern is a design pattern that restricts the instantiation of a class to one object. This is useful when exactly one object is needed to coordinate actions across the system. Classically, you can implement the Singleton pattern by creating a class with a method that creates a new instance of the class only if one doesn't already exist. If an instance already exists, it simply returns a reference to that object.

Singletons differ from static classes (or objects) in that we can delay their initialization because they require certain information that may not be available during initialization time. Any code that is unaware of a previous reference to the Singleton class cannot easily retrieve it. This is because it is neither the object nor "class" that a

Singleton returns; it's a structure. Think of how closured variables aren't actually closures—the function scope that provides the closure is the closure.

ES2015+ allows us to implement the Singleton pattern to create a global instance of a JavaScript class that is instantiated once. You can expose the Singleton instance through a module export. This makes access to it more explicit and controlled and differentiates it from other global variables. You cannot create a new class instance but can read/modify the instance using public get and set methods defined in the class.

We can implement a Singleton as follows:

```javascript
// Instance stores a reference to the Singleton
let instance;

// Private methods and variables
const privateMethod = () => {
    console.log('I am private');
  };
const privateVariable = 'Im also private';
const randomNumber = Math.random();

// Singleton
class MySingleton {
  // Get the Singleton instance if one exists
  // or create one if it doesn't
  constructor() {
    if (!instance) {
      // Public property
      this.publicProperty = 'I am also public';
      instance = this;
    }

    return instance;
  }

  // Public methods
  publicMethod() {
    console.log('The public can see me!');
  }

  getRandomNumber() {
    return randomNumber;
  }
}
// [ES2015+] Default export module, without name
export default MySingleton;


// Instance stores a reference to the Singleton
let instance;
```

```
// Singleton
class MyBadSingleton {
    // Always create a new Singleton instance
    constructor() {
        this.randomNumber = Math.random();
        instance = this;

        return instance;
    }

    getRandomNumber() {
        return this.randomNumber;
    }
}

export default MyBadSingleton;


// Usage:
import MySingleton from './MySingleton';
import MyBadSingleton from './MyBadSingleton';

const singleA = new MySingleton();
const singleB = new MySingleton();
console.log(singleA.getRandomNumber() === singleB.getRandomNumber());
// true

const badSingleA = new MyBadSingleton();
const badSingleB = new MyBadSingleton();
console.log(badSingleA.getRandomNumber() !== badSingleB.getRandomNumber());
// true

// Note: as we are working with random numbers, there is a mathematical
// possibility both numbers will be the same, however unlikely.
// The preceding example should otherwise still be valid.
```

What makes the Singleton is the global access to the instance. The GoF book describes the *applicability* of the Singleton pattern as follows:

- There must be exactly one instance of a class, and it must be accessible to clients from a well-known access point.

- The sole instance should be extensible by subclassing, and clients should be able to use an extended instance without modifying their code.

The second of these points refers to a case where we might need code, such as:

```
constructor() {
    if (this._instance == null) {
        if (isFoo()) {
            this._instance = new FooSingleton();
```

```
        } else {
            this._instance = new BasicSingleton();
        }
    }

    return this._instance;
}
```

Here, the `constructor` becomes a little like a Factory method, and we don't need to update each point in our code accessing it. `FooSingleton` (in this example) would be a subclass of `BasicSingleton` and implement the same interface.

Why is deferring execution considered significant for a Singleton? In C++, it serves as isolation from the unpredictability of the dynamic initialization order, returning control to the programmer.

It is essential to note the difference between a static instance of a class (object) and a Singleton. While you can implement a Singleton as a static instance, it can also be constructed lazily, without the need for resources or memory until it is needed.

Suppose we have a static object that we can initialize directly. In that case, we need to ensure the code is always executed in the same order (e.g., in case `objCar` needs `objWheel` during its initialization), and this doesn't scale when you have a large number of source files.

Both Singletons and static objects are useful but shouldn't be overused—the same way we shouldn't overuse other patterns.

In practice, it helps to use the Singleton pattern when exactly one object is needed to coordinate others across a system. The following is one example that uses the pattern in this context:

```javascript
// options: an object containing configuration options for the Singleton
// e.g., const options = { name: "test", pointX: 5};
class Singleton {
    constructor(options = {}) {
        // set some properties for our Singleton
        this.name = 'SingletonTester';
        this.pointX = options.pointX || 6;
        this.pointY = options.pointY || 10;
    }
}

// our instance holder
let instance;

// an emulation of static variables and methods
const SingletonTester = {
    name: 'SingletonTester',
    // Method for getting an instance. It returns
    // a Singleton instance of a Singleton object
```

```
    getInstance(options) {
      if (instance === undefined) {
        instance = new Singleton(options);
      }

      return instance;
    },
  };

  const singletonTest = SingletonTester.getInstance({
    pointX: 5,
  });

  // Log the output of pointX just to verify it is correct
  // Outputs: 5
  console.log(singletonTest.pointX);
```

While the Singleton has valid uses, often, when we find ourselves needing it in JavaScript, it's a sign that we may need to reevaluate our design. Unlike C++ or Java, where you have to define a class to create an object, JavaScript allows you to create objects directly. Thus, you can create one such object directly instead of defining a Singleton class. In contrast, using Singleton classes in JavaScript has some disadvantages:

Identifying Singletons can be difficult.
> If you're importing a large module, you will be unable to recognize that a particular class is a Singleton. As a result, you may accidentally use it as a regular class to instantiate multiple objects and incorrectly update it instead.

Challenging to test.
> Singletons can be more difficult to test due to issues ranging from hidden dependencies, difficulty creating multiple instances, difficulty in stubbing dependencies, and so on.

Need for careful orchestration.
> An everyday use case for Singletons would be to store data that will be required across the global scope, such as user credentials or cookie data that can be set once and consumed by multiple components. Implementing the correct execution order becomes essential so that data is always consumed after it becomes available and not the other way around. This may become challenging as the application grows in size and complexity.

State Management in React

Developers using React for web development can rely on the global state through state management tools such as Redux or React Context instead of Singletons. Unlike Singletons, these tools provide a read-only state rather than the mutable state.

Although the downsides to having a global state don't magically disappear by using these tools, we can at least ensure that the global state is mutated the way we intend it to because components cannot update it directly.

The Prototype Pattern

The GoF refers to the Prototype pattern as one that creates objects based on a template of an existing object through cloning.

We can think of the Prototype pattern as being based on prototypal inheritance, where we create objects that act as prototypes for other objects. The prototype object is effectively used as a blueprint for each object the constructor creates. For example, if the prototype of the constructor function used contains a property called name (as per the code sample that follows), then each object created by that constructor will also have this same property. Refer to Figure 7-3 for an illustration.

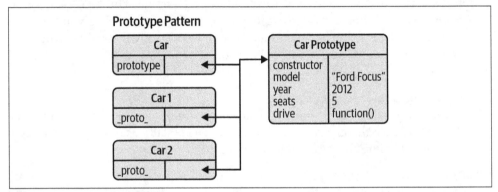

Figure 7-3. Prototype pattern

Reviewing the definitions for this pattern in existing (non-JavaScript) literature, we *may* find references to classes once again. The reality is that prototypal inheritance avoids using classes altogether. There isn't a "definition" object nor a core object in theory; we're simply creating copies of existing functional objects.

One of the benefits of using the Prototype pattern is that we're working with the prototypal strengths JavaScript has to offer natively rather than attempting to imitate features of other languages. With other design patterns, this isn't always the case.

Not only is the pattern an easy way to implement inheritance, but it can also come with a performance boost. When defining functions in an object, they're all created by reference (so all child objects point to the same functions), instead of creating individual copies.

With ES2015+, we can use classes and constructors to create objects. While this ensures that our code looks cleaner and follows object-oriented analysis and design

(OOAD) principles, the classes and constructors get compiled down to functions and prototypes internally. This ensures that we are still working with the prototypal strengths of JavaScript and the accompanying performance boost.

For those interested, real prototypal inheritance, as defined in the ECMAScript 5 standard, requires the use of `Object.create` (which we looked at earlier in this section). To review, `Object.create` creates an object with a specified prototype and optionally contains specified properties (e.g., `Object.create( prototype, optionalDescriptorObjects )`).

We can see this demonstrated in the following example:

```
const myCar = {
    name: 'Ford Escort',

    drive() {
        console.log("Weeee. I'm driving!");
    },

    panic() {
        console.log('Wait. How do you stop this thing?');
    },
};

// Use Object.create to instantiate a new car
const yourCar = Object.create(myCar);

// Now we can see that one is a prototype of the other
console.log(yourCar.name);
```

`Object.create` also allows us to easily implement advanced concepts such as differential inheritance, where objects are able to directly inherit from other objects. We saw earlier that `Object.create` allows us to initialize object properties using the second supplied argument. For example:

```
const vehicle = {
    getModel() {
        console.log(`The model of this vehicle is...${this.model}`);
    },
};

const car = Object.create(vehicle, {
    id: {
        value: MY_GLOBAL.nextId(),
        // writable:false, configurable:false by default
        enumerable: true,
    },

    model: {
        value: 'Ford',
        enumerable: true,
```

```
    },
  });
```

Here, you can initialize the properties on the second argument of `Object.create` using an object literal with a syntax similar to that used by the `Object.defineProperties` and `Object.defineProperty` methods that we looked at previously.

It is worth noting that prototypal relationships can cause trouble when enumerating properties of objects and (as Crockford recommends) wrapping the contents of the loop in a `hasOwnProperty()` check.

If we wish to implement the Prototype pattern without directly using `Object.create`, we can simulate the pattern as per the previous example as follows:

```
class VehiclePrototype {
  constructor(model) {
    this.model = model;
  }

  getModel() {
    console.log(`The model of this vehicle is... ${this.model}`);
  }

  clone() {}
}

class Vehicle extends VehiclePrototype {
  constructor(model) {
    super(model);
  }

  clone() {
    return new Vehicle(this.model);
  }
}

const car = new Vehicle('Ford Escort');
const car2 = car.clone();
car2.getModel();
```

 This alternative does not allow the user to define read-only properties in the same manner (as the `vehiclePrototype` may be altered if not careful).

A final alternative implementation of the Prototype pattern could be the following:

```
const beget = (() => {
  class F {
```

```
        constructor() {}
    }

    return proto => {
        F.prototype = proto;
        return new F();
    };
})();
```

One could reference this method from the `vehicle` function. However, note that `vehicle` here emulates a constructor since the Prototype pattern does not include any notion of initialization beyond linking an object to a prototype.

The Factory Pattern

The Factory pattern is another creational pattern for creating objects. It differs from the other patterns in its category because it doesn't explicitly require us to use a constructor. Instead, a Factory can provide a generic interface for creating objects, where we can specify the type of Factory object we want to create (Figure 7-4).

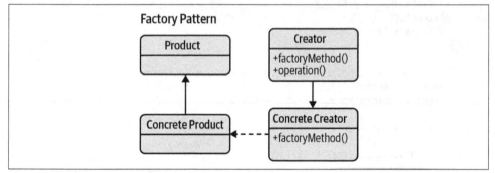

Figure 7-4. Factory pattern

Imagine a UI factory where we want to create a type of UI component. Rather than creating this component directly using the new operator or another creational constructor, we ask a Factory object for a new component instead. We inform the Factory what type of object is required (e.g., "Button", "Panel"), and it instantiates it and returns it to us for use.

This is particularly useful if the object creation process is relatively complex, e.g., if it strongly depends on dynamic factors or application configuration.

The following example builds upon our previous snippets using the Constructor pattern logic to define cars. It demonstrates how a `VehicleFactory` may be implemented using the Factory pattern:

```javascript
// Types.js - Classes used behind the scenes
// A class for defining new cars
class Car {
  constructor({ doors = 4, state = 'brand new', color = 'silver' } = {}) {
    this.doors = doors;
    this.state = state;
    this.color = color;
  }
}

// A class for defining new trucks
class Truck {
  constructor({ state = 'used', wheelSize = 'large', color = 'blue' } = {}) {
    this.state = state;
    this.wheelSize = wheelSize;
    this.color = color;
  }
}

// FactoryExample.js
// Define a vehicle factory
class VehicleFactory {
  constructor() {
    this.vehicleClass = Car;
  }

  // Our Factory method for creating new Vehicle instances
  createVehicle(options) {
    const { vehicleType, ...rest } = options;

    switch (vehicleType) {
      case 'car':
        this.vehicleClass = Car;
        break;
      case 'truck':
        this.vehicleClass = Truck;
        break;
      // defaults to VehicleFactory.prototype.vehicleClass (Car)
    }

    return new this.vehicleClass(rest);
  }
}

// Create an instance of our factory that makes cars
const carFactory = new VehicleFactory();
const car = carFactory.createVehicle({
  vehicleType: 'car',
  color: 'yellow',
  doors: 6,
});
```

```
// Test to confirm our car was created using the vehicleClass/prototype Car
// Outputs: true
console.log(car instanceof Car);
// Outputs: Car object of color "yellow", doors: 6 in a "brand new" state
console.log(car);
```

We have defined the car and truck classes with constructors that set properties relevant to the respective vehicle. The VehicleFactory can create a new vehicle object, Car, or Truck based on the vehicleType passed.

There are two possible approaches to building trucks using the VehicleFactory class.

In Approach 1, we modify a VehicleFactory instance to use the Truck class:

```
const movingTruck = carFactory.createVehicle({
    vehicleType: 'truck',
    state: 'like new',
    color: 'red',
    wheelSize: 'small',
});

// Test to confirm our truck was created with the vehicleClass/prototype Truck

// Outputs: true
console.log(movingTruck instanceof Truck);

// Outputs: Truck object of color "red", a "like new" state
// and a "small" wheelSize
console.log(movingTruck);
```

In Approach 2, we subclass VehicleFactory to create a factory class that builds Trucks:

```
class TruckFactory extends VehicleFactory {
    constructor() {
        super();
        this.vehicleClass = Truck;
    }
}
const truckFactory = new TruckFactory();
const myBigTruck = truckFactory.createVehicle({
    state: 'omg...so bad.',
    color: 'pink',
    wheelSize: 'so big',
});

// Confirms that myBigTruck was created with the prototype Truck
// Outputs: true
console.log(myBigTruck instanceof Truck);

// Outputs: Truck object with the color "pink", wheelSize "so big"
// and state "omg. so bad"
console.log(myBigTruck);
```

When to Use the Factory Pattern

The Factory pattern can be beneficial when applied to the following situations:

- When our object or component setup involves a high level of complexity.

- When we need a convenient way to generate different instances of objects depending on the environment we are in.

- When we're working with many small objects or components that share the same properties.

- When composing objects with instances of other objects that need only satisfy an API contract (aka, duck typing) to work. This is useful for decoupling.

When Not to Use the Factory Pattern

When applied to the wrong type of problem, this pattern can introduce a large amount of unnecessary complexity to an application. Unless providing an interface for object creation is a design goal for the library or framework we are writing, I would suggest sticking to explicit constructors to avoid undue overhead.

Since the process of object creation is effectively abstracted behind an interface, this can also introduce problems with unit testing, depending on just how complex this process might be.

Abstract Factories

It's also worthwhile to be aware of the Abstract Factory pattern, which aims to encapsulate a group of individual factories with a common goal. It separates the details of implementing a set of objects from their general usage.

You can use an Abstract Factory when a system must be independent of how the objects it creates are generated, or it needs to work with multiple types of objects.

An example that is both simple and easier to understand is a vehicle factory, which defines ways to get or register vehicle types. The Abstract Factory can be named `AbstractVehicleFactory`. The Abstract Factory will allow the definition of types of vehicles like `car` or `truck`, and concrete factories will implement only classes that fulfill the vehicle contract (e.g., `Vehicle.prototype.drive` and `Vehicle.prototype.breakDown`):

```
class AbstractVehicleFactory {
  constructor() {
    // Storage for our vehicle types
    this.types = {};
  }

  getVehicle(type, customizations) {
```

```
    const Vehicle = this.types[type];
    return Vehicle ? new Vehicle(customizations) : null;
  }

  registerVehicle(type, Vehicle) {
    const proto = Vehicle.prototype;
    // only register classes that fulfill the vehicle contract
    if (proto.drive && proto.breakDown) {
      this.types[type] = Vehicle;
    }
    return this;
  }
}

// Usage:
const abstractVehicleFactory = new AbstractVehicleFactory();
abstractVehicleFactory.registerVehicle('car', Car);
abstractVehicleFactory.registerVehicle('truck', Truck);

// Instantiate a new car based on the abstract vehicle type
const car = abstractVehicleFactory.getVehicle('car', {
  color: 'lime green',
  state: 'like new',
});

// Instantiate a new truck in a similar manner
const truck = abstractVehicleFactory.getVehicle('truck', {
  wheelSize: 'medium',
  color: 'neon yellow',
});
```

Structural Patterns

Structural patterns deal with class and object composition. For example, the concept of inheritance allows us to compose interfaces and objects so that they can obtain new functionality. Structural patterns provide the best methods and practices to organize classes and objects.

Following are the JavaScript structural patterns that we will discuss in this section:

- "The Facade Pattern" on page 66
- "The Mixin Pattern" on page 68
- "The Decorator Pattern" on page 73
- "Flyweight" on page 82

The Facade Pattern

When we put up a facade, we present an outward appearance to the world, which may conceal a very different reality. This inspired the name for the next pattern we'll review—the Facade pattern. This pattern provides a convenient higher-level interface to a larger body of code, hiding its true underlying complexity. Think of it as simplifying the API being presented to other developers, a quality that almost always improves usability (see Figure 7-5).

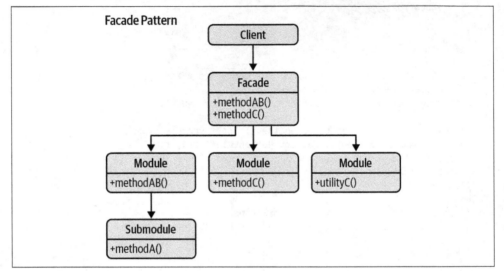

Figure 7-5. Facade pattern

Facades are a structural pattern that can often be seen in JavaScript libraries such as jQuery where, although an implementation may support methods with a wide range of behaviors, only a "facade," or limited abstraction of these methods, is presented to the public for use.

This allows us to interact with the Facade directly rather than the subsystem behind the scenes. Whenever we use jQuery's `$(el).css()` or `$(el).animate()` methods, we're using a Facade: the simpler public interface that lets us avoid manually calling the many internal methods in jQuery core required to get some behavior working. This also circumvents the need to interact manually with DOM APIs and maintain state variables.

The jQuery core methods should be considered intermediate abstractions. The more immediate burden to developers is that the DOM API and Facades make the jQuery library so easy to use.

To build on what we've learned, the Facade pattern simplifies a class's interface and decouples the class from the code that uses it. This allows us to interact indirectly with subsystems in a way that can sometimes be less error-prone than accessing the subsystem directly. A Facade's advantages include ease of use and often a small-sized footprint in implementing the pattern.

Let's take a look at the pattern in action. This is an unoptimized code example, but here we're using a Facade to simplify an interface for listening to events across browsers. We do this by creating a common method that does the task of checking for the existence of features so that it can provide a safe and cross-browser-compatible solution:

```javascript
const addMyEvent = (el, ev, fn) => {
    if (el.addEventListener) {
      el.addEventListener(ev, fn, false);
    } else if (el.attachEvent) {
      el.attachEvent(`on${ev}`, fn);
    } else {
      el[`on${ev}`] = fn;
    }
};
```

In a similar manner, we're all familiar with jQuery's `$(document).ready(…)`. Internally, this is powered by a method called `bindReady()`, which is doing this:

```javascript
function bindReady() {
    // Use the handy event callback
    document.addEventListener('DOMContentLoaded', DOMContentLoaded, false);
    // A fallback to window.onload, that will always work
    window.addEventListener('load', jQuery.ready, false);
}
```

This is another example of a Facade where the rest of the world uses the limited interface exposed by `$(document).ready(…)`, and the more complex implementation powering it is kept hidden from sight.

Facades don't just have to be used on their own, however. You can also integrate them with other patterns, such as the Module pattern. As we can see next, our instance of the Module pattern contains a number of methods that have been privately defined. A Facade is then used to supply a much simpler API for accessing these methods:

```javascript
// privateMethods.js
const _private = {
  i: 5,
  get() {
    console.log(`current value: ${this.i}`);
  },
  set(val) {
    this.i = val;
  },
  run() {
    console.log('running');
```

```
    },
    jump() {
      console.log('jumping');
    },
  };

  export default _private;

  // module.js
  import _private from './privateMethods.js';

  const module = {
    facade({ val, run }) {
      _private.set(val);
      _private.get();
      if (run) {
        _private.run();
      }
    },
  };

  export default module;

  // index.js
  import module from './module.js';

  // Outputs: "current value: 10" and "running"
  module.facade({
    run: true,
    val: 10,
  });
```

In this example, calling `module.facade()` will trigger a set of private behavior within the module, but the users aren't concerned with this. We've made it much easier for them to consume a feature without worrying about implementation-level details.

The Mixin Pattern

In traditional programming languages such as C++ and Lisp, Mixins are classes that offer functionality that a subclass or group of subclasses can easily inherit for function reuse.

Subclassing

We have already introduced the ES2015+ features that allow us to extend a base or superclass and call the methods in the superclass. The child class that extends the superclass is known as a subclass.

Subclassing refers to inheriting properties for a new object from a base or superclass object. A subclass can still define its methods, including those that override methods initially defined in the superclass. The method in the subclass can invoke an overridden method in the superclass, known as method chaining. Similarly, it can invoke the superclass's constructor, which is known as constructor chaining.

To demonstrate subclassing, we first need a base class that can have new instances of itself created. Let's model this around the concept of a person:

```
class Person{
    constructor(firstName, lastName) {
        this.firstName = firstName;
        this.lastName = lastName;
        this.gender = "male";
    }
}
// a new instance of Person can then easily be created as follows:
const clark = new Person( 'Clark', 'Kent' );
```

Next, we'll want to specify a new class that's a subclass of the existing Person class. Let us imagine we want to add distinct properties to distinguish a Person from a Superhero while inheriting the properties of the Person superclass. As superheroes share many common traits with ordinary people (e.g., name, gender), this should ideally adequately illustrate how subclassing works:

```
class Superhero extends Person {
    constructor(firstName, lastName, powers) {
        // Invoke the superclass constructor
        super(firstName, lastName);
        this.powers = powers;
    }
}

// A new instance of Superhero can be created as follows

const SuperMan = new Superhero('Clark','Kent', ['flight','heat-vision']);
console.log(SuperMan);

// Outputs Person attributes as well as power
```

The Superhero constructor creates an instance of the Superhero class, which is an extension of the Person class. Objects of this type have attributes of the classes above it in the chain. If we had set default values in the Person class, Superhero could override any inherited values with values specific to its class.

Mixins

In JavaScript, we can look at inheriting from Mixins to collect functionality through extension. Each new class we define can have a superclass from which it can inherit methods and properties. Classes can also define their own properties and methods. We can leverage this fact to promote function reuse, as shown in Figure 7-6.

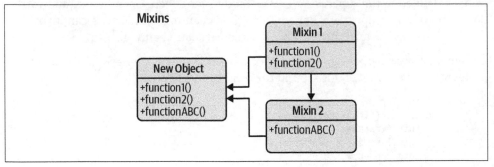

Figure 7-6. Mixins

Mixins allow objects to borrow (or inherit) functionality from them with minimal complexity. Thus, Mixins are classes with attributes and methods that can be easily shared across several other classes.

While JavaScript classes cannot inherit from multiple superclasses, we can still mix functionality from various classes. A class in JavaScript can be used as an expression as well as a statement. As an expression, it returns a new class each time it's evaluated. The extends clause can also accept arbitrary expressions that return classes or constructors. These features enable us to define a Mixin as a function that accepts a superclass and creates a new subclass from it.

Imagine that we define a Mixin containing utility functions in a standard JavaScript class as follows:

```
const MyMixins = superclass =>
    class extends superclass {
        moveUp() {
            console.log('move up');
        }
        moveDown() {
            console.log('move down');
        }
        stop() {
            console.log('stop! in the name of love!');
        }
    };
```

Here, we created a `MyMixins` function that can extend a dynamic superclass. We will now create two classes, `CarAnimator` and `PersonAnimator`, from which `MyMixins` can extend and return a subclass with methods defined in `MyMixins` and those in the class being extended:

```
// A skeleton carAnimator constructor
class CarAnimator {
    moveLeft() {
        console.log('move left');
    }
}
// A skeleton personAnimator constructor
class PersonAnimator {
    moveRandomly() {
        /*...*/
    }
}

// Extend MyMixins using CarAnimator
class MyAnimator extends MyMixins(CarAnimator) {}

// Create a new instance of carAnimator
const myAnimator = new MyAnimator();
myAnimator.moveLeft();
myAnimator.moveDown();
myAnimator.stop();

// Outputs:
// move left
// move down
// stop! in the name of love!
```

As we can see, this makes mixing similar behavior into classes reasonably trivial.

The following example has two classes: a `Car` and a `Mixin`. What we're going to do is augment (another way of saying extend) the `Car` so that it can inherit specific methods defined in the `Mixin`, namely `driveForward()` and `driveBackward()`.

This example will demonstrate how to augment a constructor to include functionality without the need to duplicate this process for every constructor function we may have:

```
// Car.js
class Car {
  constructor({ model = 'no model provided', color = 'no color provided' }) {
    this.model = model;
    this.color = color;
  }
}

export default Car;

// Mixin.js and index.js remain unchanged

// index.js
import Car from './Car.js';
import Mixin from './Mixin.js';
```

```
class MyCar extends Mixin(Car) {}

// Create a new Car
const myCar = new MyCar({});

// Test to make sure we now have access to the methods
myCar.driveForward();
myCar.driveBackward();

// Outputs:
// drive forward
// drive backward

const mySportsCar = new MyCar({
  model: 'Porsche',
  color: 'red',
});

mySportsCar.driveSideways();

// Outputs:
// drive sideways
```

Advantages and Disadvantages

Mixins assist in decreasing functional repetition and increasing function reuse in a system. Where an application is likely to require shared behavior across object instances, we can easily avoid duplication by maintaining this shared functionality in a Mixin and thus focusing on implementing only the functionality in our system, which is truly distinct.

That said, the downsides to Mixins are a little more debatable. Some developers feel that injecting functionality into a class or an object prototype is a bad idea as it leads to both prototype pollution and a level of uncertainty regarding the origin of our functions. In large systems, this may well be the case.

Even with React, Mixins were often used to add functionality to components before the introduction of ES6 classes. The React team discourages Mixins (*https://oreil.ly/RCMzS*) because it adds unnecessary complexity to a component, making it hard to maintain and reuse. The React team encouraged using higher-order components and Hooks instead (*https://oreil.ly/f1216*).

I would argue that solid documentation can assist in minimizing the amount of confusion regarding the source of mixed-in functions. Still, as with every pattern, we should be okay if we take care during implementation.

The Decorator Pattern

Decorators are a structural design pattern that aims to promote code reuse. Like Mixins, you can think of them as another viable alternative to object subclassing.

Classically, decorators offered the ability to add behavior to existing classes in a system dynamically. The idea was that the *decoration* itself wasn't essential to the base functionality of the class. Otherwise, we could bake it into the *superclass* itself.

We can use them to modify existing systems where we wish to add additional features to objects without heavily changing the underlying code that uses them. A common reason developers use them is that their applications may contain features requiring many distinct types of objects. Imagine defining hundreds of different object constructors for, say, a JavaScript game (see Figure 7-7).

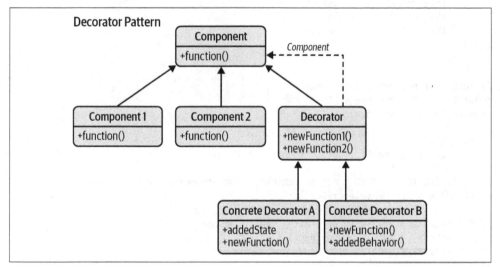

Figure 7-7. Decorator pattern

The object constructors could represent distinct player types, each with differing capabilities. A *Lord of the Rings* game could require constructors for Hobbit, Elf, Orc, Wizard, Mountain Giant, Stone Giant, and so on, but there could easily be hundreds of these. If we then factored in capabilities, imagine having to create subclasses for each combination of capability types, e.g., HobbitWithRing, HobbitWithSword, HobbitWithRingAndSword, and so on. This isn't practical and certainly isn't manageable when we factor in an increasing number of different abilities.

The Decorator pattern isn't heavily tied to how objects are created but instead focuses on the problem of extending their functionality. Rather than just relying on prototypal inheritance, we work with a single base class and progressively add decorator objects that provide additional capabilities. The idea is that rather than subclassing, we add (decorate) properties or methods to a base object, so it's a little more streamlined.

We can use JavaScript classes to create the base classes that can be decorated. Adding new attributes or methods to object instances of the class in JavaScript is a straightforward process. With this in mind, we can implement a simplistic decorator, as shown in Examples 7-4 and 7-5.

Example 7-4. Decorating constructors with new functionality

```
// A vehicle constructor
class Vehicle {
    constructor(vehicleType) {
        // some sane defaults
        this.vehicleType = vehicleType || 'car';
        this.model = 'default';
        this.license = '00000-000';
    }
}

// Test instance for a basic vehicle
const testInstance = new Vehicle('car');
console.log(testInstance);

// Outputs:
// vehicle: car, model:default, license: 00000-000

// Let's create a new instance of vehicle, to be decorated
const truck = new Vehicle('truck');

// New functionality we're decorating vehicle with
truck.setModel = function(modelName) {
    this.model = modelName;
};

truck.setColor = function(color) {
    this.color = color;
};

// Test the value setters and value assignment works correctly
truck.setModel('CAT');
truck.setColor('blue');

console.log(truck);

// Outputs:
// vehicle:truck, model:CAT, color: blue

// Demonstrate "vehicle" is still unaltered
const secondInstance = new Vehicle('car');
console.log(secondInstance);
```

```
// Outputs:
// vehicle: car, model:default, license: 00000-000
```

Here, `truck` is an instance of the class `Vehicle`, and we also decorate it with additional methods `setColor` and `setModel`.

This type of simplistic implementation is functional, but it doesn't demonstrate all the strengths that decorators offer. For this, we're going to go through my variation of the Coffee example from an excellent book called *Head First Design Patterns* by Freeman et al., which is modeled around a MacBook purchase.

Example 7-5. Decorating objects with multiple decorators

```
// The constructor to decorate
class MacBook {
    constructor() {
        this.cost = 997;
        this.screenSize = 11.6;
    }
    getCost() {
        return this.cost;
    }
    getScreenSize() {
        return this.screenSize;
    }
}

// Decorator 1
class Memory extends MacBook {
    constructor(macBook) {
        super();
        this.macBook = macBook;
    }

    getCost() {
        return this.macBook.getCost() + 75;
    }
}

// Decorator 2
class Engraving extends MacBook {
    constructor(macBook) {
        super();
        this.macBook = macBook;
    }

    getCost() {
        return this.macBook.getCost() + 200;
    }
}
```

```
// Decorator 3
class Insurance extends MacBook {
    constructor(macBook) {
        super();
        this.macBook = macBook;
    }

    getCost() {
        return this.macBook.getCost() + 250;
    }
}

// init main object
let mb = new MacBook();

// init decorators
mb = new Memory(mb);
mb = new Engraving(mb);
mb = new Insurance(mb);

// Outputs: 1522
console.log(mb.getCost());

// Outputs: 11.6
console.log(mb.getScreenSize());
```

In this example, our decorators are overriding the MacBook superclass object's .cost() function to return the current price of the MacBook plus the cost of the upgrade.

It's considered decoration because the original MacBook objects constructor methods that are not overridden (e.g., screenSize()), as well as any other properties we may define as a part of the MacBook, remain unchanged and intact.

There isn't a defined interface in the previous example. We're shifting away from the responsibility of ensuring an object meets an interface when moving from the creator to the receiver.

Pseudoclassical Decorators

We're now going to examine a variation of the Decorator first presented in a Java-Script form in *Pro JavaScript Design Patterns* (PJDP) by Dustin Diaz and Ross Harmes.

Unlike some of the previous examples, Diaz and Harmes stick more closely to how decorators are implemented in other programming languages (such as Java or C++) using the concept of an "interface," which we will define in more detail shortly.

This particular variation of the Decorator pattern is provided for reference purposes. If you find it overly complex, I recommend opting for one of the straightforward implementations covered earlier.

Interfaces

PJDP describes the Decorator pattern as one that is used to transparently wrap objects inside other objects of the same interface. An interface is a way of defining the methods an object *should* have. However, it doesn't directly specify how you should implement those methods. Interfaces can also optionally indicate what parameters the methods take.

So, why would we use an interface in JavaScript? The idea is that they're self-documenting and promote reusability. In theory, interfaces make code more stable by ensuring any change to the interface must also be propagated to the objects implementing them.

What follows is an example of an implementation of interfaces in JavaScript using duck-typing. This approach helps determine whether an object is an instance of a constructor/object based on the methods it implements:

```
// Create interfaces using a predefined Interface
// constructor that accepts an interface name and
// skeleton methods to expose.

// In our reminder example summary() and placeOrder()
// represent functionality the interface should
// support
const reminder = new Interface('List', ['summary', 'placeOrder']);

const properties = {
    name: 'Remember to buy the milk',
    date: '05/06/2040',
    actions: {
        summary() {
            return 'Remember to buy the milk, we are almost out!';
        },
        placeOrder() {
            return 'Ordering milk from your local grocery store';
        },
    },
};

// Now create a constructor implementing these properties
// and methods

class Todo {
    constructor({ actions, name }) {
```

```
    // State the methods we expect to be supported
    // as well as the Interface instance being checked
    // against

    Interface.ensureImplements(actions, reminder);

    this.name = name;
    this.methods = actions;
  }
}

// Create a new instance of our Todo constructor

const todoItem = new Todo(properties);

// Finally test to make sure these function correctly

console.log(todoItem.methods.summary());
console.log(todoItem.methods.placeOrder());

// Outputs:
// Remember to buy the milk, we are almost out!
// Ordering milk from your local grocery store
```

Both classic JavaScript and ES2015+ do not support interfaces. However, we can create our Interface class. In the previous example, `Interface.ensureImplements` provides strict functionality checking, and you can find code for both this and the `Interface` constructor (*https://oreil.ly/JbbLL*).

The main concern with interfaces is that JavaScript does not have built-in support for them, which may lead to attempts at emulating features from other languages that might not be an ideal fit. However, you can utilize TypeScript if you really need interfaces, as it provides built-in support for them. Lightweight interfaces can be used without a significant performance cost in JavaScript, and we will explore *abstract* decorators using this same concept in the following section.

Abstract Decorators

To demonstrate the structure of this version of the Decorator pattern, we're going to imagine we have a superclass that models a MacBook once again and a store that allows us to "decorate" our MacBook with a number of enhancements for an additional fee.

Enhancements can include upgrades to 4 GB or 8 GB of RAM (this can be much higher now, of course!), engraving, Parallels, or a case. Now, if we were to model this using an individual subclass for each combination of enhancement options, it might look something like this:

```
const MacBook = class {
    //...
};

const MacBookWith4GBRam = class {};
const MacBookWith8GBRam = class {};
const MacBookWith4GBRamAndEngraving = class {};
const MacBookWith8GBRamAndEngraving = class {};
const MacBookWith8GBRamAndParallels = class {};
const MacBookWith4GBRamAndParallels = class {};
const MacBookWith8GBRamAndParallelsAndCase = class {};
const MacBookWith4GBRamAndParallelsAndCase = class {};
const MacBookWith8GBRamAndParallelsAndCaseAndInsurance = class {};
const MacBookWith4GBRamAndParallelsAndCaseAndInsurance = class {};
```

...and so on.

This solution would be impractical because a new subclass would be required for every possible combination of enhancements that are available. As we would prefer to keep things simple, without maintaining a large set of subclasses, let's look at how we can use decorators to solve this problem better.

Rather than requiring all of the combinations we saw earlier, we will create only five new decorator classes. Methods called on these enhancement classes would be passed on to our MacBook class.

In the following example, decorators transparently wrap around their components and can be interchanged as they use the same interface. Here's the interface we're going to define for the MacBook:

```
const MacBook = new Interface('MacBook', [
    'addEngraving',
    'addParallels',
    'add4GBRam',
    'add8GBRam',
    'addCase',
]);

// A MacBook Pro might thus be represented as follows:
class MacBookPro {
    // implements MacBook
}

// ES2015+: We still could use Object.prototype for adding new methods,
// because internally we use the same structure

MacBookPro.prototype = {
    addEngraving() {},
    addParallels() {},
    add4GBRam() {},
    add8GBRam() {},
    addCase() {},
```

```
    getPrice() {
        // Base price
        return 900.0;
    },
};
```

To make it easier for us to add many more options as needed later on, an abstract decorator class is defined with default methods required to implement the MacBook interface, which the rest of the options will subclass. Abstract Decorators ensure that we can decorate a base class independently with as many decorators as needed in different combinations (remember the example earlier?) without needing to derive a class for every possible combination:

```
// MacBook decorator abstract decorator class

class MacBookDecorator {
    constructor(macbook) {
        Interface.ensureImplements(macbook, MacBook);
        this.macbook = macbook;
    }

    addEngraving() {
        return this.macbook.addEngraving();
    }

    addParallels() {
        return this.macbook.addParallels();
    }

    add4GBRam() {
        return this.macbook.add4GBRam();
    }

    add8GBRam() {
        return this.macbook.add8GBRam();
    }

    addCase() {
        return this.macbook.addCase();
    }

    getPrice() {
        return this.macbook.getPrice();
    }
}
```

In this sample, the MacBook Decorator accepts an object (a MacBook) to use as our base component. It uses the MacBook interface we defined earlier, and each method is just calling the same method on the component. We can now create our option classes for what can be added by using the MacBook Decorator:

```
// Let's now extend (decorate) the CaseDecorator
// with a MacBookDecorator

class CaseDecorator extends MacBookDecorator {
    constructor(macbook) {
        super(macbook);
    }

    addCase() {
        return `${this.macbook.addCase()}Adding case to macbook`;
    }

    getPrice() {
        return this.macbook.getPrice() + 45.0;
    }
}
```

We are overriding the addCase() and getPrice() methods that we want to decorate, and we're achieving this by first calling these methods on the original MacBook and then simply appending a string or numeric value (e.g., 45.00) to them accordingly.

As there's been quite a lot of information presented in this section so far, let's try to bring it all together in a single example that will hopefully highlight what we have learned:

```
// Instantiation of the macbook
const myMacBookPro = new MacBookPro();

// Outputs: 900.00
console.log(myMacBookPro.getPrice());

// Decorate the macbook
const decoratedMacBookPro = new CaseDecorator(myMacBookPro);

// This will return 945.00
console.log(decoratedMacBookPro.getPrice());
```

As decorators can modify objects dynamically, they're a perfect pattern for changing existing systems. Occasionally, it's just simpler to create decorators around an object instead of maintaining individual subclasses for each object type. This makes maintaining applications that may require many subclassed objects significantly more straightforward.

You can find a functional version of this example on JSBin (*https://oreil.ly/wNgs6*).

Advantages and Disadvantages

Developers enjoy using this pattern as it can be used transparently and is somewhat flexible. As we've seen, objects can be wrapped or "decorated" with new behavior and continue to be used without worrying about the base object being modified. In a broader context, this pattern also avoids us needing to rely on large numbers of sub-classes to get the same benefits.

There are, however, drawbacks that we should be aware of when implementing the pattern. It can significantly complicate our application architecture if poorly managed, as it introduces many small but similar objects into our namespace. The concern is that other developers unfamiliar with the pattern may have difficulty grasping why it's being used, making it hard to manage.

Sufficient commenting or pattern research should assist with the latter. However, as long as we handle how widely we use the Decorator in our applications, we should be fine on both counts.

Flyweight

The Flyweight pattern is a classical structural solution for optimizing code that is repetitive, slow, and inefficiently shares data. It aims to minimize the use of memory in an application by sharing as much data as possible with related objects (e.g., application configuration, state, and so on—see Figure 7-8).

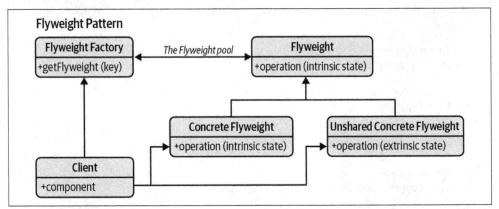

Figure 7-8. Flyweight pattern

Paul Calder and Mark Linton first conceived the pattern in 1990 and named it after the boxing weight class that includes fighters weighing less than 112 lb. The name Flyweight is derived from this weight classification because it refers to the small weight (memory footprint) the pattern aims to help us achieve.

In practice, Flyweight data sharing can involve taking several similar objects or data constructs used by many objects and placing this data into a single external object. We can pass this object to those depending on this data rather than storing identical data across each one.

Using Flyweights

There are two ways in which you can apply the Flyweight pattern. The first is at the data layer, where we deal with the concept of sharing data between large quantities of similar objects stored in memory.

You can also apply the Flyweight at the DOM layer as a central event manager to avoid attaching event handlers to every child element in a parent container with similar behavior.

Traditionally, the Flyweight pattern has been used most at the data layer, so we'll take a look at this first.

Flyweights and Sharing Data

For this application, we need to be aware of a few more concepts around the classical Flyweight pattern. In the Flyweight pattern, there's a concept of two states: intrinsic and extrinsic. Intrinsic information may be required by internal methods in our objects, without which they absolutely cannot function. Extrinsic information can, however, be removed and stored externally.

You can replace objects with the same intrinsic data with a single shared object created by a factory method. This allows us to reduce the overall quantity of implicit data being stored quite significantly.

The benefit is that we can keep an eye on objects that have already been instantiated so that new copies are only ever created if the intrinsic state differs from the object we already have.

We use a manager to handle the extrinsic states. You can implement this in various ways, but one approach is to have the manager object contain a central database of the extrinsic states and the flyweight objects to which they belong.

Implementing Classical Flyweights

The Flyweight pattern hasn't been heavily used in JavaScript recently, so many of the implementations we might use for inspiration come from the Java and C++ worlds.

Our first look at flyweights in code is my JavaScript implementation of the Java sample of the Flyweight pattern from Wikipedia (*https://oreil.ly/6rtiJ*).

This implementation makes use of three types of flyweight components:

Flyweight
Corresponds to an interface through which flyweights are able to receive and act on extrinsic states.

Concrete flyweight

Actually implements the flyweight interface and stores the intrinsic states. Concrete flyweights need to be sharable and capable of manipulating the extrinsic state.

Flyweight factory

Manages flyweight objects and creates them too. It ensures that our flyweights are shared and manages them as a group of objects that can be queried if we require individual instances. If an object has already been created in the group, it returns it. Otherwise, it adds a new object to the pool and returns it.

These correspond to the following definitions in our implementation:

- `CoffeeOrder`: Flyweight
- `CoffeeFlavor`: Concrete flyweight
- `CoffeeOrderContext`: Helper
- `CoffeeFlavorFactory`: Flyweight factory
- `testFlyweight`: Utilization of our Flyweights

Duck punching "implements"

Duck punching allows us to extend the capabilities of a language or solution without necessarily needing to modify the runtime source. As this next solution requires a Java keyword (`implements`) for implementing interfaces and isn't found in JavaScript natively, let's first duck-punch it.

`Function.prototype.implementsFor` works on an object constructor and will accept a parent class (function) or object and either inherit from this using normal inheritance (for functions) or virtual inheritance (for objects):

```
// Utility to simulate implementation of an interface
class InterfaceImplementation {
  static implementsFor(superclassOrInterface) {
    if (superclassOrInterface instanceof Function) {
      this.prototype = Object.create(superclassOrInterface.prototype);
      this.prototype.constructor = this;
      this.prototype.parent = superclassOrInterface.prototype;
    } else {
      this.prototype = Object.create(superclassOrInterface);
      this.prototype.constructor = this;
      this.prototype.parent = superclassOrInterface;
    }
    return this;
  }
}
```

We can use this to patch the lack of an `implements` keyword by explicitly having a function inherit an interface. Next, `CoffeeFlavor` implements the `CoffeeOrder` interface and must contain its interface methods for us to assign the functionality powering these implementations to an object:

```
// CoffeeOrder interface
const CoffeeOrder = {
  serveCoffee(context) {},
  getFlavor() {},
};

class CoffeeFlavor extends InterfaceImplementation {
  constructor(newFlavor) {
    super();
    this.flavor = newFlavor;
  }

  getFlavor() {
    return this.flavor;
  }

  serveCoffee(context) {
    console.log(`Serving Coffee flavor ${this.flavor} to
      table ${context.getTable()}`);
  }
}

// Implement interface for CoffeeOrder
CoffeeFlavor.implementsFor(CoffeeOrder);

const CoffeeOrderContext = (tableNumber) => ({
  getTable() {
    return tableNumber;
  },
});

class CoffeeFlavorFactory {
  constructor() {
    this.flavors = {};
    this.length = 0;
  }

  getCoffeeFlavor(flavorName) {
    let flavor = this.flavors[flavorName];
    if (!flavor) {
      flavor = new CoffeeFlavor(flavorName);
      this.flavors[flavorName] = flavor;
      this.length++;
    }
    return flavor;
  }
```

```
    getTotalCoffeeFlavorsMade() {
      return this.length;
    }
}

// Sample usage:
const testFlyweight = () => {
  const flavors = [];
  const tables = [];
  let ordersMade = 0;
  const flavorFactory = new CoffeeFlavorFactory();

  function takeOrders(flavorIn, table) {
    flavors.push(flavorFactory.getCoffeeFlavor(flavorIn));
    tables.push(CoffeeOrderContext(table));
    ordersMade++;
  }

  // Place orders
  takeOrders('Cappuccino', 2);
  // ...

  // Serve orders
  for (let i = 0; i < ordersMade; ++i) {
    flavors[i].serveCoffee(tables[i]);
  }

  console.log(' ');
  console.log(`total CoffeeFlavor objects made:
    ${flavorFactory.getTotalCoffeeFlavorsMade()}`);
};

testFlyweight();
```

Converting Code to Use the Flyweight Pattern

Next, let's continue our look at Flyweights by implementing a system to manage all books in a library. You could list the essential metadata for each book as follows:

- ID
- Title
- Author
- Genre
- Page count
- Publisher ID
- ISBN

We'll also require the following properties to track which member has checked out a particular book, the date they've checked it out, and the expected return date:

- checkoutDate
- checkoutMember
- dueReturnDate
- availability

We create a Book class to represent each book as follows before any optimization using the Flyweight pattern. The constructor takes in all the properties related directly to the book and those required for tracking it:

```
class Book {
  constructor(
    id,
    title,
    author,
    genre,
    pageCount,
    publisherID,
    ISBN,
    checkoutDate,
    checkoutMember,
    dueReturnDate,
    availability
  ) {
    this.id = id;
    this.title = title;
    this.author = author;
    this.genre = genre;
    this.pageCount = pageCount;
    this.publisherID = publisherID;
    this.ISBN = ISBN;
    this.checkoutDate = checkoutDate;
    this.checkoutMember = checkoutMember;
    this.dueReturnDate = dueReturnDate;
    this.availability = availability;
  }

  getTitle() {
    return this.title;
  }

  getAuthor() {
    return this.author;
  }

  getISBN() {
    return this.ISBN;
```

```
    }

    // For brevity, other getters are not shown
    updateCheckoutStatus(
      bookID,
      newStatus,
      checkoutDate,
      checkoutMember,
      newReturnDate
    ) {
      this.id = bookID;
      this.availability = newStatus;
      this.checkoutDate = checkoutDate;
      this.checkoutMember = checkoutMember;
      this.dueReturnDate = newReturnDate;
    }

    extendCheckoutPeriod(bookID, newReturnDate) {
      this.id = bookID;
      this.dueReturnDate = newReturnDate;
    }

    isPastDue(bookID) {
      const currentDate = new Date();
      return currentDate.getTime() > Date.parse(this.dueReturnDate);
    }
  }
```

This probably works fine initially for small collections of books. However, as the library expands to include a more extensive inventory with multiple versions and copies of each book, we may find the management system running more slowly. Using thousands of book objects may overwhelm the available memory, but we can optimize our system using the Flyweight pattern to improve this.

We can now separate our data into intrinsic and extrinsic states: data relevant to the book object (title, author, etc.) is intrinsic, while the checkout data (checkoutMember, dueReturnDate, etc.) is considered extrinsic. Effectively, this means that only one Book object is required for each combination of book properties. It's still a considerable number of objects, but significantly fewer than we had previously.

An instance of the following book metadata combination will be created for all required copies of the book object with a particular title/ISBN:

```
// Flyweight optimized version
class Book {
  constructor({ title, author, genre, pageCount, publisherID, ISBN }) {
    this.title = title;
    this.author = author;
    this.genre = genre;
    this.pageCount = pageCount;
```

```
      this.publisherID = publisherID;
      this.ISBN = ISBN;
  }
}
```

As we can see, the extrinsic states have been removed. Everything to do with library checkouts will be moved to a manager, and as the object data is now segmented, we can use a factory for instantiation.

A Basic Factory

Let's now define a very basic factory. We will have it check if a book with a particular title has been previously created inside the system—if it has, we'll return it; if not, a new book will be created and stored so that it can be accessed later. This ensures that we create only a single copy of each unique intrinsic piece of data:

```
// Book Factory Singleton
const existingBooks = {};

class BookFactory {
  createBook({ title, author, genre, pageCount, publisherID, ISBN }) {
    // Find if a particular book + metadata combination already exists
    // !! or (bang bang) forces a boolean to be returned
    const existingBook = existingBooks[ISBN];
    if (!!existingBook) {
      return existingBook;
    } else {
      // if not, let's create a new instance of the book and store it
      const book = new Book({ title, author, genre, pageCount, publisherID,
        ISBN });
      existingBooks[ISBN] = book;
      return book;
    }
  }
}
```

Managing the Extrinsic States

Next, we need to store the states that were removed from the Book objects somewhere—luckily, a manager (which we'll be defining as a Singleton) can be used to encapsulate them. Combinations of a Book object and the library member who's checked it out will be called Book record. Our manager will be storing both and will include checkout-related logic we stripped out during our Flyweight optimization of the Book class:

```
// BookRecordManager Singleton
const bookRecordDatabase = {};

class BookRecordManager {
  // add a new book into the library system
```

```
addBookRecord({ id, title, author, genre, pageCount, publisherID, ISBN,
    checkoutDate, checkoutMember, dueReturnDate, availability }) {
  const bookFactory = new BookFactory();
  const book = bookFactory.createBook({ title, author, genre, pageCount,
    publisherID, ISBN });
  bookRecordDatabase[id] = {
    checkoutMember,
    checkoutDate,
    dueReturnDate,
    availability,
    book,
  };
}

updateCheckoutStatus({ bookID, newStatus, checkoutDate, checkoutMember,
    newReturnDate }) {
  const record = bookRecordDatabase[bookID];
  record.availability = newStatus;
  record.checkoutDate = checkoutDate;
  record.checkoutMember = checkoutMember;
  record.dueReturnDate = newReturnDate;
}

extendCheckoutPeriod(bookID, newReturnDate) {
  bookRecordDatabase[bookID].dueReturnDate = newReturnDate;
}

isPastDue(bookID) {
  const currentDate = new Date();
  return currentDate.getTime() >
    Date.parse(bookRecordDatabase[bookID].dueReturnDate);
}
}
```

The result of these changes is that all of the data extracted from the Book *class* is now being stored in an attribute of the BookManager Singleton (BookDatabase)—something considerably more efficient than the large number of objects we were previously using. Methods related to book checkouts are also now based here as they deal with extrinsic rather than intrinsic data.

This process does add a little complexity to our final solution. However, it's a minor concern compared to the performance issues that we have tackled. Data-wise, if we have 30 copies of the same book, we are now storing it only once. Also, every function takes up memory. With the Flyweight pattern, these functions exist in one place (on the manager) and not on every object, thus saving on memory use. For the unoptimized version of Flyweight mentioned previously, we store just a link to the function object as we used the Book constructor's prototype. Still, if we implemented it another way, functions would be created for every book instance.

The Flyweight Pattern and the DOM

The DOM supports two approaches that allow objects to detect events—either top-down (event capture) or bottom-up (event bubbling).

In event capture, the event is first captured by the outer-most element and propagated to the inner-most element. In event bubbling, the event is captured and given to the inner-most element and then propagated to the outer elements.

Gary Chisholm wrote one of the best metaphors for describing Flyweights in this context, and it goes a little like this:

> Try to think of the flyweight in terms of a pond. A fish opens its mouth (the event), bubbles rise to the surface (the bubbling), a fly sitting on the top flies away when the bubble reaches the surface (the action). In this example we can easily transpose the fish opening its mouth to a button being clicked, the bubbles as the bubbling effect, and the fly flying away to some function being run.

Bubbling was introduced to handle situations in which a single event (e.g., a click) may be handled by multiple event handlers defined at different levels of the DOM hierarchy. Where this happens, event bubbling executes event handlers defined for specific elements at the lowest level possible. From there on, the event bubbles up to containing elements before going to those even higher up.

Flyweights can be used to further tweak the event-bubbling process, as we will see in "Example: Centralized Event Handling".

Example: Centralized Event Handling

For our first practical example, imagine we have several similar elements in a document with similar behavior executed when a user action (e.g., click, mouse-over) is performed against them.

Usually, when constructing our accordion component, menu, or other list-based widgets, we bind a click event to each link element in the parent container (e.g., $('ul li a').on(…)). Instead of binding the click to multiple elements, we can easily attach a Flyweight to the top of our container, which can listen for events coming from below. These can then be handled using logic as simple or complex as required.

As the types of components mentioned often have the same repeating markup for each section (e.g., each section of an accordion), there's a good chance the behavior of each element clicked will be pretty similar and relative to similar classes nearby. We'll use this information to construct a basic accordion using the Flyweight in Example 7-6.

A `stateManager` namespace is used here to encapsulate our Flyweight logic, while jQuery is used to bind the initial click to a container `div`. An `unbind` event is first applied to ensure that no other logic on the page attaches similar handles to the container.

To establish exactly what child element in the container is clicked, we use a `target` check, which provides a reference to the element that was clicked, regardless of its parent. We then use this information to handle the `click` event without actually needing to bind the event to specific children when our page loads.

Example 7-6. Centralized event handling

```
<div id="container">
    <div class="toggle">More Info (Address)
      <span class="info">
        This is more information
      </span>
    </div>
    <div class="toggle">Even More Info (Map)
      <span class="info">
        <iframe src="MAPS_URL"></iframe>
      </span>
    </div>
  </div>

  <script>
    (function() {
      const stateManager = {
        fly() {
          const self = this;
          $('#container')
            .off()
            .on('click', 'div.toggle', function() {
              self.handleClick(this);
            });
        },
        handleClick(elem) {
          $(elem)
            .find('span')
            .toggle('slow');
        },
      };

    // Initialize event listeners
    stateManager.fly();
  })();
  </script>
```

The benefit here is that we're converting many independent actions into shared ones (potentially saving on memory).

Behavioral Patterns

Behavioral patterns help define the communication between objects. They help to improve or streamline the communication between disparate objects in a system.

Following are the JavaScript behavioral patterns that we will discuss in this section:

- "The Observer Pattern" on page 93
- "The Mediator Pattern" on page 110
- "The Command Pattern" on page 117

The Observer Pattern

The Observer pattern allows you to notify one object when another object changes without requiring the object to know about its dependents. Often this is a pattern where an object (known as a subject) maintains a list of objects depending on it (observers), automatically notifying them of any changes to its state. In modern frameworks, the Observer pattern is used to inform components of state changes. Figure 7-9 illustrates this.

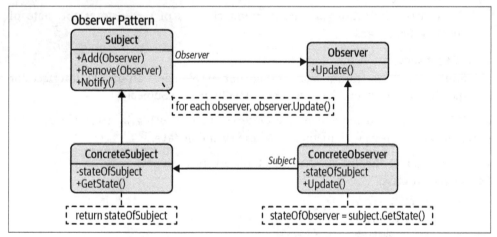

Figure 7-9. Observer pattern

When a subject needs to notify observers about something interesting happening, it broadcasts a notification to the observers (which can include specific data related to the topic). When an observer no longer wishes to be notified of changes by the subject, they can be removed from the list of observers.

It's helpful to refer back to published definitions of design patterns that are language agnostic to get a broader sense of their usage and advantages over time. The definition of the Observer pattern provided in the GoF book, *Design Patterns: Elements of Reusable Object-Oriented Software*, is:

> One or more observers are interested in the state of a subject and register their interest with the subject by attaching themselves. When something changes in our subject that the observer may be interested in, a notify message is sent which calls the update method in each observer. When the observer is no longer interested in the subject's state, they can simply detach themselves.

We can now expand on what we've learned to implement the Observer pattern with the following components:

Subject
   Maintains a list of observers, facilitates adding or removing observers

Observer
   Provides an update interface for objects that need to be notified of a Subject's changes in state

ConcreteSubject
   Broadcasts notifications to observers on changes of state, stores the state of ConcreteObservers

ConcreteObserver
   Stores a reference to the ConcreteSubject, implements an update interface for the observer to ensure the state is consistent with the Subject's

ES2015+ allows us to implement the Observer pattern using JavaScript classes for observers and subjects with methods for notify and update.

First, let's model the list of dependent observers a subject may have using the ObserverList class:

```
class ObserverList {
    constructor() {
        this.observerList = [];
    }

    add(obj) {
        return this.observerList.push(obj);
    }

    count() {
        return this.observerList.length;
    }

    get(index) {
        if (index > -1 && index < this.observerList.length) {
```

```
            return this.observerList[index];
        }
    }

    indexOf(obj, startIndex) {
        let i = startIndex;

        while (i < this.observerList.length) {
            if (this.observerList[i] === obj) {
                return i;
            }
            i++;
        }

        return -1;
    }

    removeAt(index) {
        this.observerList.splice(index, 1);
    }
}
```

Next, let's model the Subject class that can add, remove, or notify observers on the observer list:

```
class Subject {
    constructor() {
        this.observers = new ObserverList();
    }

    addObserver(observer) {
        this.observers.add(observer);
    }

    removeObserver(observer) {
        this.observers.removeAt(this.observers.indexOf(observer, 0));
    }

    notify(context) {
        const observerCount = this.observers.count();
        for (let i = 0; i < observerCount; i++) {
            this.observers.get(i).update(context);
        }
    }
}
```

We then define a skeleton for creating new observers. We will overwrite the Update functionality here later with custom behavior:

```
// The Observer
class Observer {
    constructor() {}
    update() {
```

```
      // ...
   }
}
```

In our sample application using the previous observer components, we now define:

- A button for adding new observable checkboxes to the page.
- A control checkbox will act as a subject, notifying other checkboxes that they should update to the checked state.
- A container for the new checkboxes added.

We then define ConcreteSubject and ConcreteObserver handlers to add new observers to the page and implement the updating interface. For this, we use inheritance to extend our subject and observer classes. The ConcreteSubject class encapsulates a checkbox and generates a notification when the main checkbox is clicked. ConcreteObserver encapsulates each of the observing checkboxes and implements the Update interface by changing the checked value of the checkboxes. What follows are the inline comments on how these work together in the context of our example.

Here is the HTML code:

```
<button id="addNewObserver">Add New Observer checkbox</button>
<input id="mainCheckbox" type="checkbox"/>
<div id="observersContainer"></div>
```

Here is an example:

```
// References to our DOM elements

// Concrete Subject
class ConcreteSubject extends Subject {
   constructor(element) {
     // Call the constructor of the super class.
     super();
     this.element = element;

     // Clicking the checkbox will trigger notifications to its observers
     this.element.onclick = () => {
       this.notify(this.element.checked);
     };
   }
}

// Concrete Observer

class ConcreteObserver extends Observer {
   constructor(element) {
     super();
     this.element = element;
   }
```

```
    // Override with custom update behavior
    update(value) {
      this.element.checked = value;
    }
  }

  // References to our DOM elements
  const addBtn = document.getElementById('addNewObserver');
  const container = document.getElementById('observersContainer');
  const controlCheckbox = new ConcreteSubject(
    document.getElementById('mainCheckbox')
  );

  const addNewObserver = () => {
    // Create a new checkbox to be added
    const check = document.createElement('input');
    check.type = 'checkbox';
    const checkObserver = new ConcreteObserver(check);

    // Add the new observer to our list of observers
    // for our main subject
    controlCheckbox.addObserver(checkObserver);

    // Append the item to the container
    container.appendChild(check);
  };

  addBtn.onclick = addNewObserver;
}
```

In this example, we looked at how to implement and utilize the Observer pattern, covering the concepts of a Subject, Observer, ConcreteSubject, and ConcreteObserver.

Differences Between the Observer and Publish/Subscribe Pattern

While it's helpful to be aware of the Observer pattern, quite often in the JavaScript world, we'll find it commonly implemented using a variation known as the Publish/Subscribe pattern. Although the two patterns are pretty similar, there are differences worth noting.

The Observer pattern requires that the observer (or object) wishing to receive topic notifications must subscribe this interest to the object firing the event (the subject), as seen in Figure 7-10.

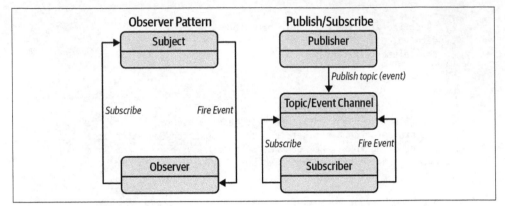

Figure 7-10. Publish/Subscribe

The Publish/Subscribe pattern, however, uses a topic/event channel that sits between the objects wishing to receive notifications (subscribers) and the object firing the event (the publisher). This event system allows code to define application-specific events, which can pass custom arguments containing values needed by the subscriber. The idea here is to avoid dependencies between the subscriber and publisher.

This differs from the Observer pattern because it allows any subscriber implementing an appropriate event handler to register for and receive topic notifications broadcast by the publisher.

Here is an example of how one might use the Publish/Subscribe pattern if provided with a functional implementation powering publish(), subscribe(), and unsubscribe() behind the scenes:

```html
<!-- Add this HTML to your page -->
<div class="messageSender"></div>
<div class="messagePreview"></div>
<div class="newMessageCounter"></div>
// A simple Publish/Subscribe implementation
const events = (function () {
  const topics = {};
  const hOP = topics.hasOwnProperty;

  return {
    subscribe: function (topic, listener) {
      if (!hOP.call(topics, topic)) topics[topic] = [];
      const index = topics[topic].push(listener) - 1;

      return {
        remove: function () {
          delete topics[topic][index];
        },
      };
    },
```

```
    publish: function (topic, info) {
      if (!hOP.call(topics, topic)) return;
      topics[topic].forEach(function (item) {
        item(info !== undefined ? info : {});
      });
    },
  };
})();

// A very simple new mail handler
// A count of the number of messages received
let mailCounter = 0;

// Initialize subscribers that will listen out for a topic
// with the name "inbox/newMessage".
// Render a preview of new messages
const subscriber1 = events.subscribe('inbox/newMessage', (data) => {
  // Log the topic for debugging purposes
  console.log('A new message was received:', data);

  // Use the data that was passed from our subject
  // to display a message preview to the user
  document.querySelector('.messageSender').innerHTML = data.sender;
  document.querySelector('.messagePreview').innerHTML = data.body;
});

// Here's another subscriber using the same data to perform
// a different task.
// Update the counter displaying the number of new
// messages received via the publisher
const subscriber2 = events.subscribe('inbox/newMessage', (data) => {
  document.querySelector('.newMessageCounter').innerHTML = ++mailCounter;
});

events.publish('inbox/newMessage', {
  sender: 'hello@google.com',
  body: 'Hey there! How are you doing today?',
});

// We could then at a later point unsubscribe our subscribers
// from receiving any new topic notifications as follows:
// subscriber1.remove();
// subscriber2.remove();
```

The general idea here is the promotion of loose coupling. Rather than single objects calling on the methods of other objects directly, they instead subscribe to a specific task or activity of another object and are notified when it occurs.

Advantages

The Observer and Publish/Subscribe patterns encourage us to think hard about the relationships between different application parts. They also help us identify layers containing direct relationships that could be replaced with sets of subjects and observers. This effectively could be used to break down an application into smaller, more loosely coupled blocks to improve code management and potential for reuse.

Further motivation for using the Observer pattern is in situations where we need to maintain consistency between related objects without making classes tightly coupled. For example, when an object needs to be able to notify other objects without making assumptions regarding those objects.

Dynamic relationships can exist between observers and subjects when using either pattern. This provides excellent flexibility that may not be as easy to implement when disparate parts of our application are tightly coupled.

While it may not always be the best solution to every problem, these patterns remain one of the best tools for designing decoupled systems and should be considered an essential tool in any JavaScript developer's utility belt.

Disadvantages

Consequently, some of the issues with these patterns actually stem from their main benefits. In Publish/Subscribe, by decoupling publishers from subscribers, it can sometimes become difficult to obtain guarantees that particular parts of our applications are functioning as we may expect.

For example, publishers may assume that one or more subscribers are listening to them. Say that we're using such an assumption to log or output errors regarding some application process. If the subscriber performing the logging crashes (or for some reason fails to function), the publisher won't have a way of seeing this due to the decoupled nature of the system.

Another drawback of the pattern is that subscribers are entirely ignorant of the existence of each other and are blind to the cost of switching publishers. Due to the dynamic relationship between subscribers and publishers, it can be difficult to track an update dependency.

Publish/Subscribe Implementations

Publish/Subscribe fits in very well in JavaScript ecosystems, primarily because, at the core, ECMAScript implementations are event-driven. This is particularly true in browser environments, as the DOM uses events as its main interaction API for scripting.

That said, neither ECMAScript nor DOM provides core objects or methods for creating custom event systems in implementation code (except for perhaps the DOM3 CustomEvent, which is bound to the DOM and is thus not generically applicable).

An example Publish/Subscribe implementation

To better appreciate how many of the ordinary JavaScript implementations of the Observer pattern might work, let's take a walkthrough of a minimalist version of Publish/Subscribe I released on GitHub under a project called "pubsubz" (*https://oreil.ly/yPPfE*). This demonstrates the core concepts of subscribe and publish, and the idea of unsubscribing.

I've opted to base our examples on this code as it sticks closely to the method signatures and implementation approach I expect to see in a JavaScript version of the classic Observer pattern:

```
class PubSub {
    constructor() {
        // Storage for topics that can be broadcast
        // or listened to
        this.topics = {};

        // A topic identifier
        this.subUid = -1;
    }

    publish(topic, args) {
        if (!this.topics[topic]) {
            return false;
        }

        const subscribers = this.topics[topic];
        let len = subscribers ? subscribers.length : 0;

        while (len--) {
            subscribers[len].func(topic, args);
        }

        return this;
    }

    subscribe(topic, func) {
        if (!this.topics[topic]) {
            this.topics[topic] = [];
        }

        const token = (++this.subUid).toString();
        this.topics[topic].push({
            token,
            func,
        });
```

```
            return token;
        }

        unsubscribe(token) {
            for (const m in this.topics) {
                if (this.topics[m]) {
                    for (let i = 0, j = this.topics[m].length; i < j; i++) {
                        if (this.topics[m][i].token === token) {
                            this.topics[m].splice(i, 1);

                            return token;
                        }
                    }
                }
            }
            return this;
        }
    }

    const pubsub = new PubSub();

    pubsub.publish('/addFavorite', ['test']);
    pubsub.subscribe('/addFavorite', (topic, args) => {
        console.log('test', topic, args);
    });
```

Here we have defined a basic PubSub class that contains:

- A list of topics with subscribers who have subscribed to it.
- The Subscribe method creates a new subscriber to a topic using the function to be called when publishing a topic and a unique token.
- The Unsubscribe method removes a subscriber from the list based on the token value passed. The Publish method publishes content on a given topic to all its subscribers by calling the registered function.

Using our implementation

We can now use the implementation to publish and subscribe to events of interest, as shown in Example 7-7.

Example 7-7. Using our implementation

```
// Another simple message handler

// A simple message logger that logs any topics and data received through our
// subscriber
const messageLogger = (topics, data) => {
    console.log(`Logging: ${topics}: ${data}`);
};
```

```
// Subscribers listen for topics they have subscribed to and
// invoke a callback function (e.g., messageLogger) once a new
// notification is broadcast on that topic
const subscription = pubsub.subscribe('inbox/newMessage', messageLogger);

// Publishers are in charge of publishing topics or notifications of
// interest to the application. e.g.:

pubsub.publish('inbox/newMessage', 'hello world!');

// or
pubsub.publish('inbox/newMessage', ['test', 'a', 'b', 'c']);

// or
pubsub.publish('inbox/newMessage', {
    sender: 'hello@google.com',
    body: 'Hey again!',
});

// We can also unsubscribe if we no longer wish for our subscribers
// to be notified
pubsub.unsubscribe(subscription);

// Once unsubscribed, this for example won't result in our
// messageLogger being executed as the subscriber is
// no longer listening
pubsub.publish('inbox/newMessage', 'Hello! are you still there?');
```

UI notifications

Next, let's imagine we have a web application responsible for displaying real-time stock information.

The application might have a grid displaying the stock stats and a counter indicating the last update point. The application must update the grid and counter when the data model changes. In this scenario, our subject (which will be publishing topics/notifications) is the data model, and our subscribers are the grid and counter.

When our subscribers are notified that the model has changed, they can update themselves accordingly.

In our implementation, our subscriber will listen to the topic newDataAvailable to find out if new stock information is available. If a new notification is published to this topic, it will trigger gridUpdate to add a new row to our grid containing this information. It will also update the *last updated* counter to log the last time that data was added (Example 7-8).

Example 7-8. UI notifications

```javascript
// Return the current local time to be used in our UI later
getCurrentTime = () => {
    const date = new Date();
    const m = date.getMonth() + 1;
    const d = date.getDate();
    const y = date.getFullYear();
    const t = date.toLocaleTimeString().toLowerCase();

    return `${m}/${d}/${y} ${t}`;
};

  // Add a new row of data to our fictional grid component
  const addGridRow = data => {
    // ui.grid.addRow( data );
    console.log(`updated grid component with:${data}`);
  };

  // Update our fictional grid to show the time it was last
  // updated
  const updateCounter = data => {
    // ui.grid.updateLastChanged( getCurrentTime() );
    console.log(`data last updated at: ${getCurrentTime()} with ${data}`);
  };

  // Update the grid using the data passed to our subscribers
  const gridUpdate = (topic, data) => {
    if (data !== undefined) {
      addGridRow(data);
      updateCounter(data);
    }
  };


// Create a subscription to the newDataAvailable topic
const subscriber = pubsub.subscribe('newDataAvailable', gridUpdate);

// The following represents updates to our data layer. This could be
// powered by ajax requests that broadcast that new data is available
// to the rest of the application.

// Publish changes to the gridUpdated topic representing new entries
pubsub.publish('newDataAvailable', {
  summary: 'Apple made $5 billion',
  identifier: 'APPL',
  stockPrice: 570.91,
});

pubsub.publish('newDataAvailable', {
  summary: 'Microsoft made $20 million',
  identifier: 'MSFT',
```

```
    stockPrice: 30.85,
});
```

Decoupling applications using Ben Alman's Pub/Sub implementation

In the following movie rating example, we'll use Ben Alman's jQuery implementation of Publish/Subscribe (*https://oreil.ly/w9ECl*) to demonstrate how we can decouple a UI. Notice how submitting a rating only has the effect of publishing the fact that new user and rating data is available.

It's left up to the subscribers to those topics to delegate what happens with that data. In our case, we're pushing that new data into existing arrays and then rendering them using the Lodash library's `.template()` method for templating.

Example 7-9 has the HTML/Templates code.

Example 7-9. HTML/Templates code for Pub/Sub

```html
<script id="userTemplate" type="text/html">
    <li><%- name %></li>
</script>


<script id="ratingsTemplate" type="text/html">
    <li><strong><%- title %></strong> was rated <%- rating %>/5</li>
</script>


<div id="container">

    <div class="sampleForm">
        <p>
            <label for="twitter_handle">Twitter handle:</label>
            <input type="text" id="twitter_handle" />
        </p>
        <p>
            <label for="movie_seen">Name a movie you've seen this year:</label>
            <input type="text" id="movie_seen" />
        </p>
        <p>

            <label for="movie_rating">Rate the movie you saw:</label>
            <select id="movie_rating">
                  <option value="1">1</option>
                   <option value="2">2</option>
                   <option value="3">3</option>
                   <option value="4">4</option>
                   <option value="5" selected>5</option>

            </select>
        </p>
```

```
        <p>
            <button id="add">Submit rating</button>
        </p>
    </div>


    <div class="summaryTable">
        <div id="users"><h3>Recent users</h3></div>
        <div id="ratings"><h3>Recent movies rated</h3></div>
    </div>

</div>
```

The JavaScript code is in Example 7-10.

Example 7-10. JavaScript code for Pub/Sub

```javascript
;($ => {
    // Pre-compile templates and "cache" them using closure
    const userTemplate = _.template($('#userTemplate').html());

    const ratingsTemplate = _.template($('#ratingsTemplate').html());

    // Subscribe to the new user topic, which adds a user
    // to a list of users who have submitted reviews
    $.subscribe('/new/user', (e, data) => {
      if (data) {
        $('#users').append(userTemplate(data));
      }
    });

    // Subscribe to the new rating topic. This is composed of a title and
    // rating. New ratings are appended to a running list of added user
    // ratings.
    $.subscribe('/new/rating', (e, data) => {
      if (data) {
        $('#ratings').append(ratingsTemplate(data));
      }
    });

    // Handler for adding a new user
    $('#add').on('click', e => {
      e.preventDefault();

      const strUser = $('#twitter_handle').val();
      const strMovie = $('#movie_seen').val();
      const strRating = $('#movie_rating').val();

      // Inform the application a new user is available
```

```
    $.publish('/new/user', {
      name: strUser,
    });

    // Inform the app a new rating is available
    $.publish('/new/rating', {
      title: strMovie,
      rating: strRating,
    });
  });
})(jQuery);
```

Decoupling an Ajax-based jQuery application

In our final example, we'll take a practical look at how decoupling our code using Pub/Sub early in the development process can save us some potentially painful refactoring later.

Often in Ajax-heavy applications, we want to achieve more than just one unique action once we've received a response to a request. We could add all of the post-request logic into a success callback, but there are drawbacks to this approach.

Highly coupled applications sometimes increase the effort required to reuse functionality due to the increased interfunction/code dependency. Keeping our post-request logic hardcoded in a callback might be okay if we just try to grab a result set once. However, it's not as appropriate when we want to make further Ajax calls to the same data source (and different end behavior) without rewriting parts of the code multiple times. Rather than going back through each layer that calls the same data source and generalizing them later on, we can use Pub/Sub from the start and save time.

Using observers, we can also easily separate application-wide notifications regarding different events down to whatever level of granularity we're comfortable with—something that can be less elegantly done using other patterns.

Notice how in our upcoming sample, one topic notification is made when a user indicates that he wants to make a search query. Another is made when the request returns and actual data is available for consumption. It's left up to the subscribers to then decide how to use knowledge of these events (or the data returned). The benefits of this are that, if we wanted, we could have 10 different subscribers using the data returned in different ways, but as far as the Ajax layer is concerned, it doesn't care. Its sole duty is to request and return data and then pass it on to whoever wants to use it. This separation of concerns can make the overall design of our code a little cleaner.

The HTML/Templates code is shown in Example 7-11.

Example 7-11. HTML/Templates code for Ajax

```html
<form id="flickrSearch">

    <input type="text" name="tag" id="query"/>

    <input type="submit" name="submit" value="submit"/>

</form>


<div id="lastQuery"></div>

<ol id="searchResults"></ol>


<script id="resultTemplate" type="text/html">
    <% _.each(items, function( item ){ %>
        <li><img src="<%= item.media.m %>"/></li>
    <% });%>
</script>
```

Example 7-12 shows the JavaScript code.

Example 7-12. JavaScript code for Ajax

```javascript
($ => {
    // Pre-compile template and "cache" it using closure
    const resultTemplate = _.template($('#resultTemplate').html());

    // Subscribe to the new search tags topic
    $.subscribe('/search/tags', (e, tags) => {
      $('#lastQuery').html(`Searched for: ${tags}`);
    });

    // Subscribe to the new results topic
    $.subscribe('/search/resultSet', (e, results) => {
      $('#searchResults')
        .empty()
        .append(resultTemplate(results));
    });

    // Submit a search query and publish tags on the /search/tags topic
    $('#flickrSearch').submit(function(e) {
      e.preventDefault();
      const tags = $(this)
        .find('#query')
        .val();
```

```
  if (!tags) {
    return;
  }

  $.publish('/search/tags', [$.trim(tags)]);
});

// Subscribe to new tags being published and perform a search query
// using them. Once data has returned publish this data for the rest
// of the application to consume. We used the destructuring assignment
// syntax that makes it possible to unpack values from data structures
// into distinct variables.

$.subscribe('/search/tags', (e, tags) => {
  $.getJSON(
    'http://api.flickr.com/services/feeds/photos_public.gne?jsoncallback=?',
    {
      tags,
      tagmode: 'any',
      format: 'json',
    },
    // The destructuring assignment as function parameter
    ({ items }) => {
      if (!items.length) {
        return;
      }
      //shorthand property names in object creation,
      // if variable name equal to object key
      $.publish('/search/resultSet', { items });
    }
  );
});
})(jQuery);
```

Observer pattern in the React ecosystem

A popular library that uses the observable pattern is RxJS. The RxJS documentation (*https://oreil.ly/JH3lY*) states that:

> ReactiveX combines the Observer pattern with the Iterator pattern and functional programming with collections to fill the need for an ideal way of managing sequences of events.

With RxJS, we can create observers and subscribe to certain events! Let's look at an example from their documentation, which logs whether a user was dragging in the document:

```
import ReactDOM from "react-dom";
import { fromEvent, merge } from "rxjs";
import { sample, mapTo } from "rxjs/operators";

import "./styles.css";
```

```
merge(
  fromEvent(document, "mousedown").pipe(mapTo(false)),
  fromEvent(document, "mousemove").pipe(mapTo(true))
)
  .pipe(sample(fromEvent(document, "mouseup")))
  .subscribe(isDragging => {
    console.log("Were you dragging?", isDragging);
  });

ReactDOM.render(
  <div className="App">Click or drag anywhere and check the console!</div>,
  document.getElementById("root")
);
```

The Observer pattern helps decouple several different scenarios in application design. If you haven't been using it, I recommend picking up one of the prewritten implementations mentioned here and giving it a try. It's one of the easier design patterns to get started with but also one of the most powerful.

The Mediator Pattern

The Mediator pattern is a design pattern that allows one object to notify a set of other objects when an event occurs. The difference between the Mediator and Observer patterns is that the Mediator pattern allows one object to be notified of events that occur in other objects. In contrast, the Observer pattern allows one object to subscribe to multiple events that occur in other objects.

In the section on the Observer pattern, we discussed a way of channeling multiple event sources through a single object. This is also known as Publish/Subscribe or Event Aggregation. It's common for developers to think of mediators when faced with this problem, so let's explore how they differ.

The dictionary refers to a mediator as a neutral party that assists in negotiations and conflict resolution.[1] In our world, a mediator is a behavioral design pattern that allows us to expose a unified interface through which the different parts of a system may communicate.

If it appears that a system has too many direct relationships between components, it may be time to have a central point of control that components communicate through instead. The mediator promotes loose coupling by ensuring that interactions between components are managed centrally instead of having components refer to each other explicitly. This can help us decouple systems and improve the potential for component reusability.

---

1 Wikipedia (*https://oreil.ly/OUcDc*); Dictionary.com (*https://oreil.ly/uM9-f*).

A real-world analogy could be a typical airport traffic control system. A tower (mediator) handles what planes can take off and land because all communications (notifications being listened out for or broadcast) take place from the aircraft to the control tower rather than from plane to plane. A centralized controller is key to the success of this system, and that's the role a mediator plays in software design (Figure 7-11).

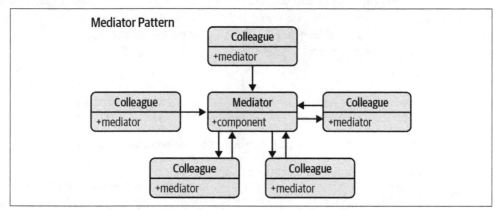

Figure 7-11. Mediator pattern

Another analogy would be DOM event bubbling and event delegation. If all subscriptions in a system are made against the document rather than individual nodes, the document effectively serves as a Mediator. Instead of binding to the events of the individual nodes, a higher-level object is given the responsibility of notifying subscribers about interaction events.

When it comes to the Mediator and Event Aggregator patterns, sometimes it may look like the patterns are interchangeable due to implementation similarities. However, the semantics and intent of these patterns are very different.

And even if the implementations both use some of the same core constructs, I believe there is a distinct difference between them. They should not be interchanged or confused in communication because of their differences.

A Simple Mediator

A mediator is an object that coordinates interactions (logic and behavior) between multiple objects. It decides when to call which objects based on the actions (or inaction) of other objects and input.

You can write a mediator using a single line of code:

```
const mediator = {};
```

Yes, of course, this is just an object literal in JavaScript. Once again, we're talking about semantics here. The mediator's purpose is to control the workflow between objects; we really don't need anything more than an object literal to do this.

The following example shows a basic implementation of a `mediator` object with some utility methods that can trigger and subscribe to events. The `orgChart` object here is a mediator that assigns actions to be taken on the occurrence of a particular event. Here, a manager is assigned to the employee on completing the details of a new employee, and the employee record is saved:

```
const orgChart = {
    addNewEmployee() {
        // getEmployeeDetail provides a view that users interact with
        const employeeDetail = this.getEmployeeDetail();

        // when the employee detail is complete, the mediator (the 'orgchart'
        // object) decides what should happen next
        employeeDetail.on('complete', employee => {
            // set up additional objects that have additional events, which are
            // used by the mediator to do additional things
            const managerSelector = this.selectManager(employee);
            managerSelector.on('save', employee => {
                employee.save();
            });
        });
    },
    // ...
};
```

I've often referred to this type of object as a "workflow" object in the past, but the truth is that it is a mediator. It is an object that handles the workflow between many other objects, aggregating the responsibility of that workflow knowledge into a single object. The result is a workflow that is easier to understand and maintain.

Similarities and Differences

There are, without a doubt, similarities between the event aggregator and mediator examples that I've shown here. The similarities boil down to two primary items: events and third-party objects. These differences are superficial at best, though. When we dig into the pattern's intent and see that the implementations can be dramatically different, the nature of the patterns becomes more apparent.

Events

Both the event aggregator and mediator use events in the examples shown. An event aggregator obviously deals with events—it's in the name, after all. The mediator only uses events because it makes life easy when dealing with modern JavaScript web app frameworks. There is nothing that says a mediator must be built with events. You can build a mediator with callback methods by handing the mediator reference to the child object or using several other means.

The difference, then, is why these two patterns are both using events. The event aggregator, as a pattern, is designed to deal with events. The mediator, though, uses them only because it's convenient.

Third-party objects

By design, the event aggregator and mediator employ a third-party object to streamline interactions. The event aggregator itself is a third party to the event publisher and the event subscriber. It acts as a central hub for events to pass through. The mediator is also a third party to other objects, though. So where is the difference? Why don't we call an event aggregator a mediator? The answer primarily depends on where the application logic and workflow are coded.

In the case of an event aggregator, the third-party object is there only to facilitate the pass-through of events from an unknown number of sources to an unknown number of handlers. All workflow and business logic that needs to be kicked off is put directly into the object that triggers the events and the objects that handle the events.

In the mediator's case, the business logic and workflow are aggregated into the mediator itself. The mediator decides when an object should have its methods called and attributes updated based on factors the mediator knows about. It encapsulates the workflow and process, coordinating multiple objects to produce the desired system behavior. The individual objects involved in this workflow know how to perform their task. But the mediator tells the objects when to perform the tasks by making decisions at a higher level than the individual objects.

An event aggregator facilitates a "fire and forget" model of communication. The object triggering the event doesn't care if there are any subscribers. It just fires the event and moves on. A mediator might use events to make decisions, but it is definitely not "fire and forget." A mediator pays attention to a known set of inputs or activities so that it can facilitate and coordinate other behavior with a known set of actors (objects).

Relationships: When to use which

Understanding the similarities and differences between an event aggregator and a mediator is essential for semantic reasons. It's equally important to know when to use which pattern. The basic semantics and intent of the patterns inform the question of when, but experience in using the patterns will help you understand the more subtle points and nuanced decisions that must be made.

Event Aggregator Use

In general, an event aggregator is used when you either have too many objects to listen to directly or have entirely unrelated objects.

When two objects already have a direct relationship—for example, a parent view and a child view—there may be a benefit in using an event aggregator. Have the child view trigger an event, and the parent view can handle the event. This is most commonly seen in Backbone's Collection and Model in JavaScript framework terms, where all Model events are bubbled up to and through its parent Collection. A Collection often uses model events to modify the state of itself or other models. Handling "selected" items in a collection is an excellent example.

jQuery's on() method as an event aggregator is a great example of too many objects to listen to. If you have 10, 20, or 200 DOM elements that can trigger a "click" event, it might be a bad idea to set up a listener on all of them individually. This could quickly deteriorate the performance of the application and user experience. Instead, using jQuery's on() method allows us to aggregate all events and reduce the overhead of 10, 20, or 200 event handlers down to 1.

Indirect relationships are also a great time to use event aggregators. In modern applications, it is ubiquitous to have multiple view objects that need to communicate but have no direct relationship. For example, a menu system might have a view that handles the menu item clicks. But we don't want the menu to be directly tied to the content views showing all the details and information when a menu item is clicked—having the content and menu coupled together would make the code difficult to maintain in the long run. Instead, we can use an event aggregator to trigger menu:click:foo events and have a "foo" object handle the click event to show its content on the screen.

Mediator Use

A mediator is best applied when two or more objects have an indirect working relationship, and business logic or workflow needs to dictate the interactions and coordination of these objects. A wizard interface is an excellent example of this, as shown in the orgChart example. Multiple views facilitate the entire workflow of the wizard. Rather than tightly coupling the view together by having them reference each other directly, we can decouple them and more explicitly model the workflow between them by introducing a mediator.

The mediator extracts the workflow from the implementation details and creates a more natural abstraction at a higher level, showing us at a much faster glance what that workflow is. We no longer have to dig into the details of each view in the workflow to see what the workflow is.

Event Aggregator (Pub/Sub) and Mediator Together

The crux of the difference between an event aggregator and a mediator, and why these pattern names should not be interchanged, is best illustrated by showing how they can be used together. The menu example for an event aggregator is the perfect place to introduce a mediator.

Clicking a menu item may trigger a series of changes throughout an application. Some of these changes will be independent of others, and using an event aggregator makes sense. Some of these changes may be internally related, though, and may use a mediator to enact those changes.

A mediator could then be set up to listen to the event aggregator. It could run its logic and process to facilitate and coordinate many objects related to each other but unrelated to the original event source:

```
const MenuItem = MyFrameworkView.extend({
    events: {
        'click .thatThing': 'clickedIt',
    },

    clickedIt(e) {
        e.preventDefault();

        // assume this triggers "menu:click:foo"
        MyFramework.trigger(`menu:click:${this.model.get('name')}`);
    },
});

// ... somewhere else in the app

class MyWorkflow {
    constructor() {
        MyFramework.on('menu:click:foo', this.doStuff, this);
    }

    static doStuff() {
        // instantiate multiple objects here.
        // set up event handlers for those objects.
        // coordinate all of the objects into a meaningful workflow.
    }
}
```

In this example, when the `MenuItem` with the right model is clicked, the `menu:click:foo` event will be triggered. An instance of the `MyWorkflow` class will handle this specific event and coordinate all of the objects it knows about to create the desired user experience and workflow.

We have thus combined an event aggregator and a mediator to create a meaningful experience in both code and application. We now have a clean separation between the menu and the workflow through an event aggregator, and we are still keeping the workflow clean and maintainable through a mediator.

Mediator/Middleware in Modern JavaScript

Express.js (*https://oreil.ly/JFzNB*) is a popular web application server framework. We can add callbacks to certain routes that the user can access.

Say we want to add a header to the request if the user hits the root (/). We can add this header in a middleware callback:

```
const app = require("express")();

app.use("/", (req, res, next) => {
  req.headers["test-header"] = 1234;
  next();
});
```

The `next()` method calls the next callback in the request-response cycle. We'd create a chain of middleware functions that sit between the request and the response or vice versa. We can track and modify the request object all the way to the response through one or multiple middleware functions.

The middleware callbacks will be invoked whenever the user hits a root endpoint (/):

```
const app = require("express")();
const html = require("./data");

  app.use(
    "/",
    (req, res, next) => {
      req.headers["test-header"] = 1234;
      next();
    },
    (req, res, next) => {
      console.log(`Request has test header: ${!!req.headers["test-header"]}`);
      next();
    }
  );

  app.get("/", (req, res) => {
    res.set("Content-Type", "text/html");
    res.send(Buffer.from(html));
  });

  app.listen(8080, function() {
    console.log("Server is running on 8080");
  });
```

Mediator Versus Facade

We will be covering the Facade pattern shortly, but for reference purposes, some developers may also wonder whether there are similarities between the Mediator and Facade patterns. They both abstract the functionality of existing modules, but there are some subtle differences.

The Mediator centralizes communication between modules where these modules explicitly reference it. In a sense, this is multidirectional. The Facade, however, defines a more straightforward interface to a module or system but doesn't add any additional functionality. Other modules in the system aren't directly aware of the concept of a facade and could be considered unidirectional.

The Command Pattern

The Command pattern aims to encapsulate method invocation, requests, or operations into a single object and allows us to both parameterize and pass method calls that can be executed at our discretion. In addition, it enables us to decouple objects invoking the action from the objects that implement them, giving us greater flexibility in swapping out concrete *classes* (objects).

Concrete classes are best explained in terms of class-based programming languages and are related to the idea of abstract classes. An *abstract* class defines an interface but doesn't necessarily provide implementations for all its member functions. It acts as a base class from which others are derived. A derived class that implements the missing functionality is called a *concrete* class (see Figure 7-12). Base and concrete classes can be implemented in JavaScript (ES2015+) using the `extends` keyword applicable to the JavaScript classes.

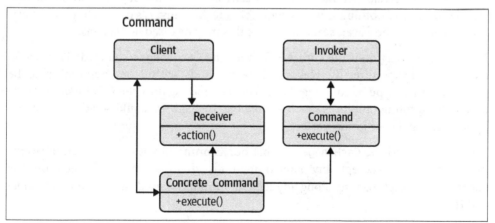

Figure 7-12. Command pattern

The general idea behind the Command pattern is that it provides a means to separate the responsibilities of issuing commands from anything executing commands, delegating this responsibility to different objects instead.

Implementation-wise, simple command objects bind the action and the object wishing to invoke the action. They consistently include an execution operation (such as run() or execute()). All command objects with the same interface can easily be swapped as needed, which is one of the vital benefits of the pattern.

To demonstrate the Command pattern, we will create a simple car purchasing service:

```
const CarManager = {
      // request information
      requestInfo(model, id) {
          return `The information for ${model} with ID ${id} is foobar`;
      },

      // purchase the car
      buyVehicle(model, id) {
          return `You have successfully purchased Item ${id}, a ${model}`;
      },

      // arrange a viewing
      arrangeViewing(model, id) {
          return `You have booked a viewing of ${model} ( ${id} ) `;
      },
  };
```

The CarManager object is our command object responsible for issuing commands to request information about a car, buy a car, and arrange a viewing. It would be trivial to invoke our CarManager methods by directly accessing the object. It would be forgivable to assume nothing is wrong with this—technically, it's completely valid JavaScript. There are, however, scenarios where this may be disadvantageous.

For example, imagine if the core API behind the CarManager changed. This would require all objects directly accessing these methods within our application to be modified. It is a type of coupling that effectively goes against the OOP methodology of loosely coupling objects as much as possible. Instead, we could solve this problem by abstracting the API away further.

Let's now expand the CarManager so that our Command pattern application results in the following: accept any named methods that can be performed on the CarManager object, passing along any data that might be used, such as the car model and ID.

Here is what we would like to be able to achieve:

```
CarManager.execute('buyVehicle', 'Ford Escort', '453543');
```

As per this structure, we should now add a definition for the `carManager.execute` method as follows:

```
carManager.execute = function(name) {
    return (
        carManager[name] &&
        carManager[name].apply(carManager, [].slice.call(arguments, 1))
    );
};
```

Our final sample calls would thus look as follows:

```
carManager.execute('arrangeViewing', 'Ferrari', '14523');
carManager.execute('requestInfo', 'Ford Mondeo', '54323');
carManager.execute('requestInfo', 'Ford Escort', '34232');
carManager.execute('buyVehicle', 'Ford Escort', '34232');
```

Summary

With that, we can conclude our discussion of traditional design patterns you can use when designing classes, objects, and modules. I have tried incorporating an ideal mix of creational, structural, and behavioral patterns. We have also studied patterns created for classic OOP languages such as Java and C++ and adapted them for JavaScript.

These patterns will help us design many domain-specific objects (e.g., shopping cart, vehicle, or book) that make up our applications' business model. In the next chapter, we will look at the larger picture of how we can structure applications so that this model delivers to the other application layers, such as the view or the presenter.

CHAPTER 8

JavaScript MV* Patterns

Object design and application architecture are the two principal aspects of application design. We have covered patterns that relate to the first in the previous chapter. In this chapter, we're going to review three fundamental architectural patterns: MVC (Model-View-Controller), MVP (Model-View-Presenter), and MVVM (Model-View-ViewModel). In the past, these patterns were heavily used for structuring desktop and server-side applications. Now they have been adapted for JavaScript too.

As most JavaScript developers currently using these patterns opt to utilize various libraries or frameworks for implementing an MVC/MV*-like structure, we will compare how these solutions differ in their interpretation of MVC compared to classical takes on these patterns.

 You can easily distinguish the Model and View layers in most modern browser-based UI design frameworks based on MVC/MVVM. However, the third component varies in both name and function. The * in MV* thus represents whatever form the third component takes in the different frameworks.

MVC

MVC is an architectural design pattern that encourages improved application organization through a separation of concerns. It enforces the isolation of business data (Models) from UIs (Views), with a third component (Controllers) traditionally managing logic and user input. Trygve Reenskaug (*https://oreil.ly/N9Dt5*) originally designed the pattern while working on Smalltalk-80 (*https://oreil.ly/6gft1*) (1979), where it was initially called Model-View-Controller-Editor. MVC was later described in depth in 1995's *Design Patterns: Elements of Reusable Object-Oriented Software* (aka the "GoF" book), which played a role in popularizing its use.

Smalltalk-80 MVC

It's essential to understand what the original MVC pattern was aiming to solve, as it has mutated quite heavily since its origin. Back in the 1970s, GUIs were few and far between. A concept known as Separated Presentation (*https://oreil.ly/yTX-F*) became famous as a means to make a clear division between domain objects that modeled ideas in the real world (e.g., a photo, a person) and the presentation objects that were rendered to the users' screen.

The Smalltalk-80 implementation of MVC took this concept further and aimed to separate the application logic from the UI. The idea was that decoupling these parts of the application would also allow the reuse of Models for other interfaces in the application. There are some interesting points worth noting about Smalltalk-80's MVC architecture:

- A Model represented domain-specific data and was ignorant of the UI (Views and Controllers). When a Model changed, it would inform its observers.

- A View represented the current state of a Model. The Observer pattern was used to let the View know whenever the Model was updated or modified.

- The View took care of the presentation, but there wasn't just a single View and Controller—a View-Controller pair was required for each section or element displayed on the screen.

- The Controller's role in this pair was handling user interaction (such as key presses and actions such as clicks) and making decisions for the View.

Developers are sometimes surprised when they learn that the Observer pattern (nowadays commonly implemented as the Publish/Subscribe variation) was included as a part of MVC's architecture decades ago. In Smalltalk-80's MVC, the View observes the Model. As mentioned in the bullet point, anytime the Model changes, the Views react. A simple example of this is an application backed by stock market data. For the application to be helpful, any change to the data in our Models should result in the View being refreshed instantly.

Martin Fowler (*https://oreil.ly/yTX-F*) has done an excellent job of writing about the origins of MVC over the years. If you're interested in some further historical information about Smalltalk-80's, I recommend reading his work.

MVC for JavaScript Developers

We've reviewed the 1970s, but let us return to the present. In modern times, the MVC pattern has been used with a diverse range of programming languages and application types, including those of most relevance to us: JavaScript. JavaScript now has several frameworks boasting support for MVC (or variations of it, which we refer to as the MV* family), allowing developers to add structure to their applications easily.

The first among these frameworks include Backbone, Ember.js, and AngularJS. More recently, React, Angular, and Vue.js ecosystems have been used to implement variations of the MV* family of patterns. Given the importance of avoiding "spaghetti" code, a term that describes code that is very difficult to read or maintain due to its lack of structure, the modern JavaScript developer must understand what this pattern provides. This allows us to effectively appreciate what these frameworks enable us to do differently (Figure 8-1).

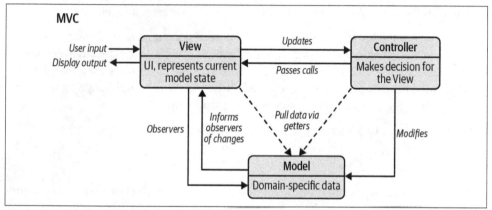

Figure 8-1. MVC pattern

MVC comprises three core components, described in the following sections.

Models

Models manage the data for an application. They are concerned with neither the UI nor presentation layers but represent unique data forms that an application may require. When a Model changes (e.g., when it is updated), it will typically notify its observers (e.g., Views, a concept we will cover shortly) that a change has occurred so that it may react accordingly.

To understand Models further, let us imagine we have a photo gallery application. In a photo gallery, the concept of a photo would merit its own Model, as it represents a unique kind of domain-specific data. Such a Model may contain related attributes such as a caption, image source, and additional metadata. You would store a specific photo in an instance of a Model, and a Model may also be reusable.

The built-in capabilities of Models vary across frameworks. However, it is pretty standard for them to support the validation of attributes, where attributes represent the properties of the Model, such as a Model identifier. When using Models in real-world applications, we generally also desire Model persistence. Persistence allows us to edit and update Models with the knowledge that their most recent state will be saved in either memory, local storage, or synchronized with a database.

In addition, a Model may have multiple Views observing it. If, say, our photo Model contained metadata, such as its location (longitude and latitude), friends who were present in the photo (a list of identifiers), and a list of tags, a developer may decide to provide a single View to display each of these three facets.

It is not uncommon for MVC/MV* frameworks to provide a means to group Models as a collection. Managing Models in groups allows us to write application logic based on notifications from the group whenever any of the Models in the group is changed. This avoids the need to observe individual Model instances manually.

Older texts on MVC may also refer to a notion of Models managing application *state*. In JavaScript applications, the *state* has a different connotation, typically referring to the current "state"—i.e., view or subview (with specific data) on a user's screen at a fixed point. The state is regularly discussed when looking at single-page applications (SPAs), where the concept of state needs to be simulated.

So to summarize, Models are primarily concerned with business data.

Views

Views are a visual representation of Models that present a filtered view of their current state. While Smalltalk Views are about painting and maintaining a bitmap, JavaScript Views build and organize a collection of DOM elements.

A View typically observes a Model and is notified when the Model changes, allowing the View to update itself accordingly. Design pattern literature commonly refers to Views as "dumb," given that their knowledge of Models and Controllers in an application is limited.

Users can interact with Views, including the ability to read and edit (i.e., get or set the attribute values in) Models. Because the View is the presentation layer, we generally present the ability to edit and update in a user-friendly fashion. For example, in the photo gallery application we discussed earlier, we could facilitate Model editing through an "edit" View where a user who selected a specific photo could edit its metadata.

The actual task of updating the Model falls to the Controllers (which we will cover shortly).

Let's explore Views a little further using a conventional JavaScript sample implementation. Now we can see a function that creates a single photo View, consuming both a Model and a Controller instance.

We define a `render()` utility within our View, which is responsible for rendering the contents of the `photoModel` using a JavaScript templating engine (Lodash templating) and updating the contents of our View, referenced by `photoEl`.

The `photoModel` then adds our `render()` callback as one of its subscribers so that we can trigger the View to update when the Model changes using the Observer pattern.

One may wonder where user interaction comes into play here. When users click on any element within the View, it's not the View's responsibility to know what to do next. It relies on a Controller to make this decision for it. Our sample implementation achieves this by adding an event listener to `photoEl`, which will delegate handling the click behavior back to the Controller, passing the Model information along with it in case it's needed.

The architecture's benefit is that each component plays its role in making the application function as needed:

```js
const buildPhotoView = (photoModel, photoController) => {
  const base = document.createElement( "div" );
  const photoEl = document.createElement( "div" );

  base.appendChild(photoEl);

  const render = () => {
        // We use Lodash's template method
        // which generates the HTML for our photo entry
        photo entry
        photoEl.innerHTML = _.template("#photoTemplate", {
            src: photoModel.getSrc()
        });
  };

  photoModel.addSubscriber( render );

  photoEl.addEventListener( "click", () => {
    photoController.handleEvent( "click", photoModel );
  });

  const show = () => {
    photoEl.style.display = "";
  };

  const hide = () => {
    photoEl.style.display = "none";
  };

  return {
    showView: show,
    hideView: hide
  };
};
```

Templating

It would be worthwhile to briefly touch upon JavaScript templating while discussing JavaScript frameworks that support MVC/MV*. As mentioned in the previous section, templating is related to Views.

It has long been considered (and proven) a performance bad practice to manually create large blocks of HTML markup in memory through string concatenation. Developers have fallen prey to inefficient iterations through their data, wrapping it in nested divs and using outdated techniques such as document.write to inject the generated "template" into the DOM. This typically means including scripted markup inline with our standard markup. The markup can quickly become difficult to read, and, more importantly, a non-trivial application with such code can be a maintenance disaster.

Modern JavaScript templating solutions have moved toward using tagged template literals, which are a powerful feature of ES6 (ECMAScript 2015). Tagged template literals allow you to create reusable templates using JavaScript's template literal syntax, along with a custom processing function that can be used to manipulate and populate the template with data. This approach eliminates the need for additional templating libraries and provides a clean, maintainable way to create dynamic HTML content.

Variables within tagged template literals can be easily interpolated using the ${variable} syntax, which is more concise and easier to read than traditional variable delimiters like {{name}}. This makes it simpler to maintain clean Models and templates while allowing the framework to handle most of the work for populating templates from Models. This has many benefits, particularly when opting to store templates externally. This can give way to templates being dynamically loaded on an as-needed basis when building larger applications.

Examples 8-1 and 8-2 are two examples of JavaScript templates. One has been implemented using tagged template literals, and another using Lodash's templates.

Example 8-1. Tagged template literals code

```
// Sample data
const photos = [
  {
    caption: 'Sample Photo 1',
    src: 'photo1.jpg',
    metadata: 'Some metadata for photo 1',
  },
  {
    caption: 'Sample Photo 2',
    src: 'photo2.jpg',
    metadata: 'Some metadata for photo 2',
  },
];
```

```javascript
// Tagged template literal function
function photoTemplate(strings, caption, src, metadata) {
  return strings[0] + caption + strings[1] + src + strings[2] + metadata
    + strings[3];
}

// Define the template as a tagged template literal string
const template = (caption, src, metadata) => photoTemplate`<li class="photo">
  <h2>${caption}</h2>
  <img class="source" src="${src}"/>
  <div class="metadata">
    ${metadata}
  </div>
</li>`;

// Loop through the data and populate the template
const photoList = document.createElement('ul');
photos.forEach((photo) => {
  const photoItem = template(photo.caption, photo.src, photo.metadata);
  photoList.innerHTML += photoItem;
});

// Insert the populated template into the DOM
document.body.appendChild(photoList);
```

Example 8-2. Lodash.js templates

```html
<li class="photo">
  <h2><%- caption %></h2>
  <img class="source" src="<%- src %>"/>
  <div class="metadata">
    <%- metadata %>
  </div>
</li>
```

Note that templates are not themselves Views. A View is an object that observes a Model and keeps the visual representation up to date. A template *might* be a declarative way to specify part or even all of a View object so that the framework may generate it from the template specification.

It is also worth noting that in classical web development, navigating between independent Views required the use of a page refresh. In single-page JavaScript applications, however, once data is fetched from a server, it can be dynamically rendered in a new View within the same page without any such refresh being necessary. The navigation role thus falls to a router, which assists in managing application state (e.g., allowing users to bookmark a particular View they have navigated to). However, as routers are neither a part of MVC nor present in every MVC-like framework, I will not be going into them in greater detail in this section.

To summarize, Views represent our application data visually, and templates may be used to generate Views. Modern templating techniques, like tagged template literals, provide a clean, efficient, and maintainable way to create dynamic HTML content in JavaScript applications.

Controllers

Controllers are intermediaries between Models and Views, which are classically responsible for updating the Model when the user manipulates the View. They manage the logic and coordination between Models and Views in an application.

What Does MVC Give Us?

This separation of concerns in MVC facilitates simpler modularization of an application's functionality and enables:

- Easier overall maintenance. When the application needs to be updated, it is obvious whether the changes are data-centric, meaning changes to Models and possibly Controllers, or merely visual, meaning changes to Views.

- Decoupling Models and Views means that writing unit tests for business logic is significantly more straightforward.

- Duplication of low-level Model and Controller code (i.e., what we may have been using instead) is eliminated across the application.

- Depending on the size of the application and the separation of roles, this modularity allows developers responsible for core logic and developers working on the UIs to work simultaneously.

Smalltalk-80 MVC in JavaScript

Most modern-day JavaScript frameworks attempt to evolve the MVC paradigm to fit the differing needs of web application development. However, there has been one framework that tried to adhere to the pure form of the pattern found in Smalltalk-80. Maria.js (*https://oreil.ly/rNJLu*) by Peter Michaux offers an implementation that is faithful to MVC's origins: Models are Models, Views are Views, and Controllers are nothing but Controllers. While some developers might feel an MV* framework should address more concerns, this is a valuable reference to be aware of in case you would like a JavaScript implementation of the original MVC.

An Alternate View of MVC

At this point in the book, we should have a basic understanding of the MVC pattern, but there's still some fascinating information about it worth noting.

The GoF does not refer to MVC as a design pattern but considers it *a set of classes to build a UI*. In their view, it's a variation of three classical design patterns: the Observer, Strategy, and Composite patterns. Depending on how MVC has been implemented in a framework, it may also use the Factory and Template patterns. The GoF book mentions these patterns as useful extras when working with MVC.

As we have discussed, Models represent application data, while Views represent what the user is presented with on-screen. As such, MVC relies on the Observer pattern for some of its core communication (something that, surprisingly, isn't covered in many articles about the MVC pattern). When a Model is changed, it notifies its observers (Views) that something has been updated—this is perhaps the most crucial relationship in MVC. The observer nature of this relationship also facilitates multiple Views being attached to the same Model.

For developers interested in the decoupled nature of MVC, one of the goals of the pattern is to help define one-to-many relationships between a topic and its observers. When a topic changes, its observers are updated. Views and Controllers have a slightly different relationship. Controllers facilitate Views to respond to user input and are an example of the Strategy pattern.

Summary of MVC

Having reviewed the classical MVC pattern, we should now understand how it allows us to cleanly separate concerns in an application. We should also appreciate how JavaScript MVC frameworks may differ in their interpretation of the MVC pattern. Although quite open to variation, they still share some fundamental concepts the original pattern offers.

When reviewing a new JavaScript MVC/MV* framework, remember: it can be helpful to step back and examine how it has opted to approach the architecture (specifically, how it supports implementing Models, Views, Controllers, or other alternatives), as this can better help us grok the best way to use the framework.

MVP

Model-View-Presenter (MVP) is a derivative of the MVC design pattern that focuses on improving presentation logic. It originated at a company named Taligent (*https://oreil.ly/sKiE8*) in the early 1990s while they were working on a Model for a C++ CommonPoint environment. While both MVC and MVP target the separation of concerns across multiple components, there are some fundamental differences between them.

Here, we will focus on the version of MVP most suitable for web-based architectures.

Models, Views, and Presenters

The P in MVP stands for Presenter. It's a component that contains the UI business logic for the View. Unlike MVC, invocations from the View are delegated to the Presenters, which are decoupled from the View and instead talk to it through an interface. This has many advantages, such as being able to mock Views in unit tests (MVP pattern) (Figure 8-2).

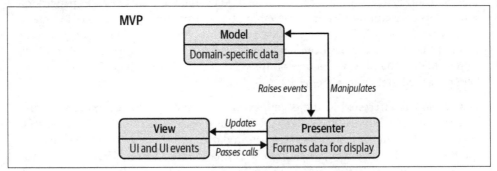

Figure 8-2. MVP pattern

The most common implementation of MVP is one that uses a passive View (a View which is, for all intents and purposes, "dumb"), containing little to no logic. MVC and MVP are different because the roles played by C and P are diverse. In MVP, the P observes Models and updates Views when Models change. The P effectively binds Models to Views, a Controller's responsibility in MVC.

Solicited by a View, Presenters perform any work related to user requests and pass data back to them. In this respect, they retrieve data, manipulate it, and determine how the data should be displayed in the View. In some implementations, the Presenter also interacts with a service layer to persist data (Models). Models may trigger events, but it's the Presenter's role to subscribe to them so that it can update the View. In this passive architecture, we have no concept of direct data binding. Views expose setters that Presenters can use to set data.

The benefit of this change from MVC is that it increases our application's testability and provides a cleaner separation between the View and the Model. This isn't, however, without its costs, as the lack of data-binding support in the pattern can often mean having to take care of this task separately.

Although a common implementation of a passive View (*https://oreil.ly/SQUNj*) is for the View to implement an interface, there are variations on it, including the use of events that can decouple the View from the Presenter a little more. As we don't have the interface construct in JavaScript, we use more of a protocol than an explicit interface here. It's technically still an API, and it's probably fair for us to refer to it as an interface from that perspective.

There is also a Supervising Controller (*https://oreil.ly/RZM34*) variation of MVP, closer to the MVC and MVVM (*https://oreil.ly/f5apN*) patterns, as it provides data binding from the Model directly from the View.

MVP or MVC?

Now that we've discussed both MVP and MVC, how do you select the most appropriate pattern for your application?

MVP is generally used in enterprise-level applications where it's necessary to reuse as much presentation logic as possible. Applications with very complex Views and a great deal of user interaction may find that MVC doesn't quite fit the bill here, as solving this problem may mean heavily relying on multiple Controllers. In MVP, all of this complex logic can be encapsulated in a Presenter, significantly simplifying maintenance.

As MVP Views are defined through an interface, and the interface is technically the only point of contact between the system and the View (other than a Presenter), this pattern also allows developers to write presentation logic without needing to wait for designers to produce layouts and graphics for the application.

MVP may be easier to unit test than MVC, depending on the implementation. The reason often cited for this is that you can use the Presenter as a complete mock of the UI so it can be unit-tested independent of other components. In my experience, this depends on the languages we are implementing MVP in (there's quite a difference between opting for MVP for a JavaScript project over one for, say, ASP.NET).

The underlying concerns we may have with MVC will likely hold for MVP, given that the differences between them are mainly semantic. As long as we cleanly separate concerns into Models, Views, and Controllers (or Presenters), we should achieve most of the same benefits regardless of the variation we choose.

Few, if any, JavaScript architectural frameworks claim to implement the MVC or MVP patterns in their classical form. Many JavaScript developers don't view MVC and MVP as mutually exclusive (we are more likely to see MVP strictly implemented in web frameworks such as ASP.NET or Google Web Toolkit). This is because we can have additional Presenter/View logic in our application and still consider it a flavor of MVC.

MVVM

MVVM (Model-View-ViewModel) is an architectural pattern based on MVC and MVP, which attempts to more clearly separate the development of UIs from that of the business logic and behavior in an application. To this end, many implementations of this pattern make use of declarative data bindings to allow a separation of work on Views from other layers.

This facilitates UI and development work occurring almost simultaneously within the same codebase. UI developers write bindings to the ViewModel within their document markup (HTML), whereas developers working on the logic for the application maintain the Model and ViewModel (Figure 8-3).

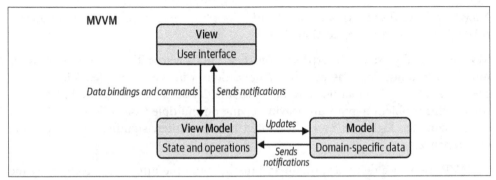

Figure 8-3. MVVM pattern

History

MVVM (by name) was initially defined by Microsoft for use with Windows Presentation Foundation (WPF) (*https://oreil.ly/1_I11*) and Silverlight (*https://oreil.ly/ve1Oh*), having been officially announced in 2005 by John Grossman in a blog post about Avalon (the codename for WPF). It also found some popularity in the Adobe Flex community as an alternative to using MVC.

Before Microsoft adopted the MVVM name, there was a movement in the community to go from MVP to MVPM: Model-View PresentationModel. Martin Fowler wrote an article on PresentationModels back in 2004 (*https://oreil.ly/78R8q*) for those interested in reading more about it. The idea of a PresentationModel had been around much longer than this article. However, it was considered a significant break for the concept and helped popularize it.

There was quite a lot of uproar in the "alt.net" circles after Microsoft announced MVVM as an alternative to MVPM. Many claimed the company's dominance in the GUI world allowed them to take over the community, renaming existing concepts as they pleased for marketing purposes. A progressive crowd recognized that while MVVM and MVPM were effectively the same ideas, they came in slightly different packages.

MVVM was originally implemented in JavaScript in the form of structural frameworks such as KnockoutJS, Kendo MVVM, and Knockback.js, with an overall positive response from the community.

Let's now review the three components that compose MVVM:

Model
> Representing the domain-specific information

View
> The UI

ViewModel
> An interface between the Model and the View

Model

As with other members of the MV* family, the Model in MVVM represents domain-specific data or information with which our application will work. A typical example of domain-specific data might be a user account (e.g., name, avatar, email) or a music track (e.g., title, year, album).

Models hold information but typically don't handle behavior. They don't format information or influence how data appears in the browser, as this isn't their responsibility. Instead, the View governs data formatting, while the behavior is considered business logic that you should encapsulate in another layer that interacts with the Model: the ViewModel.

The only exception to this rule tends to be validation, and it's acceptable for Models to validate data used to define or update existing Models (e.g., does an email address being input meet the requirements of a particular regular expression?).

View

As with MVC, the View is the only part of the application that users interact with. The View is an interactive UI that represents the state of a ViewModel. In this sense, the View is considered active rather than passive, which is also true for MVC and MVP Views. In MVC, MVP, and MVVM, a View can also be passive, but what does this mean?

A passive View only outputs a display and does not accept any user input. Such a View may also have no real knowledge of the Models in our application and could be manipulated by a Presenter. MVVM's active View contains the data bindings, events, and behaviors, which requires an understanding of the ViewModel. Although these behaviors can be mapped to properties, the View is still responsible for handling events from the ViewModel.

It's important to remember that the View isn't responsible for handling state; it keeps this in sync with the ViewModel.

ViewModel

The ViewModel can be considered a specialized Controller that acts as a data converter. It changes Model information into View information, passing commands from the View to the Model.

For example, let us imagine that we have a Model containing a `date` attribute in UNIX format (e.g., 1333832407). Rather than our Models being aware of a user's View of the date (e.g., 04/07/2012 @ 5:00 pm), where it would be necessary to convert the address to its display format, our Model holds the raw format of the data. Our View contains the formatted date, and our ViewModel acts as a middleman between the two.

In this sense, the ViewModel can be seen as more of a Model than a View, but it does handle most of the View's display logic. The ViewModel may also expose methods for helping to maintain the View's state, update the Model based on the actions on a View, and trigger events on the View.

In summary, the ViewModel sits behind our UI layer. It exposes data needed by a View (from a Model) and can be the source the View goes to for both data and actions.

Recap: The View and the ViewModel

Views and ViewModels communicate using data bindings and events. As we saw in our initial ViewModel example, the ViewModel doesn't just expose Model attributes but also provides access to other methods and features, such as validation.

Our Views handle their own UI events, mapping them to the ViewModel as necessary. Models and attributes on the ViewModel are synchronized and updated via two-way data binding.

Triggers (data triggers) also allow us to react further to changes in the state of our Model attributes.

ViewModel Versus Model

While the ViewModel may be entirely responsible for the Model in MVVM, there are some subtleties with this relationship worth noting. The ViewModel can expose a Model or Model attributes for data binding and contain interfaces for fetching and manipulating properties exposed in the View.

Pros and Cons

We now hopefully have a better appreciation for what MVVM is and how it works. Let's review the advantages and disadvantages of employing this pattern.

Advantages

- MVVM facilitates easier parallel development of a UI and the building blocks that power it.
- MVVM abstracts the View and thus reduces the quantity of business logic (or glue) required in the code behind it.
- The ViewModel can be easier to unit test than in the case of event-driven code.
- The ViewModel (being more Model than View) can be tested without UI automation and interaction concerns.

Disadvantages

- For simpler UIs, MVVM can be overkill.
- While data bindings can be declarative and nice to work with, they can be harder to debug than imperative code, where we simply set breakpoints.
- Data bindings in nontrivial applications can create a lot of bookkeeping. We also don't want to end up in a situation where bindings are heavier than the objects being bound.
- In larger applications, it can be more challenging to design the ViewModel upfront to get the necessary generalization.

MVC Versus MVP Versus MVVM

Both MVP and MVVM are derivatives of MVC. The key difference between MVC and its derivatives is the dependency each layer has on other layers and how tightly bound they are to each other.

In MVC, the View sits on top of our architecture with the Controller beside it. Models sit below the Controller, so our Views know about our Controllers, and Controllers know about Models. Here, our Views have direct access to Models. Exposing the complete Model to the View, however, may have security and performance costs, depending on the complexity of our application. MVVM attempts to avoid these issues.

In MVP, the role of the Controller is replaced with a Presenter. Presenters sit at the same level as Views, listening to events from both the View and Model and mediating the actions between them. Unlike MVVM, there isn't a mechanism for binding Views to ViewModels, so we instead rely on each View implementing an interface allowing the Presenter to interact with the View.

MVVM consequently allows us to create View-specific subsets of a Model, which can contain state and logic information, avoiding exposing the entire Model to a View. Unlike MVP's Presenter, a ViewModel is not required to reference a View. The View can bind to properties on the ViewModel, in turn exposing data contained in Models to the View. As we've mentioned, the abstraction of the View means there is less logic required in the code behind it.

However, one of the downsides to this is that a level of interpretation is needed between the ViewModel and the View, which can have performance costs. The complexity of this interpretation can also vary: it can be as simple as copying data or as complex as manipulating it to a form we would like the View to see. MVC doesn't have this problem, as the whole Model is readily available, and such manipulation can be avoided.

Modern MV* Patterns

Frameworks such as Backbone and KnockoutJS used initially to implement MVC and MVVM are no longer popular or updated. They have made way for other libraries and frameworks such as React, Vue.js, Angular, Solid, and many others. Understanding architecture from a Backbone or KnockoutJS perspective may still be relevant because it gives us a sense of where we came from and what changed with modern frameworks.

MV* patterns can always be implemented using the latest vanilla JavaScript as illustrated by this example of a list: ToDo list MVC application (*https://oreil.ly/QVYPY*). However, developers generally prefer libraries and frameworks for building larger, scalable applications.

Technically modern libraries and frameworks such as React or Vue.js form the View or the presentation layer of applications. In most cases, the frameworks are flexible about how you implement your Model and manage the state in your applications. Vue officially claims to be the ViewModel (*https://oreil.ly/UqbVh*) layer in MVVM. Here are some additional thoughts on MV* in React.

MV* and React.js

To be very clear, React is not an MVC framework. It is a JavaScript library for building UIs and is often used for creating SPAs.

React isn't considered MVC because it doesn't map well with how it has been conceived and used on the backend. React is a rendering library that ideally takes care of the View layer. It doesn't have a central Controller as an orchestrator/router, similar to MVC.

React follows a declarative approach to programming—you describe your application's desired state, and React renders the appropriate Views based on that state. You don't use React in an MVC design pattern simply because, with React, the server does not provide a "View" to the browser but "data." React parses the data on the browser to generate the actual Views. In this sense, you could say that React is a "V" (View) in the MVC pattern, but it is not an MVC framework in the traditional sense.

Another way of looking at it is that React slices the MVC vertically (by concern) instead of horizontally (by technology). You could say Components in React started as small vertically sliced encapsulated MVCs: containing state (Model), rendering (View), and control-flow logic (a localized mini-Controller).

These days, with a lot of component logic extracted into Hooks, you can see Components as Views and Hooks as Controllers. You can also consider "Model ⇒ Suspense resource, View ⇒ Component, Controller ⇒ Hook" if it helps, but don't take it too seriously.

Next.js is a framework built on top of React that makes it easy to construct server-rendered React applications. It includes features such as automatic code splitting, optimized performance, and easy deployment to production. Like React, Next.js is not an MVC framework, but when you use server-side rendering (SSR) or static site generators (SSGs), it can be like MVC. When Next.js acts as a backend, interacting with a database and providing the View to prerender it, then yes, it's MVC that is hydrated afterward with the reactive functionalities.

Summary

We have now analyzed the concepts of Model, View, Controller, Presenter, and ViewModel and where they fit in different architectural patterns. Today, we may not see these patterns applied as-is on the frontend where JavaScript is most relevant. However, they may help us figure out the overall architecture of the web application. They may also be applied to individual frontend components where the application sliced vertically may have multiple components, each with a ViewModel or Model to power the View.

By this point, we have now covered a good mix of patterns at the micro (class) as well as macro (architecture) levels. The next chapter will help us design the application flow for a modern JavaScript application. We will look at asynchronous programming patterns that can help us better manage long-running tasks on browsers.

CHAPTER 9

Asynchronous Programming Patterns

Asynchronous JavaScript programming allows you to execute long-running tasks in the background while allowing the browser to respond to events and run other code to handle these events. Asynchronous programming is relatively new in JavaScript, and the syntax to support it was not available when the first edition of this book was published.

JavaScript concepts such as `promise`, `async`, and `await` make your code tidier and easy to read without blocking the main thread. `async` functions were introduced as part of ES7 in 2016 and are now supported on all browsers. Let's look at some patterns that use these features to structure our application flows.

Asynchronous Programming

In JavaScript, synchronous code is executed in a blocking manner, meaning that the code is executed serially, one statement at a time. The following code can run only after the execution of the current statement has been completed. When you call a synchronous function, the code inside that function will execute from start to finish before the control returns to the caller.

On the other hand, asynchronous code is executed in a nonblocking manner, meaning that the JavaScript engine can switch to execute this code in the background while the currently running code is waiting on something. When you call an asynchronous function, the code inside the function will execute in the background, and the control returns to the caller immediately.

Here is an example of synchronous code in JavaScript:

```
function synchronousFunction() {
  // do something
}

synchronousFunction();
// the code inside the function is executed before this line
```

And here is an example of asynchronous code in JavaScript:

```
function asynchronousFunction() {
  // do something
}

asynchronousFunction();
// the code inside the function is executed in the background
// while control returns to this line
```

You can generally use asynchronous code to perform long-running operations without blocking the rest of your code. Asynchronous code is suitable when making network requests, reading or writing to a database, or doing any other type of I/O (input/output) operation.

Language features such as `async`, `await`, and `promise` make writing asynchronous code in JavaScript easier. They allow you to write asynchronous code in a way that looks and behaves like synchronous code, making it easier to read and understand.

Let's briefly look at the differences between callbacks, promises, and `async/await` before diving into each in more depth:

```
// using callbacks
function makeRequest(url, callback) {
  fetch(url)
    .then(response => response.json())
    .then(data => callback(null, data))
    .catch(error => callback(error));
}

makeRequest('http://example.com/', (error, data) => {
  if (error) {
    console.error(error);
  } else {
    console.log(data);
  }
});
```

In the first example, the `makeRequest` function uses a callback to return the result of the network request. The caller passes a `callback` function to `makeRequest`, which is called back with either the result(data) or an `error`:

```
// using promises
function makeRequest(url) {
  return new Promise((resolve, reject) => {
    fetch(url)
      .then(response => response.json())
      .then(data => resolve(data))
      .catch(error => reject(error));
  });
}

makeRequest('http://example.com/')
  .then(data => console.log(data))
  .catch(error => console.error(error));
```

In the second example, the makeRequest function returns a promise that resolves with the result of the network request or rejects with an error. The caller can use the then and catch methods on the returned promise to handle the result of the request:

```
// using async/await
async function makeRequest(url) {
  try {
    const response = await fetch(url);
    const data = await response.json();
    console.log(data);
  } catch (error) {
    console.error(error);
  }
}

makeRequest('http://example.com/');
```

In the third example, the makeRequest function is declared with the async keyword, which allows it to use the await keyword to wait for the result of the network request. The caller can use the try and catch keywords to handle any errors that may occur during the execution of the function.

Background

Callback functions in JavaScript can be passed to another function as an argument and executed after some asynchronous operation is completed. Callbacks were commonly used to handle the results of asynchronous operations, such as network requests or user input.

One of the main disadvantages of using callbacks is that they can lead to what is known as "callback hell"—a situation where nested callbacks become challenging to read and maintain. Consider the following example:

```
function makeRequest1(url, callback) {
  // make network request
  callback(null, response);
```

```
}

function makeRequest2(url, callback) {
  // make network request
  callback(null, response);
}

function makeRequest3(url, callback) {
  // make network request
  callback(null, response);
}

makeRequest1('http://example.com/1', (error, data1) => {
  if (error) {
    console.error(error);
    return;
  }

  makeRequest2('http://example.com/2', (error, data2) => {
    if (error) {
      console.error(error);
      return;
    }

    makeRequest3('http://example.com/3', (error, data3) => {
      if (error) {
        console.error(error);
        return;
      }

      // do something with data1, data2, data3
    });
  });
});
```

In this example, the makeRequest1 function makes a network request and then calls the callback function with the result of the request. The callback function then makes a second network request using the makeRequest2 function, which calls another callback function with its result. This pattern continues for the third network request.

Promise Patterns

Promises are a more modern approach to handling asynchronous operations in JavaScript. A promise is an object that represents the result of an asynchronous operation. It can be in three states: pending, fulfilled, or rejected. A promise is like a contract that can be settled if it is fulfilled or rejected.

You can create a promise using the Promise constructor, which takes a function as an argument. The function receives two arguments: resolve and reject. The resolve function is called when the asynchronous operation is completed successfully, and the `reject` function is called if the operation fails.

Here is an example that shows how you can use promises to make network requests:

```
function makeRequest(url) {
  return new Promise((resolve, reject) => {
    fetch(url)
      .then(response => response.json())
      .then(data => resolve(data))
      .catch(error => reject(error));
  });
}

makeRequest('http://example.com/')
  .then(data => console.log(data))
  .catch(error => console.error(error));
```

In this example, the `makeRequest` function returns a `promise` representing the network request's result. The `fetch` method is used inside the function to make the HTTP request. If the request succeeds, the promise is fulfilled with the data from the response. If it fails, the promise is rejected with the error. The caller can use the `then` and `catch` methods on the returned promise to handle the result of the request.

One of the main advantages of using promises over callbacks is that they provide a more structured and readable approach to handling asynchronous operations. This allows you to avoid "callback hell" and write code that is easier to understand and maintain.

The following sections provide additional examples that will be relevant to help you understand the different promise design patterns that you can use in JavaScript.

Promise Chaining

This pattern allows you to chain multiple promises together to create more complex async logic:

```
function makeRequest(url) {
  return new Promise((resolve, reject) => {
    fetch(url)
      .then(response => response.json())
      .then(data => resolve(data))
      .catch(error => reject(error));
  });
}

function processData(data) {
  // process data
  return processedData;
}
```

```
makeRequest('http://example.com/')
  .then(data => processData(data))
  .then(processedData => console.log(processedData))
  .catch(error => console.error(error));
```

Promise Error Handling

This pattern uses the catch method to handle errors that may occur during the execution of a promise chain:

```
makeRequest('http://example.com/')
  .then(data => processData(data))
  .then(processedData => console.log(processedData))
  .catch(error => console.error(error));
```

Promise Parallelism

This pattern allows you to run multiple promises concurrently using the Promise.all method:

```
Promise.all([
  makeRequest('http://example.com/1'),
  makeRequest('http://example.com/2')
]).then(([data1, data2]) => {
  console.log(data1, data2);
});
```

Promise Sequential Execution

This pattern allows you to run promises in sequence using the Promise.resolve method:

```
Promise.resolve()
  .then(() => makeRequest1())
  .then(() => makeRequest2())
  .then(() => makeRequest3())
  .then(() => {
    // all requests completed
  });
```

Promise Memoization

This pattern uses a cache to store the results of promise function calls, allowing you to avoid making duplicate requests:

```
const cache = new Map();

function memoizedMakeRequest(url) {
  if (cache.has(url)) {
    return cache.get(url);
```

```
  }

  return new Promise((resolve, reject) => {
    fetch(url)
      .then(response => response.json())
      .then(data => {
        cache.set(url, data);
        resolve(data);
      })
      .catch(error => reject(error));
  });
}
```

In this example, we'll demonstrate how to use the `memoizedMakeRequest` function to avoid making duplicate requests:

```
const button = document.querySelector('button');
button.addEventListener('click', () => {
  memoizedMakeRequest('http://example.com/')
    .then(data => console.log(data))
    .catch(error => console.error(error));
});
```

Now, when the button is clicked, the `memoizedMakeRequest` function will be called. If the requested URL is already in the cache, the cached data will be returned. Otherwise, a new request will be made, and the result will be cached for future requests.

Promise Pipeline

This pattern uses promises and functional programming techniques to create a pipeline of `async` transformations:

```
function transform1(data) {
  // transform data
  return transformedData;
}

function transform2(data) {
  // transform data
  return transformedData;
}

makeRequest('http://example.com/')
  .then(data => pipeline(data)
    .then(transform1)
    .then(transform2))
  .then(transformedData => console.log(transformedData))
  .catch(error => console.error(error));
```

Promise Retry

This pattern allows you to retry a promise if it fails:

```
function makeRequestWithRetry(url) {
  let attempts = 0;

  const makeRequest = () => new Promise((resolve, reject) => {
    fetch(url)
      .then(response => response.json())
      .then(data => resolve(data))
      .catch(error => reject(error));
  });

  const retry = error => {
    attempts++;
    if (attempts >= 3) {
      throw new Error('Request failed after 3 attempts.');
    }
    console.log(`Retrying request: attempt ${attempts}`);
    return makeRequest();
  };

  return makeRequest().catch(retry);
}
```

Promise Decorator

This pattern uses a higher-order function to create a decorator that can be applied to promises to add additional behavior:

```
function logger(fn) {
  return function (...args) {
    console.log('Starting function...');
    return fn(...args).then(result => {
      console.log('Function completed.');
      return result;
    });
  };
}

const makeRequestWithLogger = logger(makeRequest);

makeRequestWithLogger('http://example.com/')
  .then(data => console.log(data))
  .catch(error => console.error(error));
```

Promise Race

This pattern allows you to run multiple promises concurrently and return the result of the first one to settle:

```
Promise.race([
  makeRequest('http://example.com/1'),
  makeRequest('http://example.com/2')
]).then(data => {
  console.log(data);
});
```

async/await Patterns

async/await is a language feature that allows a programmer to write asynchronous code as if it were synchronous. It is built on top of promises, and it makes working with asynchronous code easier and cleaner.

Here is an example of how you might use async/await to make an asynchronous HTTP request:

```
async function makeRequest() {
  try {
    const response = await fetch('http://example.com/');
    const data = await response.json();
    console.log(data);
  } catch (error) {
    console.error(error);
  }
}
```

In this example, the makeRequest function is asynchronous because it uses the async keyword. Inside the function, the await keyword is used to pause the execution of the function until the fetch call resolves. If the call succeeds, the data is logged to the console. If it fails, the error is caught and logged to the console.

Let us now look at some other patterns using async.

async Function Composition

This pattern involves composing multiple async functions together to create more complex async logic:

```
async function makeRequest(url) {
  const response = await fetch(url);
  const data = await response.json();
  return data;
}
```

```
async function processData(data) {
  // process data
  return processedData;
}

async function main() {
  const data = await makeRequest('http://example.com/');
  const processedData = await processData(data);
  console.log(processedData);
}
```

async Iteration

This pattern allows you to use the for-await-of loop to iterate over an async iterable:

```
async function* createAsyncIterable() {
  yield 1;
  yield 2;
  yield 3;
}

async function main() {
  for await (const value of createAsyncIterable()) {
    console.log(value);
  }
}
```

async Error Handling

This pattern uses try-catch blocks to handle errors that may occur during the execution of an async function:

```
async function main() {
  try {
    const data = await makeRequest('http://example.com/');
    console.log(data);
  } catch (error) {
    console.error(error);
  }
}
```

async Parallelism

This pattern allows you to run multiple async tasks concurrently using the Promise.all method:

```
async function main() {
  const [data1, data2] = await Promise.all([
    makeRequest('http://example.com/1'),
    makeRequest('http://example.com/2')
```

```
  ]);

  console.log(data1, data2);
}
```

async Sequential Execution

This pattern allows you to run `async` tasks in sequence using the `Promise.resolve` method:

```
async function main() {
  let result = await Promise.resolve();

  result = await makeRequest1(result);
  result = await makeRequest2(result);
  result = await makeRequest3(result);

  console.log(result);
}
```

async Memoization

This pattern uses a cache to store the results of `async` function calls, allowing you to avoid making duplicate requests:

```
const cache = new Map();

async function memoizedMakeRequest(url) {
  if (cache.has(url)) {
    return cache.get(url);
  }

  const response = await fetch(url);
  const data = await response.json();

  cache.set(url, data);
  return data;
}
```

async Event Handling

This pattern allows you to use `async` functions to handle events:

```
const button = document.querySelector('button');

async function handleClick() {
  const response = await makeRequest('http://example.com/');
  console.log(response);
}

button.addEventListener('click', handleClick);
```

async/await Pipeline

This pattern uses `async/await` and functional programming techniques to create a pipeline of `async` transformations:

```
async function transform1(data) {
  // transform data
  return transformedData;
}

async function transform2(data) {
  // transform data
  return transformedData;
}

async function main() {
  const data = await makeRequest('http://example.com/');
  const transformedData = await pipeline(data)
    .then(transform1)
    .then(transform2);

  console.log(transformedData);
}
```

async Retry

This pattern allows you to retry an `async` operation if it fails:

```
async function makeRequestWithRetry(url) {
  let attempts = 0;

  while (attempts < 3) {
    try {
      const response = await fetch(url);
      const data = await response.json();
      return data;
    } catch (error) {
      attempts++;
      console.log(`Retrying request: attempt ${attempts}`);
    }
  }

  throw new Error('Request failed after 3 attempts.');
}
```

async/await Decorator

This pattern uses a higher-order function to create a decorator that can be applied to async functions to add additional behavior:

```
function asyncLogger(fn) {
  return async function (...args) {
    console.log('Starting async function...');
    const result = await fn(...args);
    console.log('Async function completed.');
    return result;
  };
}

@asyncLogger
async function main() {
  const data = await makeRequest('http://example.com/');
  console.log(data);
}
```

Additional Practical Examples

In addition to the patterns discussed in the previous sections, let's take a look at some practical examples of using async/await in JavaScript.

Making an HTTP Request

```
async function makeRequest(url) {
  try {
    const response = await fetch(url);
    const data = await response.json();
    console.log(data);
  } catch (error) {
    console.error(error);
  }
}
```

Reading a File from the Filesystem

```
async function readFile(filePath) {
  try {
    const fileData = await fs.promises.readFile(filePath);
    console.log(fileData);
  } catch (error) {
    console.error(error);
  }
}
```

Writing to a File on the Filesystem

```
async function writeFile(filePath, data) {
  try {
    await fs.promises.writeFile(filePath, data);
    console.log('File written successfully.');
  } catch (error) {
```

```
      console.error(error);
    }
  }
```

Executing Multiple async Operations

```
async function main() {
  try {
    const [data1, data2] = await Promise.all([
      makeRequest1(),
      makeRequest2()
    ]);
    console.log(data1, data2);
  } catch (error) {
    console.error(error);
  }
}
```

Executing Multiple async Operations in Sequence

```
async function main() {
  try {
    const data1 = await makeRequest1();
    const data2 = await makeRequest2();
    console.log(data1, data2);
  } catch (error) {
    console.error(error);
  }
}
```

Caching the Result of an async Operation

```
const cache = new Map();

async function makeRequest(url) {
  if (cache.has(url)) {
    return cache.get(url);
  }

  try {
    const response = await fetch(url);
    const data = await response.json();
    cache.set(url, data);
    return data;
  } catch (error) {
    throw error;
  }
}
```

Handling Events with async/await

```
const button = document.querySelector('button');

button.addEventListener('click', async () => {
  try {
    const data = await makeRequest('http://example.com/');
    console.log(data);
  } catch (error) {
    console.error(error);
  }
});
```

Retrying an async Operation on Failure

```
async function makeRequest(url) {
  try {
    const response = await fetch(url);
    const data = await response.json();
    return data;
  } catch (error) {
    throw error;
  }
}

async function retry(fn, maxRetries = 3, retryDelay = 1000) {
  let retries = 0;

  while (retries <= maxRetries) {
    try {
      return await fn();
    } catch (error) {
      retries++;
      console.error(error);
      await new Promise(resolve => setTimeout(resolve, retryDelay));
    }
  }

  throw new Error(`Failed after ${retries} retries.`);
}

retry(() => makeRequest('http://example.com/')).then(data => {
  console.log(data);
});
```

Creating an async/await Decorator

```
function asyncDecorator(fn) {
  return async function(...args) {
    try {
      return await fn(...args);
    } catch (error) {
```

```
      throw error;
    }
  };
}
const makeRequest = asyncDecorator(async function(url) {
  const response = await fetch(url);
  const data = await response.json();
  return data;
});

makeRequest('http://example.com/').then(data => {
  console.log(data);
});
```

Summary

This chapter covered an extensive set of patterns and examples that can be useful when writing asynchronous code for executing long-running tasks in the background. We saw how `callback` functions made way for promises and `async`/`await` to execute one or many `async` tasks.

In the next chapter, we will look at another angle of application architecture patterns. We will look at how the patterns for modular development have evolved over time.

CHAPTER 10

Modular JavaScript Design Patterns

In the world of scalable JavaScript, when we say an application is *modular*, we often mean it's composed of a set of highly decoupled, distinct pieces of functionality stored in modules. Loose coupling facilitates easier maintainability of apps by removing *dependencies* where possible. When implemented efficiently, it becomes pretty easy to see how changes to one part of a system may affect another.

In the earlier chapters, we covered the importance of modular programming and the modern way of implementing modular design patterns. While ES2015 (*https://oreil.ly/Pcc5o*) introduced native modules to JavaScript, writing modular JavaScript was still possible before 2015.

In this section, we will look at three formats for modular JavaScript using classic JavaScript (ES5) syntax: Asynchronous Module Definition (AMD), CommonJS, and Universal Module Definition (UMD). To learn more about JavaScript modules, please refer to Chapter 5, which covers ES2015+ syntax for module imports, exports, and more.

A Note on Script Loaders

It isn't easy to discuss AMD and CommonJS modules without talking about script loaders (*https://oreil.ly/ssCQT*). Script loading was a means to a goal. Modular JavaScript could be implemented only using compatible script loaders.

Several great loaders were available for handling module loading in the AMD and CommonJS formats, but I personally preferred RequireJS (*https://oreil.ly/Ri_9R*) and curl.js (*https://oreil.ly/s7QRg*).

AMD

The AMD format was introduced as a proposal for defining modules in which both the module and dependencies can be asynchronously loaded (*https://oreil.ly/iTNe3*). The overall goal for the AMD format is to provide a solution for modular JavaScript that developers could use. It has several distinct advantages, including being both asynchronous and highly flexible by nature, which removes the tight coupling one might commonly find between code and module identity. Many developers enjoyed using AMD, and one could consider it a reliable stepping stone toward JavaScript modules (*https://oreil.ly/yxADG*), which were unavailable at the time.

AMD began as a draft specification for a module format on the CommonJS list, but as it couldn't reach full consensus, further development of the format moved to the amdjs group (*https://oreil.ly/0-XeU*).

It was embraced by projects including Dojo, MooTools, and even jQuery. Although the term *CommonJS AMD format* has been seen in the wild occasionally, it's best to refer to it as just AMD or Async Module support because not all participants on the CommonJS list wished to pursue it.

> There was a time when the proposal was referred to as Modules Transport/C. However, because the spec wasn't geared toward transporting existing CommonJS modules but rather for defining modules, it made more sense to opt for the AMD naming convention.

Getting Started with Modules

The first two concepts worth noting about AMD are the ideas of a `define` method for facilitating module definition and a `require` method for handling dependency loading. `define` is used to define named or unnamed modules using the following signature:

```
define(
    module_id /*optional*/,
    [dependencies] /*optional*/,
    definition function {} /*function for instantiating the module or object*/
);
```

As we can tell by the inline comments, the `module_id` is an optional argument that is typically required only when non-AMD concatenation tools are being used (there may be some other edge cases where it's useful, too). When this argument is left out, we refer to the module as *anonymous*.

When working with anonymous modules, the idea of a module's identity is DRY (Don't repeat yourself), making it trivial to avoid duplication of filenames and code.

Because the code is more portable, it can be easily moved to other locations (or around the filesystem) without needing to alter the code itself or change its module ID. Consider the module_id similar to the concept of folder paths.

 Developers can run this same code on multiple environments using an AMD optimizer that works with a CommonJS environment such as r.js (*https://oreil.ly/48dSL*).

Back to the define signature, the dependencies argument represents an array of dependencies required by the module we are defining, and the third argument (definition function or factory function) is a function that's executed to instantiate our module. A bare bones module could be defined as in Example 10-1.

Example 10-1. Understanding AMD: define()

```
// A module_id (myModule) is used here for demonstration purposes only
define( "myModule",

    ["foo", "bar"],

    // module definition function
    // dependencies (foo and bar) are mapped to function parameters
    function ( foo, bar ) {
        // return a value that defines the module export
        // (i.e., the functionality we want to expose for consumption)

        // create your module here
        var myModule = {
            doStuff:function () {
                console.log( "Yay! Stuff" );
            }
        };

    return myModule;
});

// An alternative version could be...
define( "myModule",

    ["math", "graph"],

    function ( math, graph ) {

        // Note that this is a slightly different pattern
        // With AMD, it's possible to define modules in a few
        // different ways due to its flexibility with
        // certain aspects of the syntax
```

```
        return {
            plot: function( x, y ){
                return graph.drawPie( math.randomGrid( x, y ) );
            }
        };
});
```

On the other hand, `require` is typically used to load code in a top-level JavaScript file or within a module should we wish to fetch dependencies dynamically. An example of its usage is in Example 10-2.

Example 10-2. Understanding AMD: require()

```
// Consider "foo" and "bar" are two external modules
// In this example, the "exports" from the two modules
// loaded are passed as function arguments to the
// callback (foo and bar) so that they can similarly be accessed

require(["foo", "bar"], function ( foo, bar ) {
        // rest of your code here
        foo.doSomething();
});
```

Example 10-3 shows a dynamically loaded dependency:

Example 10-3. Dynamically loaded dependencies

```
define(function ( require ) {
    var isReady = false, foobar;

    // note the inline require within our module definition
    require(["foo", "bar"], function ( foo, bar ) {
        isReady = true;
        foobar = foo() + bar();
    });

    // we can still return a module
    return {
        isReady: isReady,
        foobar: foobar
    };
});
```

Example 10-4 shows defining an AMD-compatible plug-in.

Example 10-4. Understanding AMD: plug-ins

```
// With AMD, it's possible to load in assets of almost any kind
// including text-files and HTML. This enables us to have template
// dependencies which can be used to skin components either on
// page-load or dynamically.

define( ["./templates", "text!./template.md","css!./template.css" ],

    function( templates, template ){
        console.log( templates );
        // do something with our templates here
    }

});
```

 Although `css!` is included for loading Cascading Style Sheets (CSS) dependencies in the preceding example, it's important to remember that this approach has some caveats, such as not being able to establish when the CSS is fully loaded. Depending on how we approach our build process, it may also result in CSS being included as a dependency in the optimized file, so use CSS as a loaded dependency in such cases with caution. If you're interested in doing this, we can explore @VIISON's RequireJS CSS plug-in (*https://oreil.ly/PrLim*).

This example could simply be looked at as `requirejs(["app/myModule"], function(){})`, which indicates the loader's top-level globals are being used. This is how to kick off the top-level loading of modules with different AMD loaders. However, if a `define()` function is passed as a local require, all `require([])` examples apply to both types of loader: curl.js and RequireJS (Examples 10-5 and 10-6).

Example 10-5. Loading AMD modules using RequireJS

```
require(["app/myModule"],

    function( myModule ){
        // start the main module which in turn
        // loads other modules
        var module = new myModule();
        module.doStuff();
});
```

Example 10-6. Loading AMD modules using curl.js

```
curl(["app/myModule.js"],

    function( myModule ){
        // start the main module which in turn
        // loads other modules
        var module = new myModule();
        module.doStuff();

});
```

What follows is the code for modules with deferred dependencies:

```
<pre xmlns="http://www.w3.org/1999/xhtml" id="I_programlisting11_id234274"
data-type="programlisting" data-code-language="javascript">


// This could be compatible with jQuery's Deferred implementation,
// futures.js (slightly different syntax) or any one of a number
// of other implementations

define(["lib/Deferred"], function( Deferred ){
    var defer = new Deferred();

    require(["lib/templates/?index.html","lib/data/?stats"],
        function( template, data ){
            defer.resolve( { template: template, data:data } );
        }
    );
    return defer.promise();
});

</pre>
```

As we've seen in previous sections, design patterns can be highly effective in improving how we approach structuring solutions to common development problems. John Hann (*https://oreil.ly/SrQI5*) has given some excellent presentations about AMD module design patterns covering the Singleton, Decorator, Mediator, and others. I highly recommend checking out his slides (*https://oreil.ly/7koME*).

AMD Modules with jQuery

jQuery comes with only one file. However, given the plug-in-based nature of the library, we can demonstrate how straightforward it is to define an AMD module that uses it here:

```
// Code in app.js. baseURl set to the lib folder
// containing jquery, jquery.color, and lodash files.
define(["jquery","jquery.color","lodash"], function( $, colorPlugin, _ ){
    // Here we've passed in jQuery, the color plugin, and Lodash
```

```
    // None of these will be accessible in the global scope, but we
    // can easily reference them below.

    // Pseudorandomize an array of colors, selecting the first
    // item in the shuffled array
    var shuffleColor = _.first( _.shuffle(["#AAA","#FFF","#111","#F16"]));
    console.log(shuffleColor);

    // Animate the background color of any elements with the class
    // "item" on the page using the shuffled color
    $( ".item" ).animate( {"backgroundColor": shuffleColor } );

    // What we return can be used by other modules
    return function () {};
});
```

However, there is something missing from this example, and it's the registration concept.

Registering jQuery as an async-compatible module

One of the key features that landed in jQuery 1.7 was support for registering jQuery as an asynchronous module. A number of compatible script loaders (including RequireJS and curl) are capable of loading modules using an asynchronous module format, which means fewer hacks are required to get things working.

If a developer wants to use AMD and does not want her jQuery version leaking into the global space, she should call noConflict in their top-level module that uses jQuery. In addition, since multiple versions of jQuery can be on a page, there are special considerations that an AMD loader must account for, so jQuery only registers with AMD loaders that have recognized these concerns, which are indicated by the loader specifying define.amd.jQuery. RequireJS and curl are two loaders that do so.

The named AMD provides a robust and safe safety blanket for most use cases:

```
// Account for the existence of more than one global
// instance of jQuery in the document, cater for testing
// .noConflict()

var jQuery = this.jQuery || "jQuery",
$ = this.$ || "$",
originaljQuery = jQuery,
original$ = $;

define(["jquery"] , function ( $ ) {
    $( ".items" ).css( "background","green" );
    return function () {};
});
```

Why was AMD a better choice for writing modular JavaScript?

We have now reviewed several code samples taking us through what AMD is capable of. It appears to be more than just a typical Module pattern, but why was it a better choice for modular application development?

- Provides a clear proposal for how to approach defining flexible modules.

- Significantly cleaner than the present global namespace and `<script>` tag solutions many of us rely on. There's a clean way to declare standalone modules and dependencies they may have.

- Module definitions are encapsulated, helping us to avoid pollution of the global namespace.

- Arguably works better than some alternative solutions (e.g., CommonJS, which we'll be looking at shortly). It doesn't have issues with cross-domain, local, or debugging and doesn't rely on server-side tools to be used. Most AMD loaders support loading modules in the browser without a build process.

- Provides a "transport" approach for including multiple modules in a single file. Other approaches like CommonJS have yet to agree on a transport format.

- It's possible to lazy-load scripts if this is needed.

 Most of the points mentioned are valid for YUI's module-loading strategy.

Related reading for AMD

- The RequireJS Guide to AMD (*https://oreil.ly/uPEJg*)
- What's the Fastest Way to Load AMD Modules? (*https://oreil.ly/Z04H9*)
- AMD vs. CommonJS, What's the Better Format? (*https://oreil.ly/W4Fqi*)
- The Future Is Modules Not Frameworks (*https://oreil.ly/A9S7c*)
- AMD No Longer a CommonJS Specification (*https://oreil.ly/Tkti9*)
- On Inventing JavaScript Module Formats and Script Loaders (*https://oreil.ly/AB01l*)
- The AMD Mailing List (*https://oreil.ly/jdTYO*)

Script loaders and frameworks that support AMD

In-browser:

- RequireJS (*https://oreil.ly/Ri_9R*)
- curl.js (*https://oreil.ly/fi105*)
- Yabble (*https://oreil.ly/oBWDi*)
- PINF (*https://oreil.ly/C28-D*)
- And more

Server-side:

- RequireJS (*https://oreil.ly/Ri_9R*)
- PINF (*https://oreil.ly/TJldu*)

AMD Conclusions

Having used AMD for several projects, I conclude that it ticks a lot of the checkboxes that developers creating serious applications might desire from a better module format. It avoids the need to worry about globals, supports named modules, doesn't require server transformation to function, and is a pleasure to use for dependency management.

It's also an excellent addition for modular development using Backbone.js, ember.js, or other structural frameworks for keeping applications organized.

As AMD was heavily discussed within the Dojo and CommonJS worlds, we know it's had time to mature and evolve. We also know it's been battle-tested in the wild by a number of large companies to build nontrivial applications (IBM, BBC iPlayer), and so, if it didn't work, chances are they would have abandoned it, but they didn't.

That said, there are still areas where AMD could have been improved. Developers who have used the format for some time may feel the AMD boilerplate/wrapper code was an annoying overhead. While I share this concern, there were tools such as Volo (*https://oreil.ly/TLSYv*) that helped work around these issues, and I would argue that, on the whole, the pros with using AMD far outweighed the cons.

CommonJS

The CommonJS module proposal specifies a simple API for declaring modules server-side. Unlike AMD, it attempts to cover broader concerns such as I/O, filesystem, promises, and more.

Originally called ServerJS in a project started by Kevin Dangoor back in 2009, the format was later formalized by CommonJS (*https://oreil.ly/EUFt3*), a volunteer working group that aims to design, prototype, and standardize JavaScript APIs. They attempted to ratify standards for both modules (*https://oreil.ly/v_hsu*) and packages (*https://oreil.ly/Trgzj*).

Getting Started

From a structural perspective, a CommonJS module is a reusable piece of JavaScript that exports specific objects made available to any dependent code. Unlike AMD, there are typically no function wrappers around such modules (so we won't see define here, for example).

CommonJS modules contain two primary parts: a free variable named `exports`, which includes the objects a module wishes to make available to other modules, and a `require` function that modules can use to import the exports of other modules (Examples 10-7, 10-8, and 10-9).

Example 10-7. Understanding CommonJS: `require()` and `exports`

```
// package/lib is a dependency we require
var lib = require("package/lib");

// behavior for our module
function foo() {
  lib.log("hello world!");
}

// export (expose) foo to other modules
exports.foo = foo;
```

Example 10-8. Basic consumption of `exports`

```
// Import the module containing the foo function
var exampleModule = require("./example-10-9");

// Consume the 'foo' function from the imported module
exampleModule.foo();
```

In Example 10-8, we first import the module containing the foo function from Example 10-7 using the require() function. Then, we consume the foo function by calling it from the imported module with exampleModule.foo().

Example 10-9. AMD-equivalent of the first CommonJS example

```
// CommonJS module getting started
// AMD-equivalent of CommonJS example
// AMD module format
define(function(require){
var lib = require( "package/lib" );

// some behavior for our module
function foo(){
   lib.log( "hello world!" );
}

// export (expose) foo for other modules
return {
   foobar: foo
};
});
```

This can be done as AMD supports a simplified CommonJS wrapping (*https://oreil.ly/IzG9s*) feature.

Consuming Multiple Dependencies

app.js:

```
var modA = require( "./foo" );
var modB = require( "./bar" );

exports.app = function(){
    console.log( "Im an application!" );
}

exports.foo = function(){
    return modA.helloWorld();
}
```

bar.js:

```
exports.name = "bar";
```

foo.js:

```
require( "./bar" );
exports.helloWorld = function(){
    return "Hello World!!"
}
```

CommonJS in Node.js

The ES module format has become the standard format for encapsulating JavaScript code for reuse, but CommonJS is the default in Node.js. CommonJS modules are the original way to package JavaScript code for Node.js (*https://oreil.ly/4Bh_O*), although starting with version 13.2.0, Node.js has stable support of ES modules.

By default, Node.js treats the following as CommonJS modules:

- Files with a *.cjs* extension
- Files with a *.js* extension when the nearest parent *package.json* file contains a top-level field *type* with a value of *commonjs*
- Files with a *.js* extension when the nearest parent *package.json* file doesn't contain a top-level field *type*
- Files with an extension that is not *.mjs*, *.cjs*, *.json*, *.node*, or *.js*

Calling `require()` always uses the CommonJS module loader, while calling `import()` always uses the ECMAScript module loader irrespective of the type value configured in the nearest parent *package.json*.

Many Node.js libraries and modules are written with CommonJS. For browser support, all major browsers support the ES module syntax, and you can use import/export in frameworks like React and Vue.js. These frameworks use a transpiler like Babel to compile the import/export syntax to `require()`, which older Node.js versions natively support. Libraries written using ES6 module syntax will be transpiled to CommonJS under the hood if you run the code in Node.

Is CommonJS Suitable for the Browser?

There are developers who feel that CommonJS is better suited to server-side development, which is one reason there was a disagreement over whether AMD or CommonJS should be used as the de facto standard before ES2015. Some arguments against CommonJS were that many CommonJS APIs address server-oriented features that one would be unable to implement at a browser level in JavaScript—for example, *io*, *system*, and *js* could be considered unimplementable by the nature of their functionality.

Regardless, it's useful to know how to structure CommonJS modules so that we can better appreciate how they fit in when defining modules that may be used everywhere. Modules with applications on both the client and server include validation, conversion, and templating engines. Some developers approached choosing which format to use by opting for CommonJS when a module can be used in a server-side environment and using AMD or ES2015 if this is not the case.

ES2015 and AMD modules can define more granular things like constructors and functions. CommonJS modules can only define objects, which can be tedious to work with if we're trying to obtain constructors from them. For new projects in Node.js, ES2015 modules provide an alternative to CommonJS on the server and also ensure that the syntax is identical to the client-side code. Thus, it creates an easier route to isomorphic JavaScript, which can run in the browser or on the server.

Although it's beyond the scope of this section, you may have noticed that there were different types of `require` methods mentioned when discussing AMD and CommonJS. The concern with a similar naming convention is confusion, and the community is split on the merits of a global `require` function. John Hann's suggestion here is that rather than calling it `require`, which would probably fail to achieve the goal of informing users about the different between a global and inner `require`, it may make more sense to rename the global loader method something else (e.g., the name of the library). It's for this reason that a loader like curl.js uses `curl()` instead of `require`.

Related Reading for CommonJS

- JavaScript Growing Up (*https://oreil.ly/NeuFT*)
- The RequireJS Notes on CommonJS (*https://oreil.ly/Nb-5e*)
- Taking Baby Steps with Node.js and CommonJS—Creating Custom Modules (*https://oreil.ly/ZpO5u*)
- Asynchronous CommonJS Modules for the Browser (*https://oreil.ly/gJhQA*)
- The CommonJS Mailing List (*https://oreil.ly/rL3C2*)

AMD and CommonJS: Competing, but Equally Valid Standards

Both AMD and CommonJS are valid module formats with different end goals.

AMD adopts a browser-first approach to development, opting for asynchronous behavior and simplified backward compatibility, but it doesn't have any concept of file I/O. It supports objects, functions, constructors, strings, JSON, and many other types of modules, running natively in the browser. It's incredibly flexible.

CommonJS, on the other hand, takes a server-first approach, assuming synchronous behavior, no global *baggage*, and attempts to cater to the future (on the server). What I mean by this is that because CommonJS supports unwrapped modules, it can feel a little closer to the ES2015+ specifications, freeing us of the `define()` wrapper that AMD enforces. CommonJS modules, however, support objects only as modules.

UMD: AMD and CommonJS-Compatible Modules for Plug-ins

These solutions could be a little lacking for developers wishing to create modules that can work in browser and server-side environments. To help alleviate this, James Burke, I, and several other developers created Universal Module Definition (UMD) (*https://oreil.ly/HaHHJ*).

UMD is an experimental module format that allows the definition of modules that work in both client and server environments with all or most of the popular script-loading techniques available at the time of writing. Although the idea of (yet) another module format may be daunting, we will cover UMD briefly for thoroughness.

We began defining UMD by looking at the simplified CommonJS wrapper supported in the AMD specification. Developers wishing to write modules as if they were CommonJS modules could use the following CommonJS-compatible format:

Basic AMD hybrid format

```
define( function ( require, exports, module ){

    var shuffler = require( "lib/shuffle" );

    exports.randomize = function( input ){
        return shuffler.shuffle( input );
    }
});
```

It's essential, however, to note that a module is really only treated as a CommonJS module if it doesn't contain a dependency array and the definition function contains one parameter at minimum. This also won't work correctly on some devices (e.g., the PS3). For further information about the wrapper, see the RequireJS documentation (*https://oreil.ly/7A9k6*).

Taking this further, we wanted to provide several different patterns that worked with AMD and CommonJS and solved typical compatibility problems developers wishing to develop such modules had with other environments.

One such variation we can see next allows us to use CommonJS, AMD, or browser globals to create a module.

Using CommonJS, AMD, or browser globals to create a module

Define a module commonJsStrict, which depends on another module called b. The filename implies the module's name, and it's best practice for the filename and the exported global to have the same name.

If the module b also uses the same boilerplate type in the browser, it will create a global `.b` that is used. If we don't wish to support the browser global patch, we can remove the `root` and pass `this` as the first argument to the top function:

```
(function ( root, factory ) {
    if ( typeof exports === 'object' ) {
        // CommonJS
        factory( exports, require('b') );
    } else if ( typeof define === 'function' && define.amd ) {
        // AMD. Register as an anonymous module.
        define( ['exports', 'b'], factory);
    } else {
        // Browser globals
        factory( (root.commonJsStrict = {}), root.b );
    }
}(this, function ( exports, b ) {
    //use b in some fashion.

    // attach properties to the exports object to define
    // the exported module properties.
    exports.action = function () {};
}));
```

The UMD repository contains variations covering modules that work optimally in the browser, those best for providing exports, those optimal for CommonJS runtimes, and even those that work best for defining jQuery plug-ins, which we will look at next.

jQuery plug-ins that function in all environments

UMD provides two patterns for working with jQuery plug-ins: one that defines plug-ins that work well with AMD and browser globals and another that can also work in CommonJS environments. jQuery is not likely to be used in most CommonJS environments, so keep this in mind unless we're working with an environment that does play well with it.

We will now define a plug-in composed of a core and an extension to that core. The core plug-in is loaded into a `$.core` namespace, which can then be easily extended using plug-in extensions via the namespacing pattern. Plug-ins loaded via `script` tags automatically populate a `plugin` namespace under `core` (i.e., `$.core.plugin.methodName()`).

The pattern can be nice to work with, because plug-in extensions can access properties and methods defined in the base or, with a bit of tweaking, override default behavior so that it can be extended to do more. A loader is also not required to make any of this fully functional.

For more details of what is being done, please see the inline comments in these code samples.

usage.html:

```html
<script type="text/javascript" src="jquery.min.js"></script>
<script type="text/javascript" src="pluginCore.js"></script>
<script type="text/javascript" src="pluginExtension.js"></script>

<script type="text/javascript">

$(function(){

    // Our plug-in "core" is exposed under a core namespace in
    // this example, which we first cache
    var core = $.core;

    // Then use some of the built-in core functionality to
    // highlight all divs in the page yellow
    core.highlightAll();

    // Access the plug-ins (extensions) loaded into the "plugin"
    // namespace of our core module:

    // Set the first div in the page to have a green background.
    core.plugin.setGreen( "div:first");
    // Here we're making use of the core's "highlight" method
    // under the hood from a plug-in loaded in after it

    // Set the last div to the "errorColor" property defined in
    // our core module/plug-in. If we review the code further down,
    // we can see how easy it is to consume properties and methods
    // between the core and other plug-ins
    core.plugin.setRed("div:last");
});

</script>
```

pluginCore.js:

```javascript
// Module/plug-in core
// Note: the wrapper code we see around the module is what enables
// us to support multiple module formats and specifications by
// mapping the arguments defined to what a specific format expects
// to be present. Our actual module functionality is defined lower
// down, where a named module and exports are demonstrated.
//
// Note that dependencies can just as easily be declared if required
// and should work as demonstrated earlier with the AMD module examples.

(function ( name, definition ){
  var theModule = definition(),
      // this is considered "safe":
      hasDefine = typeof define === "function" && define.amd,
      hasExports = typeof module !== "undefined" && module.exports;
```

```
  if ( hasDefine ){ // AMD Module
    define(theModule);
  } else if ( hasExports ) { // Node.js Module
    module.exports = theModule;
  } else { // Assign to common namespaces or simply the global object (window)
    ( this.jQuery || this.ender || this.$ || this)[name] = theModule;
  }
})( "core", function () {
  var module = this;
  module.plugins = [];
  module.highlightColor = "yellow";
  module.errorColor = "red";

  // define the core module here and return the public API

  // This is the highlight method used by the core highlightAll()
  // method and all of the plug-ins highlighting elements different
  // colors
  module.highlight = function( el,strColor ){
    if( this.jQuery ){
      jQuery(el).css( "background", strColor );
    }
  }
  return {
    highlightAll:function(){
      module.highlight("div", module.highlightColor);
    }
  };

});
```

pluginExtension.js:

```
// Extension to module core

(function ( name, definition ) {
    var theModule = definition(),
        hasDefine = typeof define === "function",
        hasExports = typeof module !== "undefined" && module.exports;

    if ( hasDefine ) { // AMD Module
        define(theModule);
    } else if ( hasExports ) { // Node.js Module
        module.exports = theModule;
    } else {

        // Assign to common namespaces or simply the global object (window)
        // account for flat-file/global module extensions
        var obj = null,
            namespaces,
            scope;

        obj = null;
```

```
        namespaces = name.split(".");
        scope = ( this.jQuery || this.ender || this.$ || this );

        for ( var i = 0; i < namespaces.length; i++ ) {
            var packageName = namespaces[i];
            if ( obj && i == namespaces.length - 1 ) {
                obj[packageName] = theModule;
            } else if ( typeof scope[packageName] === "undefined" ) {
                scope[packageName] = {};
            }
            obj = scope[packageName];
        }

    }
})( "core.plugin" , function () {

    // Define our module here and return the public API.
    // This code could be easily adapted with the core to
    // allow for methods that overwrite and extend core functionality
    // in order to expand the highlight method to do more if we wish.
    return {
        setGreen: function ( el ) {
            highlight(el, "green");
        },
        setRed: function ( el ) {
            highlight(el, errorColor);
        }
    };

});
```

UMD doesn't aim to replace AMD or CommonJS but merely offers some supplemental assistance for developers wishing to get their code working in more environments today. For further information or to contribute suggestions toward this experimental format, see this GitHub page (*https://oreil.ly/H2pUf*).

Related reading for UMD and AMD

- Using AMD Loaders to Write and Manage Modular JavaScript (*https://oreil.ly/Zgs_G*)

- AMD Module Patterns: Singleton (*https://oreil.ly/IP22B*)

- Standards and Proposals for JavaScript Modules and jQuery (*https://oreil.ly/I-3jy*)

Summary

This section reviewed several options for writing modular JavaScript using different module formats before ES2015+.

These formats had several advantages over using the Module pattern alone, including avoiding the need to manage global variables, better support for static and dynamic dependency management, improved compatibility with script loaders, better compatibility for modules on the server, and more.

To conclude our discussion of classic design and architecture patterns, I want to touch on one area where we can apply patterns to structure and organize our JavaScript code in the next chapter on Namespacing patterns.

CHAPTER 11

Namespacing Patterns

In this chapter, we will explore patterns for namespacing in JavaScript. Namespaces can be considered a logical grouping of code units under a unique identifier. You can reference the identifier in many namespaces, and each identifier can contain a hierarchy of nested (or sub) namespaces.

In application development, we employ namespaces for many important reasons. JavaScript namespaces help us avoid *collisions* with other objects or variables in the global namespace. They're also handy for helping organize blocks of functionality in a codebase so that it can be more easily referenced and used.

Namespacing any serious script or application is critical because it's crucial to safeguard our code from breaking in the event of another script on the page using the *same* variable or method names we are. With the number of *third-party* tags regularly injected into pages, this can be a common problem we all need to tackle at some point in our careers. As a well-behaved "citizen" of the global namespace, it's also imperative that we try our best not to prevent other developers' scripts from executing due to the same issues.

While JavaScript doesn't have built-in support for namespaces like other languages, it does have objects and closures that you can use to achieve a similar effect.

Namespacing Fundamentals

You can find namespaces in almost any serious JavaScript application. Unless we're working with a simple code snippet, we must do our best to ensure that we're implementing namespacing correctly, as it's not just easy to pick up; it'll also avoid third-party code destroying our own. The patterns we'll be examining in this section are:

- Single global variables
- Prefix namespacing
- Object literal notation
- Nested namespacing
- Immediately invoked function
- Expressions
- Namespace injection

Single Global Variables

One popular pattern for namespacing in JavaScript is opting for a single global variable as our primary object of reference. Here's a skeleton implementation of this where we return an object with functions and properties:

```
const myUniqueApplication = (() => {
  function myMethod() {
    // code
    return;
  }

  return {
    myMethod,
  };
})();

// Usage
myUniqueApplication.myMethod();

// In this updated example, we use an immediately invoked function expression
// (IIFE) to create a unique namespace for our application, which is stored in
// the myUniqueApplication variable. The IIFE returns an object with functions
// and properties, and we can access these using dot notation
// (e.g., myUniqueApplication.myMethod()).
```

Although this works for certain situations, the biggest challenge with the single global variable pattern is ensuring that no one else has used the same global variable name as we have on the page.

Prefix Namespacing

One solution to the problem mentioned, as noted by Peter Michaux (*https://oreil.ly/o2dgF*), is to use prefix namespacing. It's a simple concept at heart, but the idea is we select a unique prefix namespace we wish to use (in this example, myApplication_) and then define any methods, variables, or other objects after the prefix as follows:

```
const myApplication_propertyA = {};
const myApplication_propertyB = {};
function myApplication_myMethod(){   //...
}
```

This effectively decreases the chances of a particular variable existing in the global scope, but remember that a uniquely named object can have the same effect.

This aside, the biggest issue with the pattern is that it can result in many global objects once our application grows. There is also a heavy reliance on our prefix not being used by any other developers in the global namespace, so be careful if opting to use this.

For more on Peter's views about the single global variable pattern, read his excellent post (*https://oreil.ly/o2dgF*).

Object Literal Notation

Object literal notation, which we also cover in the Module pattern section, can be thought of as an object containing a collection of key-value pairs with a colon separating each pair of keys and values, where keys can also represent new namespaces:

```
const myApplication = {

    // As we've seen, we can easily define functionality for
    // this object literal...
    getInfo() {
      //...
    },

    // but we can also populate it to support
    // further object namespaces containing anything
    // anything we wish:
    models : {},
    views : {
        pages : {}
    },
    collections : {}
};
```

One can also opt for adding properties directly to the namespace:

```
myApplication.foo = () => "bar"

myApplication.utils = {
    toString() {
        //...
    },
    export() {
        //...
```

```
      }
   }
```

Object literals don't pollute the global namespace but assist in organizing code and parameters logically. They are truly beneficial if you wish to create easily readable structures that you can expand to support deep nesting. Unlike simple global variables, object literals often consider tests for the existence of a variable by the same name, so the chances of a collision occurring are significantly reduced.

The following sample demonstrates several ways to check if an object namespace already exists, defining it if it doesn't:

```
// This doesn't check for existence of "myApplication" in
// the global namespace. Bad practice as we can easily
// clobber an existing variable/namespace with the same name
const myApplication = {};

// The following options *do* check for variable/namespace existence.
// If already defined, we use that instance, otherwise we assign a new
// object literal to myApplication.
//
// Option 1: var myApplication = myApplication || {};
// Option 2  if( !MyApplication ){ MyApplication = {} };
// Option 3: window.myApplication || ( window.myApplication = {} );
// Option 4: var myApplication = $.fn.myApplication = function() {};
// Option 5: var myApplication = myApplication === undefined ? {} :
// myApplication;
```

You'll often see developers opting for Option 1 or Option 2—they are both straightforward and equivalent in terms of their results.

Option 3 assumes that you're working in the global namespace, but it can also be written as:

```
myApplication || (myApplication = {});
```

This variation assumes that myApplication has already been initialized, so it's only handy for a parameter/argument scenario, as in the following example:

```
function foo() {
   myApplication || ( myApplication = {} );
}

// myApplication hasn't been initialized,
// so foo() throws a ReferenceError

foo();

// However accepting myApplication as an
// argument

function foo( myApplication ) {
   myApplication || ( myApplication = {} );
```

```
}

foo();

// Even if myApplication === undefined, there is no error
// and myApplication gets set to {} correctly
```

Option 4 can help write jQuery plug-ins where:

```
// If we were to define a new plug-in...
var myPlugin = $.fn.myPlugin = function() { ... };

// Then later rather than having to type:
$.fn.myPlugin.defaults = {};

// We can do:
myPlugin.defaults = {};
```

This results in better compression (minification) and can save on scope lookups.

Option 5 is a little similar to Option 4 but is a long form that evaluates whether myApplication is undefined inline, such that it's defined as an object if not and set to a current value for myApplication if so.

It is shown just for the sake of being thorough, but in most situations, Options 1–4 will more than suffice for most needs.

There is, of course, a great deal of variance in how and where object literals are used for organizing and structuring code. For smaller applications wishing to expose a nested API for a particular self-enclosed module, you may just find yourself using the Revealing Module pattern, which we covered earlier in the book:

```
const namespace = (() => {
    // defined within the local scope
    const privateMethod1 = () => { /* ... */ };

    const privateMethod2 = () => { /* ... */ };
    privateProperty1 = "foobar";

    return {

        // the object literal returned here can have as many
        // nested depths as we wish; however, as mentioned,
        // this way of doing things works best for smaller,
        // limited-scope applications in my personal opinion
        publicMethod1: privateMethod1,

        // nested namespace with public properties
        properties:{
            publicProperty1: privateProperty1
        },

        // another tested namespace
```

```
        utils:{
            publicMethod2: privateMethod2
        }
        ...
    }
})();
```

The benefit of using object literals here is that they offer us a very elegant key-value syntax to work with—one where we're able to easily encapsulate any distinct logic or functionality for our application in a way that clearly separates it from others and provides a solid foundation for extending our code:

```
const myConfig = {

    language: "english",

    defaults: {
        enableGeolocation: true,
        enableSharing: false,
        maxPhotos: 20
    },

    theme: {
        skin: "a",
        toolbars: {
            index: "ui-navigation-toolbar",
            pages: "ui-custom-toolbar"
        }
    }

};
```

Note that JSON is a subset of object literal notation, and there are only minor syntactical differences between it and the preceding code (e.g., JSON keys must be strings). If, for any reason, one wishes to use JSON for storing configuration data instead (e.g., for simpler storage when sending to the backend), feel free to.

Nested Namespacing

An extension of the Object Literal pattern is nested namespacing. It's another common pattern that offers a lower risk of collision because even if a namespace already exists, it's unlikely the same nested children do.

For example, something like this:

```
YAHOO.util.Dom.getElementsByClassName("test");
```

Older versions of Yahoo!'s YUI library regularly used the Nested Object Namespacing pattern. During my time as an engineer at AOL, we also used this pattern in many of our larger applications. A sample implementation of nested namespacing may look like this:

```
const myApp =  myApp || {};

// perform a similar existence check when defining nested
// children
myApp.routers = myApp.routers || {};
myApp.model = myApp.model || {};
myApp.model.special = myApp.model.special || {};

// nested namespaces can be as complex as required:
// myApp.utilities.charting.html5.plotGraph(/*..*/);
// myApp.modules.financePlanner.getSummary();
// myApp.services.social.facebook.realtimeStream.getLatest();
```

This code differs from how YUI3 approaches namespacing. YUI3 modules use a sandboxed API host object with far less and far shallower namespacing.

We can also opt to declare new nested namespaces/properties as indexed properties as follows:

```
myApp["routers"] = myApp["routers"] || {};
myApp["models"] = myApp["models"] || {};
myApp["controllers"] = myApp["controllers"] || {};
```

Both options are readable and organized and offer a relatively safe way of namespacing our application, similar to what we may be used to in other languages. The only real caveat is that it requires our browser's JavaScript engine first to locate the myApp object and then dig down until it gets to the function we actually wish to use.

This can mean more work to perform lookups; however, developers such as Juriy Zaytsev (*https://oreil.ly/hxJnZ*) have previously tested and found the performance differences between single object namespacing versus the "nested" approach quite negligible.

Immediately Invoked Function Expressions

Earlier in the book, we briefly covered the concept of an immediately invoked function expression (IIFE); an IIFE (*https://oreil.ly/KSspI*), which is effectively an unnamed function, is immediately invoked after it's been defined. If it sounds familiar, it's because you may have previously come across it referred to as a self-executing (or self-invoked) anonymous function. However, I feel Ben Alman's IIFE naming is more accurate. In JavaScript, because both variables and functions explicitly defined within such a context may be accessed only inside of it, function invocation provides an easy means to achieving privacy.

IIFEs are a popular approach to encapsulating application logic to protect it from the global namespace, but they also have their use in the world of namespacing.

Here are examples of IIFEs:

```
// an (anonymous) immediately invoked function expression
((() => { /*...*/})());

// a named immediately invoked function expression
(function foobar () { /*..*/}());

// this is technically a self-executing function which is quite different
function foobar () { foobar(); }
```

A slightly more expanded version of the first example might look like this:

```
const namespace = namespace || {};

// here a namespace object is passed as a function
// parameter, where we assign public methods and
// properties to it
(o => {
    o.foo = "foo";
    o.bar = () => "bar";
})(namespace);

console.log( namespace );
```

While readable, this example could be significantly expanded to address common development concerns such as defined levels of privacy (public/private functions and variables) as well as convenient namespace extension. Let's go through some more code:

```
// namespace (our namespace name) and undefined are passed here
// to ensure: 1. namespace can be modified locally and isn't
// overwritten outside of our function context;
// 2. the value of undefined is guaranteed as being truly
// undefined. This is to avoid issues with undefined being
// mutable pre-ES5.

;((namespace, undefined) => {
    // private properties
    const foo = "foo";

    const bar = "bar";

    // public methods and properties
    namespace.foobar = "foobar";
    namespace.sayHello = () => {
        speak( "hello world" );
```

```
    };

    // private method
    function speak(msg) {
        console.log( `You said: ${msg}` );
    };

    // check to evaluate whether "namespace" exists in the
    // global namespace - if not, assign window.namespace an
    // object literal
})(window.namespace = window.namespace || {});



// we can then test our properties and methods as follows

// public

// Outputs: foobar
console.log( namespace.foobar );

// Outputs: hello world
namespace.sayHello();

// assigning new properties
namespace.foobar2 = "foobar";

// Outputs: foobar
console.log( namespace.foobar2 );
```

Extensibility is of course key to any scalable namespacing pattern and IIFEs can be used to achieve this quite easily. In the following example, our "namespace" is once again passed as an argument to our anonymous function and is then extended (or decorated) with additional functionality:

```
// let's extend the namespace with new functionality
((namespace, undefined) => {

    // public method
    namespace.sayGoodbye = () => {
        console.log( namespace.foo );
        console.log( namespace.bar );
        speak( "goodbye" );
    }
})(window.namespace = window.namespace || {});

// Outputs: goodbye
namespace.sayGoodbye();
```

If you want to learn more about this pattern, I recommend reading Ben's IIFE post (*https://oreil.ly/KSspI*) for more information.

Namespace Injection

Namespace injection is another variation on the IIFE in which we "inject" the methods and properties for a specific namespace from within a function wrapper using this as a namespace proxy. The benefit this pattern offers is the easy application of functional behavior to multiple objects or namespaces and can come in useful when applying a set of base methods to be built on later (e.g., getters and setters).

The disadvantages of this pattern are that there may be easier or more optimal approaches to achieving this goal (e.g., deep object extension or merging), which I cover earlier in the section.

Next we can see an example of this pattern in action, where we use it to populate the behavior for two namespaces: one initially defined (utils) and another which we dynamically create as a part of the functionality assignment for utils (a new namespace called tools):

```
const myApp = myApp || {};
myApp.utils = {};

(function () {
  let val = 5;

  this.getValue = () => val;

  this.setValue = newVal => {
    val = newVal;
  }

  // also introduce a new subnamespace
  this.tools = {};

}).apply( myApp.utils );

// inject new behavior into the tools namespace
// which we defined via the utilities module

(function () {
    this.diagnose = () => "diagnosis"
}).apply( myApp.utils.tools );

// note, this same approach to extension could be applied
// to a regular IIFE, by just passing in the context as
// an argument and modifying the context rather than just
// "this"

// Usage:

// Outputs our populated namespace
console.log( myApp );
```

```
// Outputs: 5
console.log( myApp.utils.getValue() );

// Sets the value of `val` and returns it
myApp.utils.setValue( 25 );
console.log( myApp.utils.getValue() );

// Testing another level down
console.log( myApp.utils.tools.diagnose() );
```

Previously, Angus Croll has suggested using the call API to provide a natural separation between contexts and arguments (*https://oreil.ly/eBc5N*). This pattern can feel a lot more like a module creator, but as modules still offer an encapsulation solution, we'll briefly cover it for the sake of thoroughness:

```
// define a namespace we can use later
const ns = ns || {};

const ns2 = ns2 || {};

// the module/namespace creator
const creator = function( val ){

    var val = val || 0;

    this.next = () => val++;

    this.reset = () => {
        val = 0;
    }
};

creator.call( ns );

// ns.next, ns.reset now exist
creator.call( ns2 , 5000 );

// ns2 contains the same methods
// but has an overridden value for val
// of 5000
```

As mentioned, this type of pattern helps assign a similar base set of functionality to multiple modules or namespaces. I would, however, suggest using it only where explicitly declaring functionality within an object/closure as direct access doesn't make sense.

Advanced Namespacing Patterns

We'll now explore some advanced patterns and utilities that I have found invaluable when working on more extensive applications, some of which have required a rethink of traditional approaches to application namespacing. I'll note that I am not advocating the following as *the* way to namespace but rather as ways I have found to work in practice.

Automating Nested Namespacing

As we've reviewed, nested namespaces can provide an organized hierarchy of structure for a unit of code. An example of such a namespace could be the following: `application.utilities.drawing.canvas.2d`. This can also be expanded using the Object Literal pattern to be:

```
const application = {
    utilities:{
        drawing:{
            canvas:{
                paint:{
                            //...
                }
            }
        }
    }
};
```

One of the obvious challenges with this pattern is that each additional layer we wish to create requires yet another object to be defined as a child of some parent in our top-level namespace. This can become particularly laborious when multiple depths are required as our application increases in complexity.

How can this problem be better solved? In *JavaScript Patterns*, Stoyan Stefanov presents a clever approach for automatically defining nested namespaces under an existing global variable. He suggests a convenience method that takes a single string argument for a nest, parses this, and automatically populates our base namespace with the objects required.

The method he suggests using is the following, which I've updated to be a generic function for easier reuse with multiple namespaces:

```
// top-level namespace being assigned an object literal
const myApp = {};

// a convenience function for parsing string namespaces and
// automatically generating nested namespaces
function extend( ns, ns_string ) {
    const parts = ns_string.split(".");
    let parent = ns;
```

```
    let pl;

    pl = parts.length;

    for ( let i = 0; i < pl; i++ ) {
        // create a property if it doesn't exist
        if ( typeof parent[parts[i]] === "undefined" ) {
            parent[parts[i]] = {};
        }

        parent = parent[parts[i]];
    }

    return parent;
}

// Usage:
// extend myApp with a deeply nested namespace
const mod = extend(myApp, "modules.module2");

// the correct object with nested depths is output
console.log(mod);

// minor test to check the instance of mod can also
// be used outside of the myApp namespace as a clone
// that includes the extensions

// Outputs: true
console.log(mod == myApp.modules.module2);

// further demonstration of easier nested namespace
// assignment using extend
extend(myApp, "moduleA.moduleB.moduleC.moduleD");
extend(myApp, "longer.version.looks.like.this");
console.log(myApp);
```

Figure 11-1 shows the Chrome Developer Tools output. Where one would previously have had to explicitly declare the various nests for their namespace as objects, this can now be easily achieved using a single, cleaner line of code.

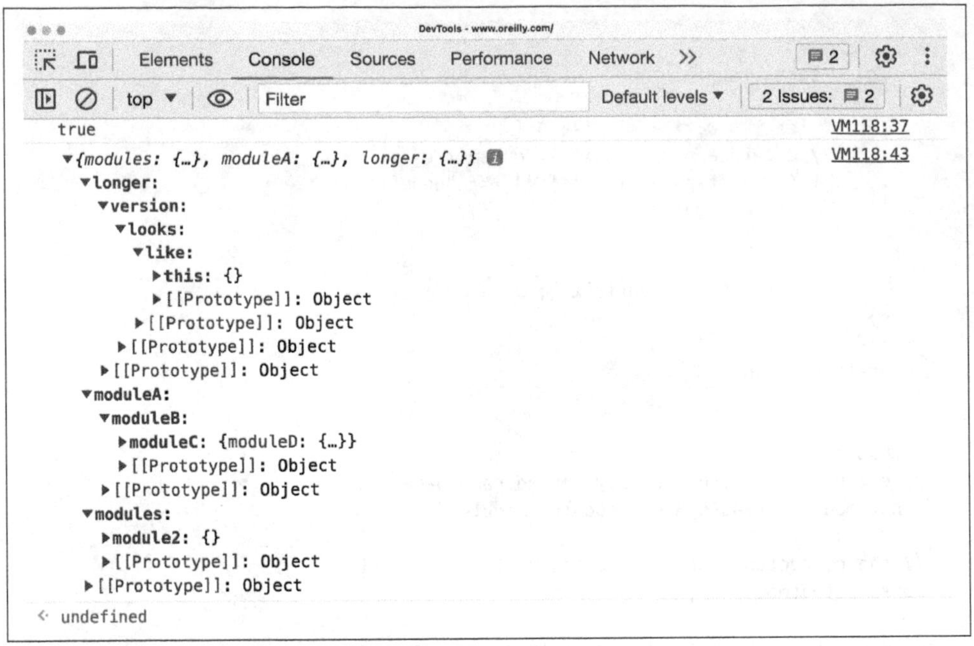

Figure 11-1. Chrome Developer Tools output

Dependency Declaration Pattern

We'll now explore a minor augmentation to the Nested Namespacing pattern, which we'll refer to as the Dependency Declaration pattern. We all know that local references to objects can decrease overall lookup times, but let's apply this to namespacing to see how it might look in practice:

```
// common approach to accessing nested namespaces
myApp.utilities.math.fibonacci( 25 );
myApp.utilities.math.sin( 56 );
myApp.utilities.drawing.plot( 98,50,60 );

// with local/cached references
const utils = myApp.utilities;

const maths = utils.math;
const drawing = utils.drawing;

// easier to access the namespace
maths.fibonacci( 25 );
maths.sin( 56 );
drawing.plot( 98, 50,60 );

// note that this is particularly performant when
// compared to hundreds or thousands of calls to nested
// namespaces vs. a local reference to the namespace
```

Working with a local variable here is almost always faster than working with a top-level global (e.g., myApp). It's also more convenient and more performant than accessing nested properties/subnamespaces on every subsequent line and can improve readability in more complex applications.

Stoyan recommends declaring localized namespaces required by a function or module at the top of our function scope (using the single-variable pattern) and calls this a Dependency Declaration pattern. One of the benefits this offers is a decrease in locating dependencies and resolving them, should we have an extendable architecture that dynamically loads modules into our namespace when required.

In my opinion, this pattern works best when working at a modular level, localizing a namespace to be used by a group of methods. Localizing namespaces on a per-function level, especially where there is significant overlap between namespace dependencies, is something I recommend avoiding where possible. Instead, define it further up and have them all access the same reference.

Deep Object Extension

An alternative approach to automatic namespacing is deep object extension. Namespaces defined using object literal notation may be easily extended (or merged) with other objects (or namespaces) such that the properties and functions of both namespaces can be accessible under the same namespace postmerge.

This is something that's been made relatively easy to accomplish with JavaScript frameworks (e.g., see jQuery's $.extend (*https://oreil.ly/WDJWX*)); however, if looking to extend objects (namespaces) using conventional JS, the following routine may be of assistance:

```
// Deep object extension using Object.assign and recursion
function extendObjects(destinationObject, sourceObject) {
  for (const property in sourceObject) {
    if (
      sourceObject[property] &&
      typeof sourceObject[property] === "object" &&
      !Array.isArray(sourceObject[property])
    ) {
      destinationObject[property] = destinationObject[property] || {};
      extendObjects(destinationObject[property], sourceObject[property]);
    } else {
      destinationObject[property] = sourceObject[property];
    }
  }
  return destinationObject;
}

// Example usage
const myNamespace = myNamespace || {};
```

```
extendObjects(myNamespace, {
  utils: {},
});

console.log("test 1", myNamespace);

extendObjects(myNamespace, {
  hello: {
    world: {
      wave: {
        test() {
          // ...
        },
      },
    },
  },
});

myNamespace.hello.test1 = "this is a test";
myNamespace.hello.world.test2 = "this is another test";
console.log("test 2", myNamespace);

myNamespace.library = {
  foo() {},
};

extendObjects(myNamespace, {
  library: {
    bar() {
      // ...
    },
  },
});

console.log("test 3", myNamespace);

const shorterNamespaceAccess = myNamespace.hello.world;
shorterNamespaceAccess.test3 = "hello again";
console.log("test 4", myNamespace);
```

This implementation is not cross-browser compatible with all
objects and should be considered a proof of concept only. One may
find the Lodash.js extend() method (*https://oreil.ly/TD1-D*) to be a
simpler, more cross-browser-friendly implementation to start with.

For developers who are going to use jQuery in their applications, one can achieve the same object namespace extensibility with `$.extend` as follows:

```
// top-level namespace
const myApplication = myApplication || {};

// directly assign a nested namespace
myApplication.library = {
  foo() {
    // ...
  },
};

// deep extend/merge this namespace with another
// to make things interesting, let's say it's a namespace
// with the same name but with a different function
// signature: $.extend( deep, target, object1, object2 )
$.extend(true, myApplication, {
  library: {
    bar() {
      // ...
    },
  },
});

console.log("test", myApplication);
```

For thoroughness, please check this (*https://oreil.ly/ZCB2C*) for jQuery `$.extend` equivalents to the rest of the namespacing experiments in this section.

Recommendation

Reviewing the namespace patterns we've explored in this section, the option that I would personally use for most larger applications is Nested Object Namespacing with the Object Literal pattern. Where possible, I would implement this using automated nested namespacing. However, this is just a personal preference.

IIFEs and single global variables may work fine for applications in the small to medium range. However, larger codebases requiring both namespaces and deep sub-namespaces require a succinct solution that promotes readability and scale. This pattern achieves all of these objectives well.

I recommend trying out some of the suggested advanced utility methods for namespace extension, as they can save time in the long run.

Summary

This chapter discussed how namespacing could help bring structure to your Java-Script and jQuery applications and prevent collisions between variables and function names. Organizing our project files in large JavaScript applications with many code files helps you better manage modules and namespaces and enhances the development experience.

We have now covered different aspects of design and architecture using plain Java-Script. We have mentioned React in passing but haven't discussed any React patterns in detail. In the next chapter, we aim to do just that.

CHAPTER 12

React.js Design Patterns

Over the years, there has been an increased demand for straightforward ways to compose UIs using JavaScript. Frontend developers look for out-of-the-box solutions provided by many different libraries and frameworks. React's popularity in this area has persevered for a long time now since its original release in 2013. This chapter will look at design patterns that are helpful in the React universe.

React (*https://oreil.ly/7Z-65*), also referred to as React.js, is an open source JavaScript library designed by Facebook to build UIs or UI components. It is, of course, not the only UI library out there. Preact (*https://oreil.ly/jXmKM*), Vue (*https://oreil.ly/ fMoMp*), Angular (*https://oreil.ly/G_Oyv*), Svelte (*https://oreil.ly/scSoT*), Lit (*https:// oreil.ly/5UgxC*), and many others are also great for composing interfaces from reusable elements. Given React's popularity, however, we have chosen it for our discussion on design patterns for the current decade.

An Introduction to React

When frontend developers talk about code, it's most often in the context of designing interfaces for the web. And the way we think of interface composition is in elements like buttons, lists, navigation, etc. React provides an optimized and simplified way of expressing interfaces in these elements. It also helps build complex and tricky interfaces by organizing your interface into three key concepts: components, props, and state.

Because React is composition-focused, it can perfectly map to the elements of your design system. So, designing for React rewards you for thinking in a modular way. It allows you to develop individual components before putting together a page or view so that you fully understand each component's scope and purpose—a process referred to as componentization.

Terminology Used

We will use the following terms frequently in this chapter. Let's quickly look at what each of them means:

React/React.js/ReactJS
> React library, created by Facebook in 2013

ReactDOM
> The `react-dom` package providing DOM-specific methods for client and server rendering

JSX
> Syntax extension to JavaScript

Redux
> Centralized state container

Hooks
> A new way to use state and other React features without writing a class

ReactNative
> The library to develop cross-platform native apps with JavaScript

webpack
> JavaScript module bundler, popular in React community

Single-page application (SPA)
> A web app that loads new content on the same page without a full page refresh/ reload.

Basic Concepts

Before we discuss React design patterns, it would be helpful to understand some basic concepts used in React:

JSX
> JSX is an extension to JavaScript that embeds template HTML in JS using XML-like syntax. It is meant to be transformed into valid JavaScript, though the semantics of that transformation are implementation-specific. JSX rose to popularity with the React library but has also seen other implementations.

Components
> Components are the building blocks of any React app. They are like JavaScript functions that accept arbitrary input (Props) and return React elements describing what should be displayed on the screen. Everything on screen in a React app is part of a component. Essentially, a React app is just components within

components within components. So developers don't build pages in React; they build components. Components let you split your UI into independent, reusable pieces. If you're used to designing pages, thinking from a component perspective might seem like a significant change. But if you use a design system or style guide, this might be a smaller paradigm shift than it looks.

Props

Props are a short form for properties, and they refer to the internal data of a component in React. They are written inside component calls and are passed into components. They also use the same syntax as HTML attributes, e.g., `prop = value`. Two things worth remembering about props are: (1) we determine the value of a prop and use it as part of the blueprint before the component is built, and (2) the value of a prop will never change, i.e., props are read-only once passed into components. You access a prop by referencing it via the `this.props` property that every component can access.

State

State is an object that holds information that may change over the component's lifetime. It is the current snapshot of data stored in a component's props. The data can change over time, so techniques to manage data changes become necessary to ensure the component looks the way engineers want it to, at just the right time—this is called state management.

Client-side rendering

In client-side rendering (CSR), the server renders only the bare bones HTML container for a page. The logic, data fetching, templating, and routing required to display content on the page are handled by JavaScript code that executes on the client. CSR became popular as a method of building SPAs. It helped to blur the difference between websites and installed applications and works best for highly interactive applications. With React by default, most of the application logic is executed on the client. It interacts with the server through API calls to fetch or save data.

Server-side rendering

SSR is one of the oldest methods of rendering web content. SSR generates the complete HTML for the page content to be rendered in response to a user request. The content may include data from a data store or external API. React can be rendered isomorphically, which means that it can function both on the browser and other platforms like the server. Thus, UI elements may be rendered on the server using React.

Hydration

In a server-rendered application, HTML for the current navigation is generated on the server and sent to the client. Since the server generated the markup, the client can quickly parse this and display it on the screen. The JavaScript required to make the UI interactive is loaded after this. The event handlers that will make UI elements like buttons interactive get attached only once the JavaScript bundle is loaded and processed. This process is called hydration. React checks the current DOM nodes and hydrates them with the corresponding JavaScript.

Creating a new app

Older documentation suggests using Create React App (CRA) to build a new client-only SPA for learning React. It is a CLI tool to create a scaffolding React app for bootstrapping a project. However, CRA offers a restricted development experience, which is too limiting for many modern web applications. React recommends using a production-grade React-powered framework such as Next.js or Remix to build new web apps or websites. These frameworks provide features that most apps and sites eventually need, such as static HTML generation, file-based routing, SPA navigations, and real client code.

React has evolved over the years. Different features introduced to the library gave rise to various ways of solving common problems. Here are some popular design patterns for React that we will look into in detail in the following sections:

- "Higher-Order Components" on page 196
- "Render Props Pattern" on page 200
- "Hooks Pattern" on page 205
- "Static Import" on page 216
- "Dynamic Import" on page 217
- "Code-Splitting" on page 221
- "PRPL Pattern" on page 224
- "Loading Prioritization" on page 226

Higher-Order Components

We may often want to use the same logic in multiple components within our application. This logic can include applying specific styling to components, requiring authorization, or adding a global state. One way to reuse the same logic in multiple components is by using the Higher-Order Component (HOC) pattern. This pattern allows us to reuse component logic throughout our application.

An HOC is a component that receives another component. The HOC can contain a specific feature that can be applied to a component we pass to it as a parameter. The HOC returns the component with the additional feature applied to it.

Say that we always wanted to add particular styling to multiple components in our application. Instead of creating a style object locally each time, we can create an HOC that adds the style objects to the component it received as a parameter:

```
function withStyles(Component) {
  return props => {
    const style = { padding: '0.2rem', margin: '1rem' }
    return <Component style={style} {...props} />
  }
}

const Button = () = <button>Click me!</button>
const Text = () => <p>Hello World!</p>

const StyledButton = withStyles(Button)
const StyledText = withStyles(Text)
```

We just created a StyledButton and StyledText component, the modified versions of the Button and Text component. They now both contain the style that got added in the withStyles HOC.

To take it further, let us look at an application that renders a list of dog images fetched from an API. When fetching the data, we want to show the user a "Loading… " screen. Instead of adding it to the DogImages component directly, we can use an HOC that adds this logic.

Let's create an HOC called withLoader. An HOC should receive a component and return that component. In this case, the withLoader HOC should receive the element which should display Loading… until the data is fetched. To make the withLoader HOC very reusable, we won't hardcode the Dog API URL in that component. Instead, we can pass the URL as an argument to the withLoader HOC, so this loader can be used on any component that needs a loading indicator while fetching data from a different API endpoint:

```
function withLoader(Element, url) {
  return props => {};
}
```

An HOC returns an element, a functional component props ⇒ {} in this case, to which we want to add the logic that allows us to display a text with Loading… as the data is still being fetched. Once the data has been fetched, the component should pass the fetched data as a prop. The complete code for withLoader looks like this:

```
import React, { useEffect, useState } from "react";

export default function withLoader(Element, url) {
  return (props) => {
    const [data, setData] = useState(null);

    useEffect(() => {
      async function getData() {
        const res = await fetch(url);
        const data = await res.json();
        setData(data);
      }

      getData();
    }, []);

    if (!data) {
      return <div>Loading...</div>;
    }

    return <Element {...props} data={data} />;
  };
}
```

We just created an HOC that can receive any component and URL:

- In the useEffect hook, the withLoader HOC fetches the data from the API endpoint that we pass as the value of url. While the data is being fetched, we return the element containing the Loading... text.

- Once the data has been fetched, we set data equal to the data that has been fetched. Since data is no longer null, we can display the element that we passed to the HOC.

Now to show the Loading... indicator on the DogImages list, we will export the "wrapped" withLoading HOC around the DogImages component. The withLoader HOC also expects the url to know which endpoint to fetch the data from. In this case, we want to add the Dog API endpoint. Since the withLoader HOC returned the element with an extra data prop, DogImages in this case, we can access the data prop in the DogImages component:

```
import React from "react";
import withLoader from "./withLoader";

function DogImages(props) {
  return props.data.message.map((dog, index) => (
    <img src={dog} alt="Dog" key={index} />
  ));
}
```

```
export default withLoader(
  DogImages,
  "https://dog.ceo/api/breed/labrador/images/random/6"
);
```

The HOC pattern allows us to provide the same logic to multiple components while keeping all the logic in one place. The withLoader HOC doesn't care about the component or URL it receives; as long as it's a valid component and a valid API endpoint, it'll simply pass the data from that API endpoint to the component that we pass.

Composing

We can also compose multiple HOCs. Let's say we also want to add functionality that shows a hovering text box when the user hovers over the DogImages list.

We must create a HOC that provides a hovering prop to the element we pass. Based on that prop, we can conditionally render the text box based on whether the user is hovering over the DogImages list.

We can now wrap the withHover HOC around the withLoader HOC:

```
export default withHover(
  withLoader(DogImages, "https://dog.ceo/api/breed/labrador/images/random/6")
);
```

The DogImages element now contains all props we passed from withHover and withLoader.

We can also use the Hooks pattern to achieve similar results in some cases. We will discuss this pattern in detail later in this chapter, but for now, let's just say that using Hooks can reduce the depth of the component tree, while using the HOC pattern, it's easy to end up with a deeply nested component tree. The best use cases for HOC are those where the following are true:

- The same uncustomized behavior needs to be used by many components throughout the application.
- The component can work standalone without the added custom logic.

Pros

Using the HOC pattern allows us to keep logic we want to reuse all in one place. This reduces the risk of accidentally spreading bugs throughout the application by duplicating code repeatedly, potentially introducing new bugs. By keeping the logic in one place, we can keep our code DRY and efficiently enforce the separation of concerns.

Cons

The prop's name that a HOC can pass to an element can cause a naming collision. For example:

```
function withStyles(Component) {
  return props => {
    const style = { padding: '0.2rem', margin: '1rem' }
    return <Component style={style} {...props} />
  }
}

const Button = () = <button style={{ color: 'red' }}>Click me!</button>
const StyledButton = withStyles(Button)
```

In this case, the `withStyles` HOC adds a prop called `style` to the element we pass to it. However, the `Button` component already had a prop called `style`, which will be overwritten! Make sure the HOC can handle accidental name collision by either renaming or merging the props:

```
function withStyles(Component) {
  return props => {
    const style = {
      padding: '0.2rem',
      margin: '1rem',
      ...props.style
    }

    return <Component style={style} {...props} />
  }
}

const Button = () = <button style={{ color: 'red' }}>Click me!</button>
const StyledButton = withStyles(Button)
```

When using multiple composed HOCs that all pass props to the element wrapped within them, it can be challenging to figure out which HOC is responsible for which prop. This can hinder debugging and scaling an application easily.

Render Props Pattern

In the section on HOCs, we saw that reusing component logic can be convenient if multiple components need access to the same data or contain the same logic.

Another way of making components reusable is by using the Render Prop pattern. A render prop is a prop on a component whose value is a function that returns a JSX element. The component itself does not render anything besides the render prop. It simply calls the render prop instead of implementing its own rendering logic.

Imagine that we have a `Title` component that should just render the value we pass. We can use a render prop for this. Let's pass the value we want the `Title` component to render to the render prop:

```
<Title render={() => <h1>I am a render prop!</h1>} />
```

We can render this data within the `Title` component by returning the invoked render prop:

```
const Title = props => props.render();
```

We have to pass a prop called `render` to the Component element, which is a function that returns a React element:

```
import React from "react";
import { render } from "react-dom";

import "./styles.css";

const Title = (props) => props.render();

render(
  <div className="App">
    <Title
      render={() => (
        <h1>
          <span role="img" aria-label="emoji">

          </span>
          I am a render prop!{" "}
          <span role="img" aria-label="emoji">

          </span>
        </h1>
      )}
    />
  </div>,
  document.getElementById("root")
);
```

The cool thing about render props is that the component receiving the prop is reusable. We can use it multiple times, passing different values to the render prop each time.

Although they're called render props, a render prop doesn't have to be called render. Any prop that renders JSX is considered a render prop. Thus we have three render props in the following example:

```
const Title = (props) => (
  <>
    {props.renderFirstComponent()}
    {props.renderSecondComponent()}
```

```
        {props.renderThirdComponent()}
    </>
);

render(
  <div className="App">
    <Title
      renderFirstComponent={() => <h1>First render prop!</h1>}
      renderSecondComponent={() => <h2> Second render prop!</h2>}
      renderThirdComponent={() => <h3>Third render prop!</h3>}
    />
  </div>,
  document.getElementById("root")
);
```

We've just seen that we can use render props to make a component reusable, as we can pass different data to the render prop each time.

A component that takes a render prop usually does much more than simply invoking the render prop. Instead, we typically want to pass data from the component that takes the render prop to the element we pass as a render prop:

```
function Component(props) {
  const data = { ... }

  return props.render(data)
}
```

The render prop can now receive this value that we passed as its argument:

```
<Component render={data => <ChildComponent data={data} />}
```

Lifting State

Before we look at another use case for the Render Props pattern, let's understand the concept of "Lifting state up" in React.

Let's say we have a temperature converter where you can provide the input in Celsius in one stateful input element. The corresponding `Fahrenheit` and `Kelvin` values are reflected instantly in two other components. For the input element to be able to share its state with other components, we will have to move the state up to the closest common ancestor of the components that need it. This is called "Lifting state up":

```
function Input({ value, handleChange }) {
  return <input value={value} onChange={e => handleChange(e.target.value)} />;
}
function Kelvin({ value = 0 }) {
  return <div className="temp">{value + 273.15}K</div>;
}

function Fahrenheit({ value = 0 }) {
  return <div className="temp">{(value * 9) / 5 + 32}°F</div>;
```

```
}

export default function App() {
  const [value, setValue] = useState("");

  return (
    <div className="App">
      <h1>Temperature Converter</h1>
      <Input value={value} handleChange={setValue} />
      <Kelvin value={value} />
      <Fahrenheit value={value} />
    </div>
  );
}
```

Lifting state is a valuable React state management pattern because sometimes we want a component to be able to share its state with sibling components. In the case of small applications with a few components, we can avoid using a state management library like Redux or React Context and use this pattern instead to lift the state up to the closest common ancestor.

Although this is a valid solution, lifting the state in larger applications with components that handle many children can be tricky. Each state change could cause a re-render of all the children, even those that don't handle the data, which could negatively affect your app's performance. We can use the Render Props pattern to work around this problem. We will change the Input component such that it can receive render props:

```
function Input(props) {
  const [value, setValue] = useState("");

  return (
    <>
      <input
        type="text"
        value={value}
        onChange={e => setValue(e.target.value)}
        placeholder="Temp in °C"
      />
      {props.render(value)}
    </>
  );
}

export default function App() {
  return (
    <div className="App">
      <h1>Temperature Converter</h1>
      <Input
        render={value => (
          <>
```

```
        <Kelvin value={value} />
        <Fahrenheit value={value} />
      </>
    )}
  />
  </div>
);
}
```

Children as a Function

Besides regular JSX components, we can pass functions as children to React components. This function is available to us through the children prop, which is technically also a render prop.

Let's change the Input component. Instead of explicitly passing the render prop, we'll pass a function as a child for the Input component:

```
export default function App() {
  return (
    <div className="App">
      <h1>Temperature Converter</h1>
      <Input>
        {value => (
          <>
            <Kelvin value={value} />
            <Fahrenheit value={value} />
          </>
        )}
      </Input>
    </div>
  );
}
```

We have access to this function through the props.children prop that's available on the Input component. Instead of calling props.render with the user input value, we'll call props.children with the value of the user input:

```
function Input(props) {
  const [value, setValue] = useState("");

  return (
    <>
      <input
        type="text"
        value={value}
        onChange={e => setValue(e.target.value)}
        placeholder="Temp in °C"
      />
      {props.children(value)}
    </>
```

```
    );
  }
```

This way, the `Kelvin` and `Fahrenheit` components have access to the value without worrying about the name of the render prop.

Pros

Sharing logic and data among several components is straightforward with the Render Props pattern. Components can be made reusable by using a render or children prop. Although the HOC pattern mainly solves the same issues, namely reusability and sharing data, the Render Props pattern solves some problems we could encounter using the HOC pattern.

The issue of naming collisions that we can run into by using the HOC pattern no longer applies by using the Render Props pattern since we don't automatically merge props. We explicitly pass the props down to the child components with the value provided by the parent component.

Since we explicitly pass props, we solve the HOC's implicit props issue. The props that should get passed down to the element are all visible in the render prop's arguments list. This way, we know exactly where specific props come from. We can separate our app's logic from rendering components through render props. The stateful component that receives a render prop can pass the data onto stateless components, which merely render the data.

Cons

React Hooks have mostly resolved the issues we tried to solve with render props. As Hooks changed how we can add reusability and data sharing to components, they can replace the Render Props pattern in many cases.

Since we can't add lifecycle methods to a render prop, we can use it only on components that don't need to alter the data they receive.

Hooks Pattern

React 16.8 introduced a new feature called Hooks (*https://oreil.ly/6qnHk*). Hooks make it possible to use React state and lifecycle methods without using an ES2015 class component. Although Hooks is not necessarily a design pattern, Hooks plays a vital role in your application design. Hooks can replace many traditional design patterns.

Let's see how class components enabled the addition of state and lifecycle methods.

Class Components

Before Hooks were introduced in React, we had to use class components to add state and lifecycle methods to components. A typical class component in React can look something like this:

```
class MyComponent extends React.Component {
  // Adding state and binding custom methods
  constructor() {
    super()
    this.state = { ... }

    this.customMethodOne = this.customMethodOne.bind(this)
    this.customMethodTwo = this.customMethodTwo.bind(this)
  }

  // Lifecycle Methods
  componentDidMount() { ...}
  componentWillUnmount() { ... }

  // Custom methods
  customMethodOne() { ... }
  customMethodTwo() { ... }

  render() { return { ... }}
}
```

A class component can contain the following:

- A state in its constructor
- Lifecycle methods such as `componentDidMount` and `componentWillUnmount` to perform side effects based on a component's lifecycle
- Custom methods to add extra logic to a class

Although we can still use class components after the introduction of React Hooks, using class components can have some downsides. For example, consider the following example where a simple `div` functions as a button:

```
function Button() {
  return <div className="btn">disabled</div>;
}
```

Instead of always displaying disabled, we want to change it to enabled and add some extra CSS styling to the button when the user clicks on it. To do that, we need to add state to the component to know whether the status is enabled or disabled. This means we'd have to refactor the functional component entirely and make it a class component that keeps track of the button's state:

```
export default class Button extends React.Component {
  constructor() {
    super();
    this.state = { enabled: false };
  }

  render() {
    const { enabled } = this.state;
    const btnText = enabled ? "enabled" : "disabled";

    return (
      <div
        className={`btn enabled-${enabled}`}
        onClick={() => this.setState({ enabled: !enabled })}
      >
        {btnText}
      </div>
    );
  }
}
```

In this example, the component is minimal, and refactoring didn't need much effort. However, your real-life components probably consist of many more lines of code, making refactoring the component much more difficult.

Besides ensuring you don't accidentally change any behavior while refactoring the component, you must also understand how ES2015+ classes work. Knowing how to refactor a component properly without accidentally changing the data flow can be challenging.

Restructuring

The standard way to share code among several components is using the HOC or Render Props pattern. Although both patterns are valid and using them is a good practice, adding those patterns at a later point in time requires you to restructure your application.

Besides restructuring your app, which is trickier the bigger your components are, having many wrapping components to share code among deeper nested components can lead to something that's best referred to as a "wrapper hell." It's not uncommon to open your dev tools and see a structure similar to the following:

```
<WrapperOne>
  <WrapperTwo>
    <WrapperThree>
      <WrapperFour>
        <WrapperFive>
          <Component>
            <h1>Finally in the component!</h1>
          </Component>
```

```
      </WrapperFive>
     </WrapperFour>
    </WrapperThree>
   </WrapperTwo>
  </WrapperOne>
```

The wrapper hell can make it difficult to understand how data flows through your application, making it harder to figure out why unexpected behavior is happening.

Complexity

As we add more logic to class components, the size of the component increases fast. Logic within that component can get tangled and unstructured, making it difficult for developers to understand where certain logic is used in the class component. This can make debugging and optimizing performance more difficult. Lifecycle methods also require quite a lot of duplication in the code.

Hooks

Class components aren't always a great feature in React. To solve the common issues that React developers can run into when using class components, React introduced React Hooks. React Hooks are functions you can use to manage a component's state and lifecycle methods. React Hooks make it possible to:

- Add state to a functional component

- Manage a component's lifecycle without having to use lifecycle methods such as `componentDidMount` and `componentWillUnmount`

- Reuse the same stateful logic among multiple components throughout the app

First, let's look at how we can add state to a functional component using React Hooks.

State Hook

React provides a Hook called `useState` that manages state within a functional component.

Let's see how a class component can be restructured into a functional component using the `useState` Hook. We have a class component called `Input`, which renders an input field. The value of input in the state updates whenever the user types anything in the input field:

```
class Input extends React.Component {
  constructor() {
    super();
    this.state = { input: "" };
```

```
      this.handleInput = this.handleInput.bind(this);
    }

    handleInput(e) {
      this.setState({ input: e.target.value });
    }

    render() {
      <input onChange={handleInput} value={this.state.input} />;
    }
  }
```

To use the `useState` Hook, we need to access React's `useState` method. The `useState` method expects an argument: this is the initial value of the state, an empty string in this case.

We can destructure two values from the `useState` method:

- The *current value* of the state
- The *method with which we can update* the state:

```
const [value, setValue] = React.useState(initialValue);
```

You can compare the first value to a class component's `this.state.[value]`. The second value can be compared to a class component's `this.setState` method.

Since we're dealing with the value of an input, let's call the current value of the state `input` and the method to update the state `setInput`. The initial value should be an empty string:

```
const [input, setInput] = React.useState("");
```

We can now refactor the `Input` class component into a stateful functional component:

```
function Input() {
  const [input, setInput] = React.useState("");

  return <input onChange={(e) => setInput(e.target.value)} value={input} />;
}
```

The input field's value is equal to the current value of the input state, just like in the class component example. When the user types in the input field, the value of the input state updates accordingly using the `setInput` method:

```
import React, { useState } from "react";

export default function Input() {
  const [input, setInput] = useState("");
```

```
      return (
        <input
          onChange={e => setInput(e.target.value)}
          value={input}
          placeholder="Type something..."
        />
      );
    }
```

Effect Hook

We've seen we can use the `useState` component to handle state within a functional component. Still, another benefit of class components was the possibility of adding lifecycle methods to a component.

With the `useEffect` Hook, we can "hook into" a component's lifecycle. The `useEffect` Hook effectively combines the `componentDidMount`, `componentDidUpdate`, and `componentWillUnmount` lifecycle methods:

```
componentDidMount() { ... }
useEffect(() => { ... }, [])

componentWillUnmount() { ... }
useEffect(() => { return () => { ... } }, [])

componentDidUpdate() { ... }
useEffect(() => { ... })
```

Let's use the input example we used in the state Hook section. Whenever the user is typing anything in the input field, the value should also be logged to the console.

We need a `useEffect` Hook that "listens" to the input value. We can do so by adding input to the dependency array of the `useEffect` Hook. The dependency array is the second argument that the `useEffect` Hook receives:

```
import React, { useState, useEffect } from "react";

export default function Input() {
  const [input, setInput] = useState("");

  useEffect(() => {
    console.log(`The user typed ${input}`);
  }, [input]);

  return (
    <input
      onChange={e => setInput(e.target.value)}
      value={input}
      placeholder="Type something..."
    />
```

```
  );
}
```

The value of the input now gets logged to the console whenever the user types a value.

Custom Hooks

Besides the built-in Hooks that React provides (useState, useEffect, useReducer, useRef, useContext, useMemo, useImperativeHandle, useLayoutEffect, useDebug Value, useCallback), we can easily create our own custom Hooks.

You may have noticed that all Hooks start with "use." It's essential to begin your Hooks with "use" for React to check if it violates the rules of Hooks.

Let's say we want to keep track of specific keys the user may press when writing the input. Our custom Hook should be able to receive the key we want to target as its argument.

We want to add a keydown and keyup event listener to the key that the user passed as an argument. If the user presses that key, meaning the keydown event gets triggered, the state within the Hook should toggle to true. Otherwise, when the user stops pressing that button, the keyup event gets triggered and the state toggles to false:

```
function useKeyPress(targetKey) {
  const [keyPressed, setKeyPressed] = React.useState(false);

  function handleDown({ key }) {
    if (key === targetKey) {
      setKeyPressed(true);
    }
  }

  function handleUp({ key }) {
    if (key === targetKey) {
      setKeyPressed(false);
    }
  }

  React.useEffect(() => {
    window.addEventListener("keydown", handleDown);
    window.addEventListener("keyup", handleUp);

    return () => {
      window.removeEventListener("keydown", handleDown);
      window.removeEventListener("keyup", handleUp);
    };
  }, []);

  return keyPressed;
}
```

We can use this custom Hook in our input application. Let's log to the console whenever the user presses the q, l, or w key:

```
import React from "react";
import useKeyPress from "./useKeyPress";

export default function Input() {
  const [input, setInput] = React.useState("");
  const pressQ = useKeyPress("q");
  const pressW = useKeyPress("w");
  const pressL = useKeyPress("l");

  React.useEffect(() => {
    console.log(`The user pressed Q!`);
  }, [pressQ]);

  React.useEffect(() => {
    console.log(`The user pressed W!`);
  }, [pressW]);

  React.useEffect(() => {
    console.log(`The user pressed L!`);
  }, [pressL]);

  return (
    <input
      onChange={e => setInput(e.target.value)}
      value={input}
      placeholder="Type something..."
    />
  );
}
```

Instead of keeping the key press logic local to the Input component, we can reuse the useKeyPress Hook with multiple components without having to rewrite the same code repeatedly.

Another great advantage of Hooks is that the community can build and share Hooks. We wrote the useKeyPress Hook ourselves, but that wasn't necessary. The Hook was already built by someone else and ready to use in our application if we had just installed it.

The following are some websites that list all the Hooks built by the community and ready to use in your application:

- React Use (*https://oreil.ly/Ya94L*)
- useHooks (*https://oreil.ly/ZMTcR*)
- Collection of React Hooks (*https://oreil.ly/jlksC*)

Additional Hooks Guidance

Like other components, special functions are used when you want to add Hooks to the code you have written. Here's a brief overview of some common Hook functions:

useState

> The useState Hook enables developers to update and manipulate state inside function components without needing to convert it to a class component. One advantage of this Hook is that it is simple and does not require as much complexity as other React Hooks.

useEffect

> The useEffect Hook is used to run code during major lifecycle events in a function component. The main body of a function component does not allow mutations, subscriptions, timers, logging, and other side effects. It could lead to confusing bugs and inconsistencies within the UI if they are allowed. The useEffect Hook prevents all of these "side effects" and allows the UI to run smoothly. It combines componentDidMount, componentDidUpdate, and componentWillUnmount, all in one place.

useContext

> The useContext Hook accepts a context object, the value returned from React.createcontext, and returns the current context value for that context. The useContext Hook also works with the React Context API to share data throughout the app without passing your app props down through various levels. Note that the argument passed to the useContext Hook must be the context object itself and any component calling the useContext always rerenders whenever the context value changes.

useReducer

> The useReducer Hook gives an alternative to setState. It is especially preferable when you have complex state logic that involves multiple subvalues or when the next state depends on the previous one. It takes on a reducer function and an initial state input and returns the current state and a dispatch function as output using array destructuring. useReducer also optimizes the performance of components that trigger deep updates.

Pros and Cons of Using Hooks

Here are some benefits of making use of Hooks:

Fewer lines of code

> Hooks allow you to group code by concern and functionality, not by lifecycle. This makes the code not only cleaner and concise but also shorter. What follows

is a comparison of a simple stateful component of a searchable product data table using React and how it looks in Hooks after using the useState keyword.

Stateful component:

```
class TweetSearchResults extends React.Component {
  constructor(props) {
    super(props);
    this.state = {
      filterText: '',
      inThisLocation: false
    };

    this.handleFilterTextChange =
              this.handleFilterTextChange.bind(this);
    this.handleInThisLocationChange =
              this.handleInThisLocationChange.bind(this);
  }

  handleFilterTextChange(filterText) {
    this.setState({
      filterText: filterText
    });
  }

  handleInThisLocationChange(inThisLocation) {
    this.setState({
      inThisLocation: inThisLocation
    })
  }

  render() {
    return (
      <div>
        <SearchBar
          filterText={this.state.filterText}
          inThisLocation={this.state.inThisLocation}
          onFilterTextChange={this.handleFilterTextChange}
          onInThisLocationChange={this.handleInThisLocationChange}
        />
        <TweetList
          tweets={this.props.tweets}
          filterText={this.state.filterText}
          inThisLocation={this.state.inThisLocation}
        />
      </div>
    );
  }
}
```

Here's the same component with Hooks:

```
const TweetSearchResults = ({tweets}) => {
  const [filterText, setFilterText] = useState('');
  const [inThisLocation, setInThisLocation] = useState(false);
  return (
    <div>
      <SearchBar
        filterText={filterText}
        inThisLocation={inThisLocation}
        setFilterText={setFilterText}
        setInThisLocation={setInThisLocation}
      />
      <TweetList
        tweets={tweets}
        filterText={filterText}
        inThisLocation={inThisLocation}
      />
    </div>
  );
}
```

Simplifies complex components

JavaScript classes can be challenging to manage, can be hard to use with hot reloading, and may need to be minified better. React Hooks solves these problems and ensures functional programming is made easy. With the implementation of Hooks, we don't need to have class components.

Reusing stateful logic

Classes in JavaScript encourage multiple levels of inheritance that quickly increase overall complexity and potential for errors. However, Hooks allow you to use state and other React features without writing a class. With React, you can always reuse stateful logic without needing to rewrite the code repeatedly. This reduces the chances of errors and allows for composition with plain functions.

Sharing nonvisual logic

Until the implementation of Hooks, React had no way of extracting and sharing nonvisual logic. This eventually led to more complexities, such as the HOC patterns and Render Props, to solve a common problem. The introduction of Hooks has solved this problem because it allows for extracting stateful logic to a simple JavaScript function.

There are, of course, some potential downsides to Hooks worth keeping in mind:

- Have to respect its rules. With a linter plug-in, knowing which rule has been broken is easier.

- Need considerable time practicing to use correctly (e.g., `useEffect`).
- Need to be aware of the wrong use (e.g., `useCallback`, `useMemo`).

React Hooks Versus Classes

When Hooks were introduced to React, it created a new problem: how do we know when to use function components with Hooks and class components? With the help of Hooks, it is possible to get state and partial lifecycle Hooks even in function components. Hooks allow you to use local state and other React features without writing a class. Here are some differences between Hooks and classes to help you decide:

- Hooks help avoid multiple hierarchies and make the code clearer. With classes, generally, when you use HOC or Render Props, you have to restructure your app with multiple hierarchies when you try to see it in DevTools.
- Hooks provide uniformity across React components. Classes confuse humans and machines due to the need to understand binding and the context in which functions are called.

Static Import

The `import` keyword allows us to import code that another module has exported. By default, all modules we're statically importing get added to the initial bundle. A module imported using the default ES2015+ import syntax, `import module from [module]`, is statically imported. In this section, we will learn the use of static imports in the React.js context.

Let's look at an example. A simple chat app contains a `Chat` component, in which we are statically importing and rendering three components: `UserProfile`, a `ChatList`, and a `ChatInput` to type and send messages. Within the `ChatInput` module, we're statically importing an `EmojiPicker` component to show the emoji picker when the user toggles the emoji. We will use webpack (*https://oreil.ly/37e9F*) to bundle our module dependencies:

```
import React from "react";

// Statically import Chatlist, ChatInput and UserInfo
import UserInfo from "./components/UserInfo";
import ChatList from "./components/ChatList";
import ChatInput from "./components/ChatInput";

import "./styles.css";

console.log("App loading", Date.now());

const App = () => (
```

```
    <div className="App">
      <UserInfo />
      <ChatList />
      <ChatInput />
    </div>
  );

  export default App;
```

The modules get executed as soon as the engine reaches the line on which we import them. When you open the console, you can see the order in which the modules were loaded.

Since the components were statically imported, webpack bundled the modules into the initial bundle. We can see the bundle that webpack creates after building the application:

Asset	main.bundle.js
Size	1.5 MiB
Chunks	main [emitted]
Chunk Names	main

Our chat application's source code gets bundled into one bundle: *main.bundle.js*. A large bundle size can significantly affect our application's loading time depending on the user's device and network connection. Before the App component can render its contents to the user's screen, it must first load and parse all modules.

Luckily, there are many ways to speed up the loading time! We don't always have to import all modules at once: there may be modules that should only get rendered based on user interaction, like the EmojiPicker in this case, or rendered further down the page. Instead of importing all components statically, we can dynamically import the modules after the App component has rendered its contents, and the user can interact with our application.

Dynamic Import

The chat application discussed in the previous section on Static Imports had four key components: UserInfo, ChatList, ChatInput, and EmojiPicker. However, only three of these components are used instantly on the initial page load: UserInfo, ChatList, and ChatInput. The EmojiPicker isn't directly visible and may only be rendered if the user clicks on the Emoji to toggle the EmojiPicker. This implies that we unnecessarily added the EmojiPicker module to our initial bundle, potentially increasing the loading time.

To solve this, we can dynamically import the `EmojiPicker` component. Instead of statically importing it, we'll import it only when we want to show the EmojiPicker. An easy way to dynamically import components in React is by using React Suspense. The `React.Suspense` component receives the component that should be dynamically loaded, making it possible for the `App` component to render its contents faster by suspending the import of the EmojiPicker module. When the user clicks on the Emoji, the `EmojiPicker` component gets rendered for the first time. The `EmojiPicker` component renders a `Suspense` component, which receives the lazily imported module: the EmojiPicker in this case. The `Suspense` component accepts a fallback prop, which receives the component that should get rendered while the suspended component is still loading!

Instead of unnecessarily adding EmojiPicker to the initial bundle, we can split it up into its own bundle and reduce the size of the initial bundle.

A smaller initial bundle size means a faster initial load: the user doesn't have to stare at a blank loading screen for as long. The fallback component lets the user know that our application hasn't frozen: they need to wait a little while for the module to be processed and executed.

Asset	Size	Chunks	Chunk names
emoji-picker.bundle.js	1.48 KiB	1 [emitted]	emoji-picker
main.bundle.js	1.33 MiB	main [emitted]	main
vendors~emoji-picker.bundle.js	171 KiB	2 [emitted]	vendors~emoji-picker

Whereas previously, the initial bundle was 1.5 MiB, we've reduced it to 1.33 MiB by suspending the import of the EmojiPicker. In the console, you can see that the Emoji-Picker gets executed once we've toggled the EmojiPicker:

```
import React, { Suspense, lazy } from "react";
  // import Send from "./icons/Send";
  // import Emoji from "./icons/Emoji";
  const Send = lazy(() =>
    import(/*webpackChunkName: "send-icon" */ "./icons/Send")
  );
  const Emoji = lazy(() =>
    import(/*webpackChunkName: "emoji-icon" */ "./icons/Emoji")
  );
  // Lazy load EmojiPicker  when <EmojiPicker /> renders
  const Picker = lazy(() =>
    import(/*webpackChunkName: "emoji-picker" */ "./EmojiPicker")
  );

  const ChatInput = () => {
    const [pickerOpen, togglePicker] = React.useReducer(state => !state, false);

    return (
```

```
      <Suspense fallback={<p id="loading">Loading...</p>}>
        <div className="chat-input-container">
          <input type="text" placeholder="Type a message..." />
          <Emoji onClick={togglePicker} />
          {pickerOpen && <Picker />}
          <Send />
        </div>
      </Suspense>
    );
  };

  console.log("ChatInput loaded", Date.now());

  export default ChatInput;
```

When building the application, we can see the different bundles that webpack created. By dynamically importing the EmojiPicker component, we reduced the initial bundle size from 1.5 MiB to 1.33 MiB! Although the user may still have to wait a while until the EmojiPicker has been fully loaded, we have improved the UX by making sure the application is rendered and interactive while the user waits for the component to load.

Loadable Components

SSR doesn't support React Suspense (yet). An excellent alternative to React Suspense is the *loadable-components* library, which you can use in SSR applications:

```
import React from "react";
import loadable from "@loadable/component";

import Send from "./icons/Send";
import Emoji from "./icons/Emoji";

const EmojiPicker = loadable(() => import("./EmojiPicker"), {
  fallback: <div id="loading">Loading...</div>
});

const ChatInput = () => {
  const [pickerOpen, togglePicker] = React.useReducer(state => !state, false);

  return (
    <div className="chat-input-container">
      <input type="text" placeholder="Type a message..." />
      <Emoji onClick={togglePicker} />
      {pickerOpen && <EmojiPicker />}
      <Send />
    </div>
  );
};

export default ChatInput;
```

Like React Suspense, we can pass the lazily imported module to the loadable, which will import the module only once the EmojiPicker module is requested. While the module is loaded, we can render a fallback component.

Although loadable components are a great alternative to React Suspense for SSR applications, they're also helpful in CSR applications to suspend module imports:

```
import React from "react";
import Send from "./icons/Send";
import Emoji from "./icons/Emoji";
import loadable from "@loadable/component";

const EmojiPicker = loadable(() => import("./components/EmojiPicker"), {
  fallback: <p id="loading">Loading...</p>
});

const ChatInput = () => {
  const [pickerOpen, togglePicker] = React.useReducer(state => !state, false);

  return (
    <div className="chat-input-container">
      <input type="text" placeholder="Type a message..." />
      <Emoji onClick={togglePicker} />
      {pickerOpen && <EmojiPicker />}
      <Send />
    </div>
  );
};

console.log("ChatInput loaded", Date.now());

export default ChatInput;
```

Import on Interaction

In the chat application example, we dynamically imported the EmojiPicker component when the user clicked on the Emoji. This type of dynamic import is called *Import on Interaction*. We triggered the component import on interaction by the user.

Import on Visibility

Besides user interaction, we often have components that need not be visible on the initial page load. An excellent example of this is lazy-loading images or components that aren't directly visible in the viewport and get loaded only once the user scrolls down. Triggering a dynamic import when the user scrolls down to a component and it becomes visible is called *Import on Visibility*.

To know whether components are currently in our viewport, we can use the IntersectionObserver API or libraries such as `react-loadable-visibility` or `react-lazyload` to add Import on Visibility to our application quickly. We can now look at the chat application example where the EmojiPicker is imported and loaded when it becomes visible to the user:

```
import React from "react";
import Send from "./icons/Send";
import Emoji from "./icons/Emoji";
import LoadableVisibility from "react-loadable-visibility/react-loadable";

const EmojiPicker = LoadableVisibility({
  loader: () => import("./EmojiPicker"),
  loading: <p id="loading">Loading</p>
});

const ChatInput = () => {
  const [pickerOpen, togglePicker] = React.useReducer(state => !state, false);

  return (
    <div className="chat-input-container">
      <input type="text" placeholder="Type a message..." />
      <Emoji onClick={togglePicker} />
      {pickerOpen && <EmojiPicker />}
      <Send />
    </div>
  );
};

console.log("ChatInput loading", Date.now());

export default ChatInput;
```

Code-Splitting

In the previous section, we saw how we could dynamically import components when needed. In a complex application with multiple routes and components, we must ensure that our code is bundled and split optimally to allow for a mix of static and dynamic imports at the right time.

You can use the route-based splitting pattern to split your code or rely on modern bundlers such as webpack or Rollup to split and bundle your application's source code.

Route-based Splitting

Specific resources may be required only on certain pages or routes, and we can request resources that are needed only for particular routes by adding route-based splitting. By combining React Suspense or *loadable-components* with libraries such as react-router, we can dynamically load components based on the current route. For example:

```
import React, { lazy, Suspense } from "react";
import { render } from "react-dom";
import { Switch, Route, BrowserRouter as Router } from "react-router-dom";

const App = lazy(() => import(/* webpackChunkName: "home" */ "./App"));
const Overview = lazy(() =>
  import(/* webpackChunkName: "overview" */ "./Overview")
);
const Settings = lazy(() =>
  import(/* webpackChunkName: "settings" */ "./Settings")
);

render(
  <Router>
    <Suspense fallback={<div>Loading...</div>}>
      <Switch>
        <Route exact path="/">
          <App />
        </Route>
        <Route path="/overview">
          <Overview />
        </Route>
        <Route path="/settings">
          <Settings />
        </Route>
      </Switch>
    </Suspense>
  </Router>,
  document.getElementById("root")
);

module.hot.accept();
```

By lazily loading the components per route, we're only requesting the bundle that contains the code necessary for the current route. Since most people are used to the fact that there may be some loading time during a redirect, it's the perfect place to load components lazily.

Bundle Splitting

When building a modern web application, bundlers such as webpack or Rollup take an application's source code and bundle this together into one or more bundles. When a user visits a website, the bundles required to display the data and features to the user are requested and loaded.

JavaScript engines such as V8 can parse and compile data requested by the user as it's being loaded. Although modern browsers have evolved to parse and compile the code as quickly and efficiently as possible, the developer is still in charge of optimizing the loading and execution time of the requested data. We want to keep the execution time as short as possible to prevent blocking the main thread.

Even though modern browsers can stream the bundle as it arrives, it can still take a significant time before the first pixel is painted on the user's device. The bigger the bundle, the longer it can take before the engine reaches the line on which the first rendering call is made. Until then, the user has to stare at a blank screen, which can be frustrating.

We want to display data to the user as quickly as possible. A larger bundle leads to an increased amount of loading time, processing time, and execution time. It would be great if we could reduce the size of this bundle to speed things up. Instead of requesting one giant bundle that contains unnecessary code, we can split the bundle into multiple smaller bundles. There are some essential metrics that we need to consider when deciding the size of our bundles.

By bundle-splitting the application, we can reduce the time it takes to load, process, and execute a bundle. This, in turn, reduces the time it takes for the first content to be painted on the user's screen, known as the First Contentful Paint (FCP). It also reduces the time for the largest component to be rendered to the screen or the Largest Contentful Paint (LCP) metric.

Although seeing data on our screen is excellent, we want to see more than just the content. To have a fully functioning application, we want users to be able to interact with it as well. The UI becomes interactive only after the bundle has been loaded and executed. The time it takes for all content to be painted on the screen and become interactive is called the Time to Interactive (TTI).

A larger bundle doesn't necessarily mean a longer execution time. It could happen that we loaded a ton of code that the user may not even use. Some parts of the bundle will get executed on only a specific user interaction, which the user may or may not do.

The engine still has to load, parse, and compile code that's not even used on the initial render before the user can see anything on their screen. Although the parsing and compilation costs can be practically ignored due to the browser's performant way of handling these two steps, fetching a larger bundle than necessary can hurt the performance of your application. Users on low-end devices or slower networks will see a significant increase in loading time before the bundle is fetched.

Instead of initially requesting parts of the code that don't have a high priority in the current navigation, we can separate this code from the code needed to render the initial page.

PRPL Pattern

Making applications accessible to a global user base can be a challenge. The application should be performant on low-end devices and in regions with poor internet connectivity. To make sure our application can load as efficiently as possible under challenging conditions, we can use the Push Render Pre-cache Lazy-load (PRPL) pattern.

The PRPL pattern focuses on four primary performance considerations:

- *Pushing* critical resources efficiently minimizes the number of roundtrips to the server and reduces loading time.
- *Rendering* the initial route as soon as possible to improve the UX.
- *Pre-caching* assets in the background for frequently visited routes to minimize the number of requests to the server and enable a better offline experience.
- *Lazily loading* routes or assets that aren't requested as frequently.

When we visit a website, the browser requests the server for the required resources. The file the entry point points to gets returned from the server, usually our application's initial HTML file. The browser's HTML parser starts to parse this data as soon as it starts receiving it from the server. If the parser discovers that more resources are needed, such as stylesheets or scripts, additional HTTP requests are sent to the server to get those resources.

Requesting resources repeatedly isn't optimal, as we are trying to minimize the number of round trips between the client and the server.

We used HTTP/1.1 for a long time to communicate between the client and the server. Although HTTP/1.1 introduced many improvements compared to HTTP/1.0, such as keeping the TCP connection between the client and the server alive before a new HTTP request gets sent with the keep-alive header, there were still some issues that had to be solved. HTTP/2 introduced significant changes compared to HTTP/1.1, allowing us to optimize the message exchange between the client and the server.

Whereas HTTP/1.1 used a newline delimited plaintext protocol in the requests and responses, HTTP/2 splits the requests and responses into smaller frames. An HTTP request that contains headers and a body field gets split into at least two frames: a headers frame and a data frame.

HTTP/1.1 had a maximum amount of six TCP connections between the client and the server. Before you can send a new request over the same TCP connection, the previous request must be resolved. If the last request takes a long time to resolve, this request is blocking the other requests from being sent. This common issue is called head-of-line blocking and can increase the loading time of specific resources.

HTTP/2 uses bidirectional streams. A single TCP connection with multiple bidirectional streams can carry multiple request and response frames between the client and the server. Once the server has received all request frames for that specific request, it reassembles them and generates response frames. These response frames are sent back to the client, which reassembles them. Since the stream is bidirectional, we can send both request and response frames over the same stream.

HTTP/2 solves head-of-line blocking by allowing multiple requests to get sent on the same TCP connection before the previous request resolves! HTTP/2 also introduced a more optimized way of fetching data, called server push. Instead of explicitly asking for resources each time by sending an HTTP request, the server can send the additional resources automatically by "pushing" these resources.

After the client has received the additional resources, the resources will get stored in the browser cache. When the resources are discovered while parsing the entry file, the browser can quickly get the resources from the cache instead of making an HTTP request to the server.

Although pushing resources reduces the time to receive additional resources, server push is not HTTP cache-aware. The pushed resources won't be available to us the next time we visit the website and will have to be requested again. To solve this, the PRPL pattern uses service workers after the initial load to cache those resources to ensure the client isn't making unnecessary requests.

As site authors, we usually know what resources are critical to fetch early on, while browsers do their best to guess this. We can help the browser by adding a preload resource hint to the critical resources.

By telling the browser that you'd like to preload a specific resource, you're telling the browser that you would like to fetch it sooner than the browser would otherwise discover it. Preloading is a great way to optimize the time it takes to load resources critical for the current route.

Although preloading resources is a great way to reduce the number of roundtrips and optimize loading time, pushing too many files can be harmful. The browser's cache is limited, and you may unnecessarily use bandwidth by requesting resources the client didn't need. The PRPL pattern focuses on optimizing the initial load. No other resources get loaded before the initial route is completely rendered.

We can achieve this by code-splitting our application into small, performant bundles. These bundles should allow users to load only the resources they need when they need them while also maximizing cache use.

Caching larger bundles can be an issue. Multiple bundles may share the same resources.

A browser needs help identifying which parts of the bundle are shared between multiple routes and cannot cache these resources. Caching resources is vital to reducing the number of round trips to the server and to making our application offline-friendly.

When working with the PRPL pattern, we need to ensure that the bundles we're requesting contain the minimal amount of resources we need at that time and are cachable by the browser. In some cases, this could mean that having no bundles at all would be more performant, and we could simply work with unbundled modules.

The benefit of dynamically requesting minimal resources by bundling an application can easily be mocked by configuring the browser and server to support HTTP/2 push and caching the resources efficiently. For browsers that don't support HTTP/2 server push, we can create an optimized build to minimize the number of roundtrips. The client doesn't have to know whether it's receiving a bundled or unbundled resource: the server delivers the appropriate build for each browser.

The PRPL pattern often uses an app shell as its main entry point, a minimal file containing most of the application's logic and shared between routes. It also includes the application's router, which can dynamically request the necessary resources.

The PRPL pattern ensures that no other resources get requested or rendered before the initial route is visible on the user's device. Once the initial route has been loaded successfully, a service worker can get installed to fetch the resources for the other frequently visited routes in the background.

Since this data is being fetched in the background, the user won't experience any delays. If a user wants to navigate to a frequently visited route cached by the service worker, the service worker can quickly get the required resources from the cache instead of sending a request to the server.

Resources for routes that aren't as frequently visited can be dynamically imported.

Loading Prioritization

The Loading Prioritization pattern encourages you to explicitly prioritize the requests for specific resources you know will be required earlier.

Preload (`<link rel="preload">`) is a browser optimization that allows critical resources (that browsers may discover late) to be requested earlier. If you are comfortable thinking about how to order the loading of your key resources manually, it can have a positive impact on loading performance and metrics in the Core Web Vitals (CWV). That said, preload is not a panacea and requires an awareness of some trade-offs:

```
<link rel="preload" href="emoji-picker.js" as="script">
  ...
```

```
    </head>
    <body>
      ...
      <script src="stickers.js" defer></script>
      <script src="video-sharing.js" defer></script>
      <script src="emoji-picker.js" defer></script>
```

When optimizing for metrics like Time to Interactive (TTI) or First Input Delay (FID), preload can be helpful to load JavaScript bundles (or chunks) necessary for interactivity. Remember that great care is needed when using preload because you want to avoid improving interactivity at the cost of delaying resources (like hero images or fonts) necessary for First Contentful Paint (FCP) or Largest Contentful Paint (LCP).

If you're trying to optimize the loading of first-party JavaScript, consider using <script defer> in the document <head> versus <body> to help with the early discovery of these resources.

Preload in Single-Page Apps

While prefetching is a great way to cache resources that may be requested sometime soon, we can preload resources that need to be used instantly. It could be a specific font used on the initial render or certain images the user sees immediately.

Say our EmojiPicker component should be visible instantly on the initial render. Although you should not include it in the main bundle, it should get loaded in parallel. Like prefetch, we can add a magic comment to inform webpack that this module should be preloaded:

```
const EmojiPicker = import(/* webpackPreload: true */ "./EmojiPicker");
```

After building the application, we can see that the EmojiPicker will be prefetched. The actual output is visible as a link tag with rel="preload" in the head of our document:

```
<link rel="prefetch" href="emoji-picker.bundle.js" as="script" />
<link rel="prefetch" href="vendors~emoji-picker.bundle.js" as="script" />
```

The preloaded EmojiPicker could be loaded in parallel with the initial bundle. Unlike prefetch, where the browser still had a say in whether it's got a good enough internet connection and bandwidth to prefetch the resource, a preloaded resource will get preloaded no matter what.

Instead of waiting until the EmojiPicker gets loaded after the initial render, the resource will be available to us instantly. As we're loading assets with more thoughtful ordering, the initial loading time may increase significantly depending on your user's device and internet connection. Only preload the resources that must be visible approximately 1 second after the initial render.

Preload + the async Hack

Should you wish for browsers to download a script as high priority but not block the parser waiting for a script, you can take advantage of the preload + async hack shown here. The preload, in this case, may delay the download of other resources, but this is a trade-off a developer has to make:

```
<link rel="preload" href="emoji-picker.js" as="script" />

<script src="emoji-picker.js" async></script>
```

Preload in Chrome 95+

The feature is slightly safer thanks to some fixes to preload's queue-jumping behavior in Chrome 95+. Pat Meenan of Chrome's new recommendations for preload suggests the following:

- Putting it in HTTP headers will jump ahead of everything else.
- Generally, preloads will load in the order the parser gets to them for anything greater than or equal to Medium, so be careful putting preloads at the beginning of the HTML.
- Font preloads are probably best toward the end of the head or the beginning of the body.
- Import preloads should be done after the script tag that needs the import (so the actual script gets loaded/parsed first).
- Image preloads will have a low priority and should be ordered relative to async scripts and other low/lowest priority tags.

List Virtualization

List virtualization helps improve the rendering performance of large lists of data. You render only visible rows of content in a dynamic list instead of the entire list. The rows rendered are only a small subset of the full list, with what is visible (the window) moving as the user scrolls. In React, you can achieve this using react-virtualized (*https://oreil.ly/3XThZ*). It's a windowing library by Brian Vaughn (*https://oreil.ly/hCqQq*) that renders only the items currently visible in a list (within a scrolling viewport). This means you don't need to pay the cost of thousands of rows of data being rendered at once.

How Does Windowing/Virtualization Work?

Virtualizing a list of items involves maintaining and moving a window around your list. Windowing in react-virtualized works by:

- Having a small container DOM element (e.g., `<ul>`) with relative positioning (window).
- Having a big DOM element for scrolling.
- Absolutely positioning children inside the container, setting their styles for top, left, width, and height.
- Rather than rendering thousands of elements from a list at once (which can cause slower initial rendering or impact scroll performance), virtualization focuses on rendering just items visible to the user.

This can help keep list rendering fast on mid- to low-end devices. You can fetch/display more items as the user scrolls, unloading previous entries and replacing them with new ones.

`react-window` (*https://oreil.ly/H_Rx7*) is a rewrite of `react-virtualized` by the same author aiming to be smaller, faster, and more tree-shakeable. In a tree-shakeable library, size is a function of which API surfaces you choose to use. I've seen approximately 20 to 30 KB (gzipped) savings using it in place of `react-virtualized`. The APIs for both packages are similar; `react-window` tends to be simpler where they differ.

The following are the main components in the case of `react-window`.

Lists

Lists render a windowed list (row) of elements meaning that only the visible rows are displayed to users. Lists use a Grid (internally) to render rows, relaying props to that inner Grid. The following code snippets show the difference between rendering lists in React versus using `react-window`.

Rendering a list of simple data (`itemsArray`) using React:

```
import React from "react";
import ReactDOM from "react-dom";

const itemsArray = [
  { name: "Drake" },
  { name: "Halsey" },
  { name: "Camila Cabello" },
  { name: "Travis Scott" },
  { name: "Bazzi" },
  { name: "Flume" },
  { name: "Nicki Minaj" },
  { name: "Kodak Black" },
  { name: "Tyga" },
  { name: "Bruno Mars" },
  { name: "Lil Wayne" }, ...
```

```
]; // our data

const Row = ({ index, style }) => (
  <div className={index % 2 ? "ListItemOdd" : "ListItemEven"} style={style}>
    {itemsArray[index].name}
  </div>
);

const Example = () => (
  <div
    style=
    class="List"
  >
    {itemsArray.map((item, index) => Row({ index }))}
  </div>
);

ReactDOM.render(<Example />, document.getElementById("root"));
```

Rendering a list using `react-window`:

```
import React from "react";
import ReactDOM from "react-dom";
import { FixedSizeList as List } from "react-window";

const itemsArray = [...]; // our data

const Row = ({ index, style }) => (
  <div className={index % 2 ? "ListItemOdd" : "ListItemEven"} style={style}>
    {itemsArray[index].name}
  </div>
);

const Example = () => (
  <List
    className="List"
    height={150}
    itemCount={itemsArray.length}
    itemSize={35}
    width={300}
  >
    {Row}
  </List>
);

ReactDOM.render(<Example />, document.getElementById("root"));
```

Grid

Grid renders tabular data with virtualization along the vertical and horizontal axes. It only renders the `Grid` cells needed to fill itself based on current horizontal/vertical scroll positions.

If we wanted to render the same list as earlier with a grid layout, assuming our input is a multidimensional array, we could accomplish this using `FixedSizeGrid` as follows:

```
import React from 'react';
import ReactDOM from 'react-dom';
import { FixedSizeGrid as Grid } from 'react-window';

const itemsArray = [
  [{},{},{},...],
  [{},{},{},...],
  [{},{},{},...],
  [{},{},{},...],
];

const Cell = ({ columnIndex, rowIndex, style }) => (
  <div
    className={
      columnIndex % 2
        ? rowIndex % 2 === 0
          ? 'GridItemOdd'
          : 'GridItemEven'
        : rowIndex % 2
          ? 'GridItemOdd'
          : 'GridItemEven'
    }
    style={style}
  >
    {itemsArray[rowIndex][columnIndex].name}
  </div>
);

const Example = () => (
  <Grid
    className="Grid"
    columnCount={5}
    columnWidth={100}
    height={150}
    rowCount={5}
    rowHeight={35}
    width={300}
  >
    {Cell}
  </Grid>
);

ReactDOM.render(<Example />, document.getElementById('root'));
```

Improvements in the Web Platform

Some modern browsers now support CSS `content-visibility` (*https://oreil.ly/l-B70*). `content-visibility:auto` allows you to skip rendering and painting off-screen content until needed. Consider trying the property out if you have a lengthy HTML document with costly rendering.

For rendering lists of dynamic content, I still recommend using a library like `react-window`. It would be hard to have a `content-visbility:hidden` version of such a library that beats a version aggressively using `display:none` or removing DOM nodes when off-screen like many list virtualization libraries may do today.

Conclusions

Again, use preload sparingly and always measure its impact on production. If the preload for your image is earlier in the document than it is, this can help browsers discover it (and order relative to other resources). When misused, preloading can cause your image to delay FCP (e.g., CSS, fonts)—the opposite of what you want. Also note that for such reprioritization efforts to be effective, it also depends on servers prioritizing requests correctly.

You may also find `<link rel="preload">` helpful for cases where you need to fetch scripts without executing them. A variety of the following web.dev articles (*https://oreil.ly/kgnfa*) touch on how to use preload to:

- Preload key scripts required for interactivity (*https://oreil.ly/bwZC9*)
- Preload your LCP image (*https://oreil.ly/4N3VO*)
- Load fonts while preventing layout shifts (*https://oreil.ly/Up2iQ*)

Summary

In this chapter, we discussed some essential considerations that drive the architecture and design of modern web applications. We also saw the different ways in which React.js design patterns address these concerns.

Earlier in this chapter, we introduced the concepts of CSR, SSR, and hydration. Java-Script can have a significant impact on page performance. The choice of rendering techniques can affect how and when the JavaScript is loaded or executed in the page lifecycle. A discussion on Rendering patterns is thus significant when discussing Java-Script patterns and the topic of our next chapter.

CHAPTER 13

Rendering Patterns

As we moved to more interactive websites, the number of events handled and the amount of content rendered on the client side grew, resulting in SPAs rendered primarily on the client, as in the case of React.js.

However, web pages can be as static or dynamic as the function they serve. We continue to serve a lot of static content on the web, for example, blog/news pages that you can generate on the server and push as-is to the clients. Static content is stateless, does not fire events, and does not need rehydration after rendering. Conversely, dynamic content (buttons, filters, search bar) has to be rewired to its events after rendering. The DOM has to be regenerated on the client side (virtual DOM). This regeneration, rehydration, and event handling functions contribute to the JavaScript sent to the client.

A Rendering pattern provides the ideal solution for rendering content for a given use case. The Rendering patterns in this table are popular:

Rendering patterns	
Client-side rendering (CSR)	HTML is rendered completely on the client
Server-side rendering (SSR)	Dynamically rendering HTML content on the server before rehydrating it on the client
Static rendering	Building a static site to render pages on the server at build time
Incremental static generation	Being able to dynamically augment or modify a static site even after the initial build (Next.js ISR, Gatsby DSG)
Streaming SSR	Breaking down server-rendered content into smaller streamed chunks
Edge rendering	Altering rendered HTML at the edge before sending it on to the client
Hybrid rendering	Combines build-time, server, and client rendering to create a more flexible approach to web development (e.g., React Server Components and Next.js App Router)
Partial hydration	Only hydrating some of your components on the client (e.g., React Server Components and Gatsby)

Progressive hydration	Controlling the order of component hydration on the client
Islands architecture	Isolated islands of dynamic behavior with multiple entry points in an otherwise static site (Astro, Eleventy)
Progressive enhancement	Making sure an app is functional even without JavaScript

This chapter introduces some of these Rendering patterns and will help you decide which pattern is most suitable for your needs. It will help you make foundational decisions such as:

- How and where do I want to render content?
- Should content be rendered on the web server, on the build server, on an edge network, or directly on the client?
- Should content be rendered all at once, partially, or progressively?

Importance of Rendering Patterns

Choosing the most suitable Rendering pattern for a given use case can make a world of difference to the developer experience (DX) you create for the engineering team and the UX you design for your end users. Choosing the correct pattern could lead to faster builds and excellent loading performance at low processing costs. On the other hand, a wrong choice of pattern can kill an app that could have brought to life a great business idea.

To create great UX, we must optimize our apps for user-centric metrics, such as the Core Web Vitals (CWV) (*https://oreil.ly/R20lq*):

Time to First Byte (TTFB)
> Time it takes for a client to receive the first byte of page content

First Contentful Paint(FCP)
> Time it takes the browser to render the first piece of content after navigation

Time to Interactive (TTI)
> Time from when the page starts loading to when it responds quickly to user input

Largest Contentful Paint (LCP)
> Time it takes to load and render the page's main content

Cumulative Layout Shift (CLS)
> Measures visual stability to avoid unexpected layout shift

First Input Delay (FID)
> Time from when the user interacts with the page to the time when the event handlers can run

The CWV metrics measure parameters most relevant to UX. Optimizing the CWV can ensure a great UX and optimal search engine optimization (SEO) for our apps.

To create a great DX for our product/engineering teams, we have to optimize our development environments by ensuring faster build times, easy rollbacks, scalable infrastructure, and many other features that help developers succeed:

Fast build times
> The project should build fast for quick iteration and deployment.

Low server costs
> The website should limit and optimize the server execution time to reduce execution costs.

Dynamic content
> The page should be able to load dynamic content performantly.

Easy rollbacks
> You can quickly revert to a previous build version and deploy it.

Reliable uptime
> Users should always be able to visit your website through operational servers.

Scalable infrastructure
> Your project may grow or shrink without facing performance issues.

Setting up a development environment based on these principles enables our development teams to build a great product efficiently.

We have now built quite a long list of expectations. But, if you choose the correct Rendering pattern, you can get most of these benefits automatically.

Rendering patterns have come a long way, from SSR and CSR to highly nuanced patterns discussed and judged today on different forums. While this can get overwhelming, it's important to remember that every pattern was designed to address specific use cases. A pattern characteristic beneficial for one use case can be detrimental in the case of another. It is also quite likely that different types of pages require different Rendering patterns on the same website.

The Chrome team has encouraged developers to consider static or SSR over a full rehydration approach. Over time, progressive loading and rendering techniques may help strike a good balance of performance and feature delivery when using a modern framework.

The following sections cover different patterns in detail.

Client-Side Rendering

We have already discussed CSR with React in the previous chapter. Here is a brief overview to help us relate it to the other Rendering patterns.

With React CSR, most of the application logic is executed on the client, and it interacts with the server through API calls to fetch or save data. Almost all of the UI is thus generated on the client. The entire web application is loaded on the first request. As the user navigates by clicking on links, no new request is generated to the server for rendering the pages. The code runs on the client to change the view/data.

CSR allows us to have an SPA that supports navigation without page refresh and provides a great UX. As the data processed to change the view is limited, routing between pages is generally faster, making the CSR application seem more responsive.

As the complexity of the page increases to show images, display data from a data store, and include event handling, the complexity and size of the JavaScript code required to render the page will also increase. CSR resulted in large JavaScript bundles, which increased the FCP and TTI of the page. Large payloads and a waterfall of network requests (e.g., for API responses) may also result in meaningful content not being rendered fast enough for a crawler to index it. This can affect the SEO of the website.

Loading and processing excess JavaScript can hurt performance. However, some interactivity and JavaScript are often required, even on primarily static websites. The rendering techniques discussed in the following sections try to find a balance between:

- Interactivity comparable to CSR applications
- SEO and performance benefits that are comparable to SSR applications

Server-Side Rendering

With SSR, we generate the HTML for every request. This approach is most suitable for pages containing highly personalized data, for example, data based on the user cookie or generally any data obtained from the user's request. It's also suitable for pages that should be render-blocking, perhaps based on the authentication state.

SSR is one of the oldest methods of rendering web content. SSR generates the complete HTML for the page content to be rendered in response to a user request. The content may include data from a data store or external API.

The connect and fetch operations are handled on the server. HTML required to format the content is also generated on the server. Thus, with SSR, we can avoid making additional round trips for data fetching and templating. As such, rendering code is not required on the client and the JavaScript corresponding to this need not be sent to the client.

With SSR, every request is treated independently and processed as a new request by the server. Even if the output of two consecutive requests is not very different, the server will process and generate it from scratch. Since the server is common to multiple users, the processing capability is shared by all active users at a given time.

A personalized dashboard is an excellent example of highly dynamic content on a page. Most of the content is based on the user's identity or authorization level that may be contained in a user cookie. This dashboard shows only when a user is authenticated and possibly shows user-specific sensitive data that should not be visible to others.

The core principle for SSR is that HTML is rendered on the server and shipped with the necessary JavaScript to rehydrate it on the client. Rehydration is regenerating the state of UI components on the client side after the server renders it. Since rehydration comes at a cost, each variation of SSR tries to optimize the rehydration process.

Static Rendering

With static rendering, the HTML for the entire page gets generated at build time and does not change until the next build. The HTML content is static and easily cacheable on a content delivery network (CDN) or an edge network. CDNs can quickly serve the prerendered cached HTML to clients when they request a specific page. This considerably cuts down the time it would otherwise take to process the request, render HTML content, and respond to a request in a typical SSR setup.

This process is most suitable for pages that do not change often and display the same data no matter who requests them. Static pages like the "About us," "Contact us," and "Blog" pages for websites, or product pages for ecommerce apps are ideal candidates for static rendering. Frameworks like Next.js, Gatsby, and VuePress support static generation.

At its core, plain static rendering does not involve any dynamic data. Let us understand it using a Next.js example:

```
// pages/about.js

export default function About() {
 return <div>
   <h1>About Us</h1>
   {/* ... */}
 </div>
}
```

When the site is built (using `next build`), this page will be prerendered into an HTML file *about.html* accessible at the route */about*.

You can have several variations of static rendering as follows:

Static generation of a listing page with dynamic data from a database
> The listing page is generated on the server with the data. This is suitable for pages where the listing itself is not very dynamic. In Next.js, you can export the function `getStaticProps()` (*https://oreil.ly/QcNhk*) in the page component for this.

Static generation of detail pages with dynamic routes
> Product pages or blog pages usually follow a fixed template with data populated in placeholders. In this case, individual pages can be generated on the server by merging the template with the dynamic data giving us several individual routes for each detailed page. The Next.js dynamic routes (*https://oreil.ly/2Bugb*) feature helps to achieve this using the `getStaticPaths()` function.

Static rendering with client-side fetch
> This pattern is helpful for a reasonably dynamic listing page that should display fresh listings always. You can still use static rendering for the website to render the UI with a skeleton component where you want to place the dynamic listing data. Then, after the page has loaded, we can fetch the data using SWR. SWR (inspired by the Stale-While-Revalidate pattern) are React Hooks for data fetching. A custom API route is used to fetch the data from the CMS and return this data. The pregenerated HTML file is sent to the client when the user requests the page. The user initially sees the skeleton UI without any data. The client fetches the data from the API route, receives the response, and shows the listings.

The key highlights of static rendering include the following:

- HTML gets generated at build time.
- Easily cacheable by CDN/Vercel Edge Network.
- Plain static rendering is best for pages that do not require request-based data.
- Static with client-side fetch is best for pages that contain data that should refresh on every page load and is contained in stable placeholder components.

Incremental Static Regeneration

ISR is a hybrid of static and SSR because it allows us to prerender only certain static pages and render the dynamic pages on-demand when the user requests them. This results in shorter build times and allows automatic invalidation of the cache and regeneration of the page after a specific interval.

ISR works on two fronts to incrementally introduce updates to an existing static site after it has been built:

Allows addition of new pages

The lazy-loading concept is used to include new pages on the website after the build. This means that the new page is generated immediately on the first request. While the generation takes place, a fallback page or a loading indicator can be shown to the user on the frontend.

Update existing pages

A suitable timeout is defined for every page. This will ensure that the page is revalidated whenever the defined timeout period has elapsed. The timeout could be set to as low as 1 second. The user will continue to see the previous version of the page until the page has finished revalidation. Thus, ISR uses the stale-while-revalidate strategy, where the user receives the cached or stale version while the revalidation takes place. The revalidation occurs entirely in the background and does not need a full rebuild.

On-Demand ISR

In this variation of ISR, the regeneration occurs on certain events rather than at fixed intervals. With regular ISR, the updated page is cached only at the edge nodes that have handled user requests for the page. On-demand ISR regenerates and redistributes the page across the edge network so that users worldwide will automatically see the most recent version of the page from the edge cache without seeing stale content. We also avoid unnecessary regenerations and serverless function calls, reducing operational costs compared to regular ISR. Thus on-demand ISR gives us performance benefits and a great DX. On-demand ISR is best for pages that should be regenerated based on specific events. It allows us to have fast and dynamic websites that are always online at a reasonable cost.

Summary of Static Rendering

Static rendering is an excellent pattern for websites where HTML can be generated at build time. We have now covered different variations of static generation, each of which is suitable for different use cases:

Plain static rendering

Best for pages that do not contain dynamic data

Static with client-side fetch

Best for pages where data should refresh on every page load and which have stable placeholder components

Incremental static regeneration

Best for pages that should be regenerated on a certain interval or on-demand

On-demand ISR
Best for pages that should be regenerated based on certain events

There are use cases where static isn't the best option. For example, SSR is ideal for highly dynamic, personalized pages that are different for every user.

Streaming SSR

With SSR or static rendering, you can reduce the amount of JavaScript so that the time taken for the page to become interactive (TTI) is closer to the time for FCP. Streaming the contents can reduce the TTI/FCP further while still server-rendering the application. Instead of generating one large HTML file containing the necessary markup for the current navigation, we can split it into smaller chunks. Node streams allow us to stream data into the response object, which means we can continuously send data down to the client. When the client receives the chunks of data, it can start rendering the contents.

React's built-in `renderToNodeStream` allows us to send our application in smaller chunks. As the client can start painting the UI when it's still receiving data, we can create a very performant first-load experience. Calling the `hydrate` method on the received DOM nodes will attach the corresponding event handlers, which makes the UI interactive.

Streaming responds well to network backpressure. If the network is clogged and unable to transfer any more bytes, the renderer gets a signal and stops streaming until the network is cleared up. Thus, the server uses less memory and is more responsive to I/O conditions. This enables your Node.js server to render multiple requests simultaneously and prevents heavier requests from blocking lighter requests for a long time. As a result, the site stays responsive even in challenging conditions.

React introduced support for streaming in React 16, released in 2016. It included the following APIs in the `ReactDOMServer` to support streaming:

`ReactDOMServer.renderToNodeStream(element)`
The output HTML from this function is the same as `ReactDOMServer.renderTo String(element)` but is in a Node.js `ReadableStream` format instead of a string. The function will only work on the server to render HTML as a stream. The client receiving this stream can call `ReactDOM.hydrate()` to hydrate the page and make it interactive.

`ReactDOMServer.renderToStaticNodeStream(element)`
This corresponds to `ReactDOMServer.renderToStaticMarkup(element)`. The HTML output is the same but in a stream format. You can use it to render static, noninteractive pages on the server and then stream them to the client.

The readable stream output by both functions can emit bytes once you start reading from it. You can achieve this by piping the readable stream to a writable stream, such as the response object. The response object progressively sends chunks of data to the client while waiting for new chunks to be rendered.

Edge SSR

Edge SSR enables you to server-render from all regions of a CDN and experience a near-zero cold boot.

Serverless functions can be used to generate the entire page server-side. The edge runtime also allows HTTP streaming so that you can stream parts of the document as soon as they are ready and hydrate these components granularly. This reduces the time to FCP.

A use case for this pattern is building region-specific listing pages for users. The majority of the page contains only static data; it's just the listings that require request-based data. Instead of server-rendering the entire page, we can now choose to render only the listing component server-side and the rest edge-side. Whereas we initially had to server-render the whole page to achieve this behavior, we can now get the excellent performance of static rendering on the edge with the dynamic benefits of SSR.

Hybrid Rendering

As the name suggests, hybrid rendering combines different approaches to focus on delivering an optimal result. It represents a mental shift in how developers approach web development, moving from a client-only starting point to a more versatile combination of rendering strategies. Pages that can be served statically will be prerendered. A dynamic strategy may be chosen for other pages in the app (e.g., ISR or SSR or CSR and streaming for subsequent navigations).

Hybrid rendering conceptually challenges traditional terminology (SPA, MPA, SSR, SSG) and emphasizes the need for new verbiage to describe modern web development practices better. A web app need not be classified as an SPA or MPA anymore. It can easily transition from one to the other based on the function served. Thus, it provides the benefits of SPAs (no server needed) while avoiding issues with static rendering (navigation without page reloads).

The shift in focus is not from writing SPAs to not writing SPAs but rather from being locked into SPAs to using whatever rendering mode makes sense for each page, thus entering the hybrid era. This shift is primarily mental, where developers start with build-time and client rendering and add server rendering as needed on a per-page basis.

As the web development landscape converges toward hybrid rendering, we see that many frameworks, both within and outside the React universe, have started supporting it. For example:

- Next.js 13 combines React Server Components and the Next.js App Router (*https://oreil.ly/UEnVf*) to demonstrate the potential of hybrid rendering.
- Astro 2.0 (*https://oreil.ly/Sbfu8*) brings the best of both static and dynamic rendering instead of choosing between SSG and SSR.
- Angular Universal 11.1 (*https://oreil.ly/g076-*) has native hybrid rendering support. It can perform prerendering (SSG) for static routes and SSR for dynamic routes.
- Nuxt 3.0 (*https://oreil.ly/gCriy*) lets you configure route rules for hybrid rendering support.

Progressive Hydration

Progressive hydration implies you can individually hydrate nodes over time so that you request only the minimum necessary JavaScript at any time. By progressively hydrating the application, we can delay the hydration of less critical parts of the page.

This way, we reduce the amount of JavaScript requested to make the page interactive and only hydrate the nodes once the user needs them, for example, when a component is visible in the viewport. Progressive hydration also helps avoid the most common SSR rehydration pitfalls, where a server-rendered DOM tree is destroyed and immediately rebuilt.

The idea behind progressive hydration is to provide excellent performance by activating your app in chunks. Any progressive hydration solution should also consider how it will impact the overall UX. You cannot have chunks of the screen popping up one after the other and blocking any activity or user input on the chunks that have already loaded. Thus, the requirements for a holistic progressive hydration implementation are as follows:

- Allows usage of SSR for all components
- Supports splitting of code into individual components or chunks
- Supports client-side hydration of these chunks in a developer-defined sequence
- Does not block user input on chunks that are already hydrated
- Allows usage of some loading indicator for chunks with deferred hydration

React concurrent mode will address all these requirements once it is available. It allows React to work on different tasks simultaneously and switch between them based on the given priority. When switching, a partially rendered tree need not be committed so that the rendering task can continue once React switches back to the same task.

Concurrent mode can be used to implement progressive hydration. In this case, the hydration of each chunk on the page becomes a task for React concurrent mode. If a task of higher priority, like user input, needs to be performed, React will pause the hydration task and switch to accepting the user input. Features like `lazy()` and `Suspense()` allow you to use declarative loading states. These can be used to show the loading indicator while chunks are lazy-loaded. `SuspenseList()` can be used to define the priority for lazy-loading components. Dan Abramov has shared a great demo (*https://oreil.ly/JHhPm*) that shows the concurrent mode in action and implements progressive hydration.

Islands Architecture

Katie Sylor-Miller and Jason Miller popularized the term Islands architecture (*https://oreil.ly/CYhom*) to describe a paradigm that aims to reduce the volume of JavaScript shipped through "islands" of interactivity that can be independently delivered on top of otherwise static HTML. Islands are a component-based architecture that suggests a compartmentalized page view with static and dynamic islands. Most pages are a combination of static and dynamic content. Usually, a page consists of static content with sprinkles of interactive regions that you can demarcate. The static regions of the page are pure noninteractive HTML and do not need hydration. The dynamic regions are a combination of HTML and scripts capable of rehydrating themselves after rendering.

The Islands architecture facilitates SSR of pages with all of their static content. However, in this case, the rendered HTML will include placeholders for dynamic content. The dynamic content placeholders contain self-contained component widgets. Each widget is similar to an app and combines server-rendered output and JavaScript to hydrate the app on the client.

Islands architecture may be confused with progressive hydration, but there are pretty distinct. In progressive hydration, the hydration architecture of the page is top-down. The page controls the scheduling and hydration of individual components. Each component has its hydration script in the Islands architecture that executes asynchronously, independent of any other script on the page. A performance issue in one component should not affect the other.

Implementing Islands

The Island architecture borrows concepts from different sources and aims to combine them optimally. Template-based static site generators such as Jekyll (*https://oreil.ly/dlxdC*) and Hugo (*https://oreil.ly/WOKTz*) support rendering static components to pages. Most modern JavaScript frameworks also support isomorphic rendering (*https://oreil.ly/mre3v*), which allows you to use the same code to render elements on the server and client.

Jason Miller's post suggests using `requestIdleCallback()` (*https://oreil.ly/x7dpf*) to implement a scheduling approach for hydrating components. A framework that supports Islands architecture should do the following:

- Support static rendering of pages on the server with zero JavaScript.
- Support embedding independent dynamic components via placeholders in static content. Each dynamic component contains its scripts and can hydrate itself using `requestIdleCallback()` as soon as the main thread is free.
- Allow isomorphic rendering of components on the server with hydration on the client to recognize the same component at both ends.

The following frameworks support this to some extent at present:

Marko
Marko (*https://oreil.ly/-l3QP*) is an open source framework developed and maintained by eBay to improve server rendering performance. It supports Islands architecture by combining streaming rendering with automatic partial hydration. HTML and other static assets are streamed to the client as soon as they are ready. Automatic partial hydration allows interactive components to hydrate themselves. Hydration code is only shipped for interactive components, which can change state on the browser. It is isomorphic, and the Marko compiler generates optimized code depending on where it will run (client or server).

Astro
Astro (*https://oreil.ly/QT77v*) is a static site builder that can generate lightweight static HTML pages from UI components built in other frameworks such as React, Preact, Svelte, Vue, and others. Components that need client-side JavaScript are loaded individually with their dependencies. Thus it provides built-in partial hydration. Astro can also lazy-load components depending on when they become visible.

Eleventy + Preact
Markus Oberlehner (*https://oreil.ly/PBckZ*) demonstrates the use of Eleventy (11ty), a static site generator with isomorphic Preact components that can be partially hydrated. It also supports lazy hydration. The component itself declaratively controls its hydration. Interactive components use a `WithHydration` wrapper so that they are hydrated on the client.

Note that Marko and Eleventy predate the definition of Islands provided by Jason but contain some of the features required to support it. Astro, however, was built based on the definition and inherently supports the Islands architecture.

Pros and Cons

Some of the potential benefits of implementing islands are as follows:

Performance
> Reduces the amount of JavaScript code shipped to the client. The code sent consists only of the script required for interactive components. This is considerably less than the script needed to re-create the virtual DOM for the entire page and rehydrate all the elements. The smaller size of JavaScript automatically corresponds to faster page loads.

SEO
> Since all the static content is rendered on the server, pages are SEO-friendly.

Prioritization of important content
> Key content (especially for blogs, news articles, and product pages) is available almost immediately to the user.

Accessibility
> Using standard static HTML links to access other pages helps to improve the accessibility of the website.

Component-based
> The design offers all advantages of component-based architecture, such as reusability and maintainability.

Despite the advantages, the concept is still in a nascent stage. The only options for developers to implement Islands are to use one of the few available frameworks or develop the architecture yourself. Migrating existing sites to Astro or Marko would require additional efforts. The architecture is also unsuitable for highly interactive pages like social media apps that would probably require thousands of islands.

React Server Components

React Server Components (RSC) (*https://oreil.ly/nYygy*) are stateless React components designed to run on the server. They aim to enable modern UX with a server-driven mental model. These zero-bundle-size components facilitate a seamless code transition experience, or "knitting", between server and client components. This differs from the SSR of components and could result in significantly smaller client-side JavaScript bundles.

RSC uses `async/await` as the primary way to fetch data from Server Components. They let you incorporate data fetching as an integral part of the component tree, allowing for top-level `await` and server-side data serialization. Components can thus be refetched regularly. An application with components that re-render when there is new data can be run on the server, limiting how much code needs to be sent to the client. This combines the rich interactivity of client-side apps with the improved performance of traditional server rendering.

RSC protocol enables the server to expose a special endpoint for the client to request parts of the component tree, allowing for SPA-like routing with MPA-like architecture. This allows merging the server component tree with the client-side tree without a loss of state and enables scaling up to more components.

Server Components are not a replacement for SSR. When paired together, they support quickly rendering in an intermediate format, then having SSR infrastructure rendering this into HTML, enabling early paints to still be fast. We SSR the Client Components, which the Server Components emit, similar to how SSR is used with other data-fetching mechanisms.

RSC provides the specification for components. Adoption of RSC depends on frameworks implementing the feature. It is technically possible to use RSC with any React framework, enabling React's own flavor of partial hydration (*https://oreil.ly/CTvSX*) with an end-state of hybrid rendering. Next.js has already introduced support through its App Router feature. The React team believes RSC will eventually be widely adopted and change the ecosystem.

Hybrid Rendering with RSC and the Next.js App Router

Next.js 13 introduced the App Router (*https://oreil.ly/2fkjH*) with new features, conventions, and support for RSC. Components in the app directory are RSC by default, promoting automatic adoption and improved performance.

RSC provide benefits such as leveraging server infrastructure and keeping large dependencies server-side, leading to better performance and reduced client-side bundle size. The Next.js App Router combines server rendering and client-side interactivity, progressively enhancing the application for a seamless user experience.

Client Components can be added to introduce client-side interactivity, similar to the functionality in Next.js 12 and earlier versions. The "use client" directive can mark components as Client Components. Components without the "use client" directive are automatically rendered as Server Components if not imported by another Client Component.

Server and Client Components can be interleaved in the same component tree, with React handling the merge of both environments. Next.js users have seen performance improvements (*https://oreil.ly/sfKEC*) after adopting RSC and the app directory in production.

Summary

This chapter introduced many patterns that attempt to balance the capabilities of CSR and SSR. Depending on the type of the application or the page type, some of the patterns may be more suitable than others. The chart in Figure 13-1 compares the highlights of different patterns and provides use cases for each.

	Classic SSR	SSR with Hydration	Streaming	Progressive Hydration	Static Generation	Incremental Static Generation	CSR
HTML generated on	Server	Server	Server	Server	Build Server	Build Server	Client
JavaScript for Hydration	No Hydration	JS for all components to be loaded for hydration	JS is streamed with HTML	JS is loaded progressively	Minimal JS	Minimal JS	No Hydration but JS for all components is required for rendering and interactivity
SPA Behaviour	Not Possible	Limited	Limited	Limited	Not Possible	Not Possible	Extensive
Crawler Readability	Full	Full	Full	Full	Full	Full	Limited
Caching	Minimum	Minimum	Minimum	Minimum	Extensive	Extensive	Minimum
TTFB	High	High	Low and consistent across page sizes	High	Low	Low	Low
TTI : FCP	TTI = FCP	TTI > FCP	TTI > FCP	TTI > FCP	TTI = FCP	TTI = FCP	TTI >> FCP
Implemented Using	Server side scripting languages like PHP	React for Server, Next.js	React for Server (React 16 onwards)	Full fledged React solution under development	Next.js	Next.js	CSR frameworks like React, Angular etc
Suitable For	Static content pages like news or encyclopedia pages	Mostly static pages with few interactive components. E.g., comments section of a blog	Mostly static pages that can be streamed in chunks. E.g., search results listing pages	Interactive pages where activation of some components may be delayed. E.g., Chatbot	Static content that does not change often. About Us or Contact us pages of websites	Huge quantities of static content that may change frequently. Blog listing or Product listing pages.	Highly Interactive apps where user experience is critical. E.g., Social media messaging and commenting

Figure 13-1. Rendering patterns

The following table from Patterns for Building JavaScript Websites in 2022 (*https://oreil.ly/Qg_h6*) offers another view pivoted by key application characteristics. It should be helpful for anyone looking for a suitable pattern for common application holotypes (*https://oreil.ly/qgaKE*).

	Portfolio	Content	Storefront	Social network	Immersive
Holotype	Personal blog	CNN	Amazon	Social network	Figma
Interactivity	Minimal	Linked articles	Purchase	Multipoint, real time	Everything
Session depth	Shallow	Shallow	Shallow to medium	Extended	Deep
Values	Simplicity	Discover-ability	Load performance	Dynamicism	Immersiveness
Routing	Server	Server, hybrid	Hybrid, transitional	Transitional, client	Client
Rendering	Static	Static, SSR	Static, SSR	SSR	CSR
Hydration	None	Progressive, partial	Partial, resumable	Any	None (CSR)
Example framework	11ty	Astro, Elder	Marko, Qwik, Hydrogen	Next, Remix	Create React App

We have now discussed some interesting React patterns for components, state management, rendering, and others. Libraries like React do not enforce a specific application structure, but there are recommended best practices for organizing your React projects. Let's explore this in the next chapter.

CHAPTER 14

Application Structure for React.js

When building small hobby projects or trying a new concept or library, developers can start adding files to a folder without a plan or organizing structure. These could include CSS, helper components, images, and pages. A single folder for all resources becomes unmanageable as the project grows. Any respectably sized codebase should be organized into an application folder structure based on logical criteria. The decision on how to structure your files and application components could be a personal/team choice. It would also generally depend on the application domain and technology used.

This chapter mainly focuses on folder structures for React.js applications that could help in better management of our projects as they grow.

Introduction

React.js itself does not provide a guideline on structuring projects but does suggest a few commonly used approaches. Let's look at these and understand their pros and cons before discussing folder structures for projects with added complexities and Next.js applications.

At the high level, you can group files in a React application in two ways (*https://oreil.ly/Tkwai*):

Group by feature
    Create folders for every application module, feature, or route.

Group by file type
    Create folders for different types of files.

Let us look at this classification in detail.

Group by Module, Feature, or Route

In this case, the file structure would mirror the business model or the application flow. For example, if you have an ecommerce application, you will have folders for product, productlist, checkout, etc. The CSS, JSX components, tests, subcomponents, or helper libraries explicitly required for the product module reside in the product folder:

```
common/
  Avatar.js
  Avatar.css
  ErrorUtils.js
  ErrorUtils.test.js
product/
  index.js
  product.css
  price.js
  product.test.js
checkout/
  index.js
  checkout.css
  checkout.test.js
```

The advantage of grouping files by feature is that if there is a change to the module, all the affected files are colocated in the same folder, and the change gets localized to a specific part of the code.

The disadvantage is common components, logic, or styles used across modules should be identified periodically to avoid repetition and promote consistency and reuse.

Group by File Type

In this type of grouping, you would create different folders for CSS, components, test files, images, libraries, etc. Thus, logically related files would reside in different folders based on the file type:

```
css/
  global.css
  checkout.css
  product.css
lib/
  date.js
  currency.js
  gtm.js
pages/
  product.js
  productlist.js
  checkout.js
```

The advantages of this approach are:

- You have a standard structure that you can reuse across projects.
- Newer team members with little knowledge of the application-specific logic can still find files for something like styles or tests.
- Common components (such as date pickers) and styles imported in different routes or modules can be changed once to ensure that the effect is seen across the application.

The disadvantages are:

- A change in logic for a specific module would likely require changes in files across different folders.
- As the number of features in the application grows, the number of files in different folders would increase, making it difficult to find a specific file.

Either of these approaches could be easy to set up for small- to mid-sized applications with a small number of files (50 to 100) per folder. For larger projects, however, you may want to go for a hybrid approach based on the logical structure of your application. Let us look at some of the possibilities.

Hybrid Grouping Based on Domain and Common Components

Here you would group all common components required across the application in a Components folder and all application flow-specific routes or features in a domain folder (*https://oreil.ly/rJQaz*) (the name could be *domain*, *pages*, or *routes*). Every folder can have subfolders for specific components and related files:

```
css/
  global.css
components/
  User/
    profile.js
    profile.test.js
    avatar.js
  date.js
  currency.js
  gtm.js
  errorUtils.js
domain/
  product/
    product.js
    product.css
    product.test.js
  checkout/
    checkout.js
    checkout.css
    checkout.test.js
```

Thus, you can combine the advantages of both "Group by file type" and "Group by feature" by colocating related files, which change together frequently and common reusable components and styles used across the application.

Depending on the complexity of the application, you can modify this to a flatter structure without subfolders or a more nested structure:

Flatter structure
   The following example illustrates a flatter structure:

```
domain/
    product.js
    product.css
    product.test.js
    checkout.js
    checkout.css
    checkout.test.js
```

Nested structure
   The following example shows a more nested structure:

```
domain/
    product/
        productType/
            features.js
            features.css
            size.js
        price/
            listprice.js
            discount.js
```

 It's best to avoid deep nesting with more than three to four levels because it becomes harder to write relative imports between folders or update those imports when the files are moved.

A variation to this approach is to create folders based on views or routes, in addition to those based on domain, as discussed here (*https://oreil.ly/WiRca*). A routing component can then coordinate the view to be displayed based on the current route. Next.js (*https://oreil.ly/6PwMu*) uses a similar structure.

Application Structure for Modern React Features

Modern React apps use different features such as Redux, stateful containers, Hooks, and Styled Components. Let's see where the code related to these would fit in the application structure proposed in the previous section.

Redux

Redux documentation strongly recommends (*https://oreil.ly/iH1aX*) colocating logic for a given feature in one place. Within a given feature folder, the Redux logic for that feature should be written as a single "slice" file, preferably using the Redux Toolkit `createSlice` API. The file bundles {`actionTypes`, `actions`, `reducer`} to a self-contained, isolated module. This is also known as the "ducks" pattern (*https://oreil.ly/ UOqb5*) (from Redux). For example, as given here (*https://oreil.ly/0gpXl*):

```
/src
    index.tsx: Entry point file that renders the React component tree
    /app
        store.ts: store setup
        rootReducer.ts: root reducer (optional)
        App.tsx: root React component
    /common: hooks, generic components, utils, etc
    /features: contains all "feature folders"
    /todos: a single feature folder
        todosSlice.ts: Redux reducer logic and associated actions
        Todos.tsx: a React component
```

Another comprehensive example that uses Redux without creating containers or Hooks is available here (*https://oreil.ly/xMZiu*).

Containers

If you have structured your code to categorize components into presentational components and stateful container components (*https://oreil.ly/JeYgI*), you can create a separate folder for the container components. Containers let you separate complex stateful logic from other aspects of the component:

```
/src
    /components
        /component1
            index.js
            styled.js

    /containers
        /container1
```

You can find a complete structure for an app with containers in the same article (*https://oreil.ly/JeYgI*).

Hooks

Hooks can fit into the hybrid structure just like any other type of code. You can have a folder at the app level for common Hooks that can be consumed by all React components. React Hooks used by only one component should remain in the component's file or a separate *hooks.js* file in the component's folder. You can find a sample structure here (*https://oreil.ly/rtT1n*):

```
/components
    /productList
        index.js
        test.js
        style.css
        hooks.js

/hooks
    /useClickOutside
      index.js
    /useData
      index.js
```

Styled Components

If you are using Styled Components instead of CSS, you can have *style.js* files instead of the component-level CSS files mentioned earlier. For example, if you have a `titlebar` component, the structure would be something like this:

```
/src/components/button/
    index.js
    style.js
```

An application-level *theme.js* file (*https://oreil.ly/OARQ8*) would contain the values for colors to be used for background and text. A globals component (*https://oreil.ly/LzmtQ*) could include definitions for common style elements that other components can use.

Other Best Practices

In addition to folder structure, some other best practices that you can consider when structuring your React applications are as follows:

- Use import aliasing (*https://oreil.ly/trM4V*) to help with long relative paths for common imports. This can be done using both Babel and webpack (*https://oreil.ly/cSkCS*) configurations.

- Wrap third-party libraries (*https://oreil.ly/Za7Yt*) with your API so that they can be swapped if required.

- Use PropTypes (*https://oreil.ly/8kL84*) with components to ensure type checking for property values.

Build performance depends on the number of files and dependencies. If you're using a bundler such as webpack, a few suggestions for improving build times may be helpful.

When using a loader (*https://oreil.ly/zXFkv*), apply it to only those modules that need to be transformed by it. For example:

```
const path = require('path');

module.exports = {
  //...
  module: {
    rules: [
      {
        test: /\.js$/,
        include: path.resolve(__dirname, 'src'),
        loader: 'babel-loader',
      },
    ],
  },
};
```

If you're using hybrid/nested folder structures, the following example from webpack (*https://oreil.ly/slT4K*) shows how to include and load files from different paths in the structure:

```
const path = require('path');

module.exports = {
  //...
  module: {
    rules: [
      {
        test: /\.css$/,
        include: [
          // Include paths relative to the current directory starting with
          // `app/styles` e.g. `app/styles.css`, `app/styles/styles.css`,
          // `app/stylesheet.css`
          path.resolve(__dirname, 'app/styles'),

          // add an extra slash to only include the content of the directory
          // `vendor/styles/`
          path.join(__dirname, 'vendor/styles/'),
        ],
      },
    ],
  },
};
```

Files that do not have an `import`, `require`, `define`, etc. to reference other modules need not be parsed for dependencies. You can avoid parsing them using the `noParse` option (*https://oreil.ly/UjYPF*).

Application Structure for Next.js Apps

Next.js (*https://oreil.ly/ZeU0P*) is a production-ready framework for scalable React apps. While you can use the hybrid structures, all the routes in the app must be grouped under the pages folder. (URL of the page = the root URL + relative path in the pages folder).

Extending the structures discussed previously, you can have folders for common components, styles, Hooks, and utility functions. Code related on account of the domain can be structured into functional components that different routes can use. Finally, you will have the pages folder for all routes. Here's an example for this based on this guide (*https://oreil.ly/AAv12*):

```
--- public/
   Favicon.ico
   images/
--- common/
    components/
      datePicker/
        index.js
        style.js
    hooks/
    utils/
    styles/
--- modules/
    auth/
      auth.js
      auth.test.js
    product/
      product.js
      product.test.js
--- pages/
    _app.js
    _document.js
    index.js
        /products
      [id].js
```

Next.js also provides examples (*https://oreil.ly/Kim4W*) for many different types of apps. You can bootstrap these using `create-next-app` to create the template folder structure provided by Next.js. For example, to create the template for a basic blog app (*https://oreil.ly/ym0kh*), use:

```
yarn create next-app --example blog my-blog
```

Summary

This chapter discussed multiple different options for structuring React projects. Depending on the size, type, and components used in the project, you can choose the one most relevant to yours. Sticking to a defined pattern for structuring a project would help you explain it to other team members and prevent projects from getting disorganized and unnecessarily complicated.

The next chapter is the concluding chapter of this book and provides additional links that might be helpful when learning about JavaScript design patterns.

CHAPTER 15

Conclusions

That's it for this introductory adventure into the world of design patterns in JavaScript and React. I hope you've found it beneficial.

Design patterns make it easy for us to build on the shoulders of developers who have defined solutions to challenging problems and architectures over several decades. The contents of this book should provide sufficient information to get you started using the patterns we covered in your scripts, plug-ins, and web applications.

We need to be aware of these patterns, but it's also essential to know how and when to use them. Study the pros and cons of each pattern before employing them. Take the time to experiment with patterns to fully appreciate what they offer and make usage judgments based on a pattern's actual value to your application.

If I've encouraged your interest in this area and you would like to learn more about design patterns, there are many excellent titles available for generic software development and, of course, JavaScript.

I am happy to recommend the following:

- *Patterns of Enterprise Application Architecture* by Martin Fowler
- *JavaScript Patterns* by Stoyan Stefanov

If you are interested in continuing your adventure into React design patterns, you may want to explore the free Patterns.dev (*https://patterns.dev*) resource by Lydia Hallie and myself.

Thanks for reading *Learning JavaScript Design Patterns*. For more educational material on learning JavaScript, please read more from me on my blog at *http://addyosmani.com* or on Twitter @addyosmani (*http://twitter.com/addyosmani*).

Until next time, the very best of luck with your adventures in JavaScript!

References

1. Hillside Engineering Design Patterns Library (*https://oreil.ly/Pffqf*).

2. Ross Harmes and Dustin Diaz, "Pro JavaScript Design Patterns" (*https://oreil.ly/RID62*).

3. Design Pattern Definitions (*https://oreil.ly/Q6tan*).

4. Patterns and Software Terminology (*https://oreil.ly/defjF*).

5. Subramanyan Murali, "Guhan, JavaScript Design Patterns" (*https://oreil.ly/3NxNQ*).

6. James Moaoriello, "What Are Design Patterns and Do I Need Them?" (*https://oreil.ly/m16E-*).

7. Alex Barnett, "Software Design Patterns" (*https://oreil.ly/bOdi1*).

8. Gunni Rode, "Evaluating Software Design Patterns" (*https://oreil.ly/hhqwh*).

9. SourceMaking Design Patterns (*https://oreil.ly/xra3I*).

10. Stoyan Stevanov, "JavaScript Patterns" (*https://oreil.ly/awdqz*).

11. Jared Spool, "The Elements of a Design Pattern" (*https://oreil.ly/qeKIq*).

12. Examples of Practical JS Design Patterns; discussion (*https://oreil.ly/wga_z*), Stack Overflow.

13. Design Patterns in jQuery (*https://oreil.ly/vXUsL*), Stack Overflow.

14. Anoop Mashudanan, "Software Designs Made Simple" (*https://oreil.ly/5PqFD*).

15. Design Patterns Explained (*https://oreil.ly/Lq6fV*).

16. Mixins explained (*https://oreil.ly/jN0zw*).

17. Working with GoF's Design Patterns in JavaScript (*https://oreil.ly/176fs*).

18. Using Object.create (*https://oreil.ly/NSjfs*).

19. t3knomanser, JavaScript Design Patterns (*https://oreil.ly/O8VfS*).

20. Working with GoF Design Patterns in JavaScript Programming (*https://oreil.ly/cerR5*).

21. JavaScript Advantages of Object Literal (*https://oreil.ly/AmJD4*), Stack Overflow.

22. Understanding proxies in jQuery (*https://oreil.ly/n5Hjx*).

23. Observer Pattern Using JavaScript (*https://oreil.ly/MJi6b*).

Index

business data primarily, 124, 133
groups of Models, 124
information not behavior except validation, 133
persistence, 123
photo gallery application, 123
   templating, 126
   View, 124
state, 124
triggers for changes in state, 134
Views, 124-125, 133
   Controllers as intermediaries, 128
   templating, 125, 126
   ViewModel state, 133
   ViewModel versus Model, 134
modular design patterns
  about, 155
    modules, 155
     (see also Module pattern; modules)
  AMD (Asynchronous Module Definition), 156-163
    AMD module design patterns, 160
  AMD and CommonJS equally valid, 167
  CommonJS, 163-167
  UMD (Universal Module Definition), 168-172
Module pattern, 40-51
  about, 40
  advantages and disadvantages, 47
  description of Module pattern, 42-46
    privacy, 42
    privacy examples, 44
  examples, 43-46
    privacy, 44
    template, 44
  Facade pattern with, 67
  further reading, 48
  history, 43
  object literals, 40-42
  React and other modern libraries, 50
  Revealing Module pattern from, 13
  variations
    declaring globals without consuming, 47
    globals passed as arguments, 46
  WeakMap object, 48
modules
  advantages of using, 25, 40
  AMD module format overview, 156

(see also AMD (Asynchronous Module Definition))
anonymous modules, 156
classes versus, 27
decoupling applications, 19, 25, 155
defer attribute, 25
importing dependencies and exporting interfaces, 20-22
loaded from remote sources, 23
modular defined, 155
  (see also modular design patterns)
module objects, 22
MVC facilitating modularization, 128
Node.js and npm support for, 24
unused modules eliminated, 25
Murphey, Rebecca, 42
MV* patterns
  about, 121
  modern MV* patterns, 136
  MVC, 121-129
  MVP, 129-131
  MVVM, 132-136
  React.js and, 136
MVC (Model-View-Controller) pattern, 121-129
  about, 121, 122
    Observer pattern in architecture, 122
    variation of Observer, Strategy, and Composite, 129
  benefits of, 128
  class set perspective, 129
  decoupling Views from Models, 128
    one-to-many relationships, 129
  Models, 123
    attributes, 123
    business data primarily, 124
    groups of Models, 124
    persistence, 123
    state, 124
    templating, 125, 126
    Views, 124-125
  MVP versus, 130
    which to use, 131
  MVP versus MVVM versus, 135
  Smalltalk-80 MVC, 121, 122
    Maria.js as faithful implementation, 128
  ToDo list in vanilla JavaScript, 136
MVP (Model-View-Presenter) pattern, 129-131
  about, 121, 129

About the Author

Addy Osmani is an engineering leader working on Google Chrome. He leads Chrome's Developer Experience teams, helping to keep the web fast and delightful to build upon. Addy has authored several open source projects as well as a number of books, including *Learning Patterns*, *Learning JavaScript Design Patterns* (O'Reilly), and *Image Optimization*. His personal blog is *addyosmani.com*.

Colophon

The animal on the cover of *Learning JavaScript Design Patterns* is the cuckoo pheasant (*Dromococcyx phasianellus*, also known as the pheasant cuckoo). The pheasant cuckoo is a bird that is native to forests from the Yucatan peninsula to Brazil and may be found as far south as Colombia.

The pheasant cuckoo has a long tail and a short, dark-brown crest. Its diet consists of insects, which it catches by making rattling sounds with its feathers and clapping its bill, then running several steps forward and pecking at the ground. Although it is an insectivore, it may also feed on small lizards and nestlings.

Like many other cuckoos, the pheasant cuckoo lays its eggs in another bird's nest. When the eggs hatch, the adoptive mother will recognize the cuckoo's offspring as her own, and the hatchlings will imprint on their adoptive mother. Acting on instinct, cuckoo hatchlings will push the host parent's eggs out of the nest to make room for themselves. Unlike the European cuckoo, however, the pheasant cuckoo is not an obligate brood parasite; it still has the ability to construct nests of its own.

The current conservation status (IUCN) of the pheasant cuckoo is "Least Concern." Many of the animals on O'Reilly covers are endangered; all of them are important to the world.

The cover illustration is by Karen Montgomery, based on a loose plate engraving, origin unknown. The cover fonts are Gilroy Semibold and Guardian Sans. The text font is Adobe Minion Pro; the heading font is Adobe Myriad Condensed; and the code font is Dalton Maag's Ubuntu Mono.